THE DAUGHTER

OF

PETER THE GREAT.

BY

R. NISBET BAIN.

AMS PRESS
NEW YORK

Elizabeth Petrovna

ætat 32

THE
DAUGHTER OF
PETER THE GREAT

A HISTORY OF RUSSIAN DIPLOMACY AND OF
THE RUSSIAN COURT UNDER THE EMPRESS
ELIZABETH PETROVNA 1741—1762. BY R.
NISBET BAIN. AUTHOR OF "THE PU-
PILS OF PETER THE GREAT" "GUS-
TAVUS III AND HIS CONTEM-
PORARIES" "CHARLES XII"
ETC. ETC.

WESTMINSTER:
ARCHIBALD CONSTABLE & Co.
2 WHITEHALL GARDENS
1899.

Reprinted from the edition of 1899, Westminister
First AMS EDITION published 1970
Manufactured in the United States of America

International Standard Book Number: 0-404-00447-4

Library of Congress Catalog Number: 72-136407

AMS PRESS INC.
NEW YORK, N.Y. 10003

LIST OF ILLUSTRATIONS.

ELIZABETH PETROVNA, ætat. 32.

Photogravure Frontispiece.

FIELD MARSHAL COUNT MÜNNICH . . . *Face Page* 22

THE GRAND DUKE PETER, ætat. 16 . . „ „ 66

THE GRAND CHANCELLOR COUNT ALEXIUS

    BESTUZHEV-RYUMIN . . . . „ „ 97

THE GRAND DUCHESS CATHERINE . . . „ „ 234

ELIZABETH PETROVNA, ætat. 52 . . . . „ „ 286

THE GRAND DUKE PETER, ætat. 33 . . „ „ 314

CONTENTS.

	PAGE
INTRODUCTION	XI
BIBLIOGRAPHY	XV
CHAPTER I.—INTRODUCTORY—PETER'S PUPILS	I

Death of Peter the Great—Danger of a reaction—Peter's pupils—Menshikov, Tolstoi, Yaguzhinsky—Their promptness—Catherine I and her difficulties—The history of Russia during the eighteenth century the history of her foreign policy—Why this was so—Ostermann—The hostility of England brings about the Austro-Russian Alliance—Peter II—Anne of Courland—Brutality of her favourite, Biren—His character—The genius of Ostermann—Russia's triumphs abroad—Münnich and Lacy—Death of Anne—Merits and defects of her government.

| CHAPTER II.—IVAN VI. Oct. 1740—Dec. 1741. | 22 |

Biren Regent—Public humiliation of the new Tsar's father—Biren's measures—His unpopularity—Discontent of the Princess Anne and of Münnich—Plot against Biren—Münnich's midnight coup-d'état—Fall of Biren—Princess Anne proclaimed Regent—Ambition and arrogance of Münnich—Foreign affairs—Death of the Emperor Charles VI—Cynical behaviour of Frederick of Prussia—Outbreak of the First Silesian War—Tergiversation of France—Convention of Nymphenburg—Treaty of Breslau—Münnich's incompetence—His resignation—Foreign policy of Ostermann—His difficulties—Hostility of France to Russia—Sweden declares war against Russia—Battle of Vilmanstrand—The Regent's fondness for Fräulein Mengden—Her liaison with Count Lynar—Dangers of the situation—Alarm of Ostermann—Character of the Marquis de la Chetardie—A ceremonial squabble—Chetardie's plot in favour of Elizabeth Petrovna—Popularity of the Tsarevna—Her hatred of Ostermann—His difficult position—And growing weariness of office.

| CHAPTER III.—THE MIDNIGHT COUP D'ÉTAT. Dec. 6th, 1741 | 50 |

Immediate causes of the Revolution of Dec. 6th, 1741—La Chetardie's misgivings—Self-confidence of the Tsarevna Elizabeth—Scene in the Winter Palace between her and the Regent—Extreme peril of Elizabeth—

Conference of the Conspirators at Elizabeth's house—The appeal to
the Grenadiers—The midnight drive to the Preobrazhensky Barracks—
Elizabeth wins over the soldiers—The march to the Winter Palace—
The Regent seized in bed—Arrest of the Ministers—Elizabeth proclaimed Empress—Enthusiasm of the people—Largesses of the new
Empress—The trial of Ostermann and Münnich —Their dignified
conduct—Tragic scene on the place of execution— The capital sentences
remitted—The fate of Ostermann, Münnich, and their associates.

CHAPTER IV.—A CROSS-FIRE OF INTRIGUE. 1741—1743 . . . 66

Infancy of Elizabeth—Project of wedding her to a French Prince—
Early years—Abilities—Unsettled state of Russia—Mr. Finch's view
of the situation—Who is to succeed Ostermann?—The new Ministers—
Alexius Cherkasky—Nikita Yurevitch Trubetskoi—Armand Lestocq—
Michael Vorontsov—Michael Bestuzhev—Alexius Bestuzhev—His early
career and character—The Swedish difficulty—La Chetardie as mediator—His effrontery—Dignified firmness of the Empress—Peace
of Abo—The treacherous despatch—Departure of La Chetardie—
The policy of the Bestuzhevs—Their immense difficulties—Elizabeth's
antipathies—Plot to ruin the Bestuzhevs—Arrest of Natalia Lopukhina—
Her character—And accomplices—The trial—The sentence—Horrible
scenes on the scaffold—Estrangement between Austria and Russia—
The Court moves to Moscow.

CHAPTER V.—THE TRIUMPH OF BESTUZHEV. 1744—1748 . . . 97

Carl Peter Ulric—His early career—Arrival in Russia—Made Grand
Duke and heir to the throne—Arrival of the Princesses of Zerbst—
Serious illness of the bride elect—Sophia Augusta becomes Catherine
Aleksyevna—The betrothal—The wedding—European Politics—Fre-
derick's dread of Russia—His intrigues against Bestuzhev—Beginning
of the Second Silesian War—La Chetardie expelled from Russia—
Bestuzhev made Grand Chancellor—Reconciliation of Austria and
Russia—Reverses of Frederick II—Frederick declares war against
Saxony—Warning protest of Elizabeth—End of the Second Silesian
War—Expulsion of "Madame Zerbst" from Russia—Quarrel between
Bestuzhev and Vorontsov—Dismissal of Mardefeld—Death of Anne
Leopoldovna—Negotiations with England—The Anglo-Russian Alli-
ance—March of the Russian troops to the Rhine—Signal triumph and
commanding position of the Grand Chancellor—Disgrace of Lestocq.

CHAPTER VI.—THE COURT OF ELIZABETH. 1742—1749 . . . 133

Elizabeth's personality—Her amiability—Equity—Indolence—Extravagant splendour of her Court—Her favourites—Alexius Razumovsky—
Cyril Razumovsky—Their amiable character—Anecdotes illustrating
their generosity—Visit of the Empress to Kiev—General character of
Elizabeth's Court—Entertainments—Opera Bouffés—The Court The-

atre—The masquerades or metamorphoses—Elizabeth in male attire—
Pilgrimages—Deterioration of morals—The rise of the Shuvalovs—
Peter Shuvalov—His abilities and vices—Immense influence—Alex-
ander Shuvalov—Ivan Shuvalov—He supersedes Razumovsky in the
Empress's favour—Alarm of Bestuzhev—The Beketov incident.

CHAPTER VII.—RUSSIA AND GREAT BRITAIN. 1749—1755 . . 161

The European situation—Antagonism of Russia and Prussia—England
opposes Russia's anti-Swedish plans—Rupture of diplomatic relations
between Russia and Prussia—Poland—The Courland question—
Saxony—Difficulties of the Grand Chancellor—Michael Bestuzhev
and Madame von Haugwitz—Estrangement between the two Bestuzhevs—England's fear of Prussia—The Anglo-Russian negotiations—
Bestuzhev's energetic efforts on behalf of England—The Conventions
of 1755.

CHAPTER VIII.—THE LEAGUE AGAINST PRUSSIA. 1756. . . . 179

The new Prussian Monarchy a menace to Europe—Kaunitz's report to
Maria Theresa as to the necessity of a new political system—The
German Neutrality Convention between Prussia and Great Britain—
Indignation in France—The Treaty of Versailles between France
and Austria—Alarm of Great Britain—Cynical levity of her policy—
Pitiable situation of Bestuzhev—Character of the Grand Duke
Peter—And of the Grand Duchess Catherine—Birth of the Grand
Duke Paul—Beginning of friendly relations between Catherine and
Bestuzhev—Illness of the Empress—Bestuzhev becomes obstructive—
Establishment of the Conference of Ministers—The Five Points—
Renewal of diplomatic relations between France and Russia—The
Mission of Mackenzie Douglas—The Mission of T. D. Bekhtyeev—
Anxiety of Great Britain—The intrigues of Hanbury Williams—
Recovery of the Empress—Russia accedes to the Treaty of Versailles—
Frederick's apprehension—Beginning of the Seven Years' War.

CHAPTER IX.—THE CAMPAIGN OF GROSSJÄGERSDORF. 1757 . . 208

Stephen Apraksin appointed the Russian Commander-in-Chief—His character—Dilatory tactics of Apraksin—Advance of the Russian Army—
Memel and Tilsit taken—Strategy of Apraksin—Battle of Grossjägersdorf—Description of an eye-witness—Retreat of Apraksin after
the victory—Demoralization of the Russian Army—The Austrian
victories—Embarrassment of Frederick—Rossbach and Leuthen—
Fresh Convention between Russia and Austria—Russia left out of
the Franco-Austrian partition treaty—The Embassy of the Marquis
de l'Hôpital to St. Petersburg—His character—The Embassy of
Michael Bestuzhev to Paris—Russia's relations with England—Sudden
and dangerous illness of Elizabeth.

PAGE

CHAPTER X.—THE FALL OF BESTUZHEV, AND THE CAMPAIGN OF
ZORNDORF. 1758. 234

Insecurity of Bestuzhev—Examination of Apraksin—Arrest of Bestuzhev—
Anxiety of Catherine—The trial of Bestuzhev—Catherine's pathetic
letter to the Empress—Her midnight interview with Elizabeth—The
Empress finally mollified—The new Commander-in-Chief, General
Fermor—The winter campaign in 1757-8—Disorganization of the
Russian army—"Letter from a traveller from Riga"—Campaign of
1758—Advance of Fermor into Prussian territory—Bombardment of
Cüstrin—Battle of Zorndorf—Subsequent operations—Elizabeth's dis-
satisfaction with Fermor—Differences with the Court of Vienna—
Firmness of Elizabeth—Opinion in France—And in England.

CHAPTER XI.—THE CAMPAIGN OF KUNERSDORF. 1759. 263

Increasing difficulties of the King of Prussia—The Conventions of Versailles, 30th and 31st. Dec.—Opening of the campaign—Advance
of Fermor—He is superseded by Peter Saltuikov—Causes of Fermor's
supersession—Character of the new Commander-in-Chief—Advance
of Saltuikov—Battle of Kay—Defeat of the Prussians—Saltuikov
reaches Frankfort—Cautious counsels—Advance of the King of
Prussia—Battle of Kunersdorf—Destruction ot the Prussian Army—
Despair of Frederick—Attempted mediation of England in his favour—
Proposed Peace Congress of the Hague—Elizabeth will not be
separated from her Allies—Dissensions between Saltuikov and Daun—
Obstinacy of Saltuikov—Angry diplomatic correspondence between
the Courts of Vienna and St. Petersburg—Dignified tone of the
Russian Empress—Maria Theresa reposes all her hopes in Elizabeth—
Choiseul and Vorontsov.

CHAPTER XII.—THE LAST YEARS OF ELIZABETH. 1760—Jan.
5th, 1762 .286

Elizabeth her own Minister of Foreign Affairs—Frederick to be crushed—
His despair—Attempts to bribe the Shuvalovs—The Austro-Russian
Conventions of May, 1760—Futile diplomacy of France—England's
apprehension of Russia's territorial aggrandizement—Saltuikov's plan
rejected—Campaign of 1760—Austrian successes—Saltuikov superseded by Buturlin—Occupation of Berlin—Battle of Torgau—General
desire for peace—Resolute attitude of Elizabeth—She rejects all
pacific overtures—Her direct and secret negotiation with Louis XV—
The question of a Peace Congress—Pitt and Golitsuin—Frederick's
projects—Campaign of 1761—The new Russian Commander-in-Chief,
A. B. Buturlin—His utter incompetency—Operations in Silesia—
Scathing rescripts of the Empress to Buturlin—Laudon and Chernuishev capture Schweidnitz—Siege and capture of Kolberg by
Rumyantsev—Frederick abandons all hope—The last illness, and
death of Elizabeth—Reflections.

INDEX. 317

INTRODUCTION.

THERE are few epochs of modern history at once so momentous and so obscure as the period of the Empress Elizabeth. The great Russian historian, Solovev, declared some thirty years ago, that although the reign of the Daughter of Peter the Great was scarcely less important than the reign of her illustrious father and marked a turning-point in the political history, not merely of Muscovy, but of Europe, it was, nevertheless, a subject less familiar to the majority of educated Russians than the semi-mythical period of Svyatoslav and Vladimir. We occidentals now stand on much the same level of ignorance as regards this most interesting and pregnant period as Russians, according to Solovev, stood thirty years ago. Incredible indeed is the want of knowledge actually prevailing amongst us, even in the best informed circles, in regard to the career and character of a Princess who was the contemporary and ally of George II, the most active friend of Maria Theresa and the most dangerous foe of Frederick II. I will venture to affirm that not one in a hundred of our historical students have ever heard of Alexius Bestuzhev whom Frederick II honoured with the title of "my great antagonist," and how many of us know the name of the Russian field-marshal who annihilated the army of the King of Prussia on the bloody field of Kunersdorf? Even German learning, on which we are apt to lean so confidently for our knowledge of continental history, fails us lamentably as soon as we cross the borders of eighteenth century Russia. I know of nothing so startling in way of blunders as the bibliographical reference to Schjörring's *play*, "*Elizabeth af Rusland*", as the best authority on the life of the Empress, appended to the article "Elizabeth, von Russland" in "Meyers Konversations-Lexikon," a publication generally regarded as a monument of accurate scholarship.

I opine that the chief cause of the almost universal ignorance of the chief events and persons of this epochmaking reign is the undeniable difficulty of the subject itself. The Court of St. Petersburg, under Elizabeth, was the focus of European diplomacy, and consequently the arena wherein conflicting ambitions met in mortal strife armed with all the weapons of chicanery and violence. There is no other period of political history with which I am acquainted wherein it is so hard to separate truth from falsehood, so hard to construct a sober, rational and coherent narrative out of the confused and confusing mass of ambiguous and contradictory documents which the enquirer has to deal with. Another difficulty is, of course, the fact that no small part of the sources is in Russian, a language still, unfortunately, almost unknown among us.

But, on the other hand, if the whole subject bristles with difficulties, it also has its compensations. The nut may be hard to crack, but it has a kernel worth the trouble. The dealings of Elizabeth and her ministers with the various Courts of Europe not only throw valuable side-lights upon many obscure points of Eighteenth Century history, but enable us to better understand the whole political situation of the period. In particular, the War of the Austrian Succession, the Seven Years' War, and the events which led up to them first become wholly intelligible when

we have fathomed the intrigues of La Chetardie and master-
ed the despatches of the Bestuzhevs. And persons as well
as things will strike us in a new light. Viewed through Russian glasses, Maria Theresa, Frederick II, Louis XV, Fleury,
Pitt, Kaunitz, and other familiar figures reveal phases of their
characters unsuspected before, and at the Court of St. Petersburg itself we are introduced to quite another world, which
possesses for us all the charm of novelty. Elizabeth herself is, indubitably, one of the most imposing and fascinating women of her day, and she brings along with her
a whole group of gay and gallant revellers and paladins
who are equally ready to share with their adored mistress
the delights of a masquerade or the perils of a *coup d'état.*

Finally, I would remind the reader that this work, as
stated on the title-page, is, principally, a history of Russian
diplomacy, during the critical years, 1740—1761, and of
the persons who inspired and controlled that diplomacy.
Though any history of those stirring times must necessarily
abound with dramatic details and vivid episodes, such incidents, though never omitted, are always subordinated to
the main purpose of the book. Nor do I profess to give
technical details of the campaigns of 1756—1761, although
I have been careful to supply from hitherto unused Russian
sources, what I trust is an intelligible summary of the chief
military events of each campaign. Those who may be
tempted to pursue the subject for themselves I refer to
the critical bibliography which follows.

R. NISBET BAIN.

October, 1899.

BIBLIOGRAPHY.

RUSSIAN SOURCES.

I.—ORIGINAL DOCUMENTS.

(1) *Iz bumag I. I. Shuvalova.* (Extracts from the papers of I. I. Shuvalov) *Sb. I. R. O.* * Vol. IX. These papers refer to the leading events of the campaigns of 1756—61, consisting, for the most part, of letters and despatches of the Russian Commanders-in-Chief addressed to I. I. Shuvalov.—(2) *Pisma Grafa A. P. Bestuzheva k Grafu M. L. Vorontsovu,* 1744—1760. (Letters of Count A. P. Bestuzhev to Count M. L. Vorontsov.) *Ark. Vor.* † Vol. II.— (3) *Dyelo o Markizye Shetardi.* (The affair of the Marquis de la Chetardie.) *Ark. Vor.* Vol. I. Letters and other documents bearing upon the expulsion of La Chetardie from Russia.—(4) *Instruktsy dlya lits naznachaemuikh sostoyat pri Velikoi Kniginye i pri Velikom Knyazye.* (Instructions for the persons attached to the Grand Duchess and the Grand Duke.) *Ark. Vor.* Vol. II. One of the most interesting and amusing documents, relating to the early married life of Peter and Catherine.—(5) *Pisma Grafa M. P. Bestuzheva k Grafu M. L. Vorontsovu.* (Letters from Count M. P. Bestuzhev to Count M. L. Vorontsov.) *Ark. Vor.* Vol. II. These letters consist of the diplomatic despatches of Michael Bestuzhev from Berlin, Dresden, Vienna and Versailles, from 1744 to 1760.— (6) *Iz chernovuikh otryetnuikh pisem Grafa M. L. Vorontsova k Grafu M. P. Bestuzhevu.* (Extracts from the rough drafts of the letters of Count M. L. Vorontsov in reply to Count M. P. Bestuzhev.) *Ark. Vor.* Vol. II.—(7) *Pisma kasayushcheyasya zagovora Markiza Bottui.* (Letters relating to the conspiracy of the Marquis

---

* Sbornik or collections of the Imperial Russian Historical Society.

† The Vorontsov Archives—a valuable collection of state documents preserved in the Archives of the Vorontsov Family, still in course of publication.

de Botta.) *Ark. Vor.* Vol. II.—(8) *Zapiski o sostoyany zdorov'ya Imperatretsui Elizavetui.* (Notes relating to the state of health of the Empress Elizabeth.) *Ark. Vor.* Vol. III.—(9) *Pisma Th. D. Bekhtyeva k Grafu M. L.Vorontsovu.* (Despatches of T. D. Bekhtyeev to Count M. L. Vorontsov.) *Ark. Vor.* Vol. III. The important documents relate to Bekhtyeev's secret mission to Versailles whither he was sent in 1756 to reopen diplomatic relations between France and Russia.—(10) *Ob arestye Lestoka.* (On the arrest of Lestocq.) *Ark. Vor.* Vol. III.—(11) *Iz bumag Elizavetinskoi Konferentsy.* (Extracts from the protocols · of Elizabeth's Council of State.) *Ark. Vor.* Vol. III. An important collection of papers bearing upon the inception of the Seven Years' War.—(12) *Zapiski Kn. Yakova Petrovicha Shakhovskago.* (Memories of Count Jacob Shakovsky.)—(13) *Zapiski A. Sh. Bolotova* (Memoirs of A. S. Bolotov). This is perhaps the most important and interesting contemporary document relating to the reign of Elizabeth. The author was an eye-witness of the earlier campaigns of the Seven Years' War and an accurate observer. His memoirs are in the epistolary style which he handles charmingly. On the other hand his ignorance of military matters, from a technical point of view, often leads him to misunderstand and misjudge.—(14) *Zapiski Minikha* (Memoirs of Münnich). This is but a fragment, yet an important one as being by an early contemporary of Elizabeth and conveying information not attainable elsewhere.

II.—RUSSIAN MONOGRAPHS, ESSAYS, ETC.

(15) Solovev: *Istorya Rossy.* Vols. XX—XXII. A monumental work, a careful study of which is absolutely indispensable to a right understanding of the period. As, however, it mainly consists of original Russian documents, perhaps I should have placed it under category I.—(16) Kostomarov: *Russkaya Istorya,* a delightful work of a more popular order than Solovev's great work. The author, however, has the irritating and unscholarly practice of rarely citing his authorities.—(18) Shcherbatov: *O povrezhdeniy nravov v Rossy* (On the degeneration of morals in Russia). A scathing attack upon the luxury of the Court of Russia in the eighteenth century. The author was a contemporary of Catherine II.—(18) Dolgoruki: *Graf A. I. Ostermann,* (A biography).—(19) Bantuish-Kamensky: *Biografy rosseskikh generalissumesov.* (Biographies of the Russian Generalissimos).—(20) *Statsdamui i Freilinui russkago dvora v XVIII stolyetiya* (Ladies in waiting and maids of honour at the Russian Court in the 18th century). A series of biographies throwing some light on the Court life of the period.—

(21) *Natalya Federovna Lopukhina.* An anonymous essay of great ability relating to the unhappy lady who was so foully victimized by Lestocq in 1743.—(22) Vasilchikov: *Semeistvo Razumovskikh* (The Family of the Razumovskys). This is, without doubt, by far the most important and intimate book relating to the Court life under Elizabeth.—(23) Ruilyaev: *Staroe Zhit'e* (Life in the olden times). A fascinating description of social life in old Russia.

DOCUMENTS IN OTHER LANGUAGES.

I.—DESPATCHES OF THE FOREIGN ENVOYS AT THE RUSSIAN COURT.

This class of documents is of value as being the testimony of contemporary observers paid to keep their eyes open and report everything. On the one hand they, as often as not, reflect the party feeling and prejudice of the writers, and therefore, especially when the envoys are fanatics or blockheads, as is sometimes the case, may be downright misleading or even absolutely worthless. On the other hand they often serve as mutual correctives. I take them seriatim, as far as possible in chronological order.—(24) *Despatches of the Saxon Minister, Pezold,* 1740—1744. Sb. of R. I. I. O. Vol. VI. A mere gossip.—(25) *Despatches of the Marquis de la Chetardie,* 1740—1742. Sb. of R. I. I. O. Vols. 92 and 96. Valuable because of the ambassador's intimate relations with Elizabeth. Misleading because he was a shallow observer, with little tact or discrimination.—(26) *Despatches of Hon. Edward Finch,* 1740—1742. Sb. of R. I. I. O. Vols. 85 and 91. Finch was a man of great ability and penetration, but the accession of Elizabeth to the throne was a disagreeable surprise to him which he could never forget or forgive, and from that moment he views everything through the spectacles of pique and jealousy.—(27) *Despatches of Cyril Wych, Lord Hyndford, Lord Tyrawley, Guy Dickens and Sir Hanbury Williams.* 12 MS. Vols. *Record Office For. State Papers, Russia,* 1742—1759. These still unpublished documents vary greatly in value. Wych is painstaking and truthful. Lord Hyndford sees things most clearly and intelligently. Williams' despatches are almost valueless. He carries party spirit to the verge of fanaticism, and repeatedly misleads his own government; his account of the state of things at the Russian Court is a caricature of the truth.

II.—ORIGINAL DOCUMENTS IN FRENCH AND GERMAN.

(28) *Early correspondence of Catherine II*, in French. 1744—1758. Gives her first impressions of Russia. So scrappy that it has evidently been mutilated before publication.—(29) *Relation* of Catherine's mother, the Princess Elizabeth of Zerbst, describing her residence in Russia, 1743—1745. An amusing document full of piquant details and petty jealousies. Both these documents will be found in Vol. VII of the Sb. of the I. R. I. O.—(30) Martens' *Recueil des traités, etc.* This great compilation is so well drawn that I need but mention it and pass on.—(31) *Politische Correspondenz Friedrichs des Grossen*, for the most part in French. Vols. I—XXI. This invaluable collection of letters and despatches, still in progress, shews us the real Frederick as no other book has ever done or can ever do. He tells his own story and we can follow his changing moods from day to day. The greater portion of this publication is posterior to Carlyle's masterpiece.—(32) A. R. Vorontsov: *Notes sur ma vie et les événements différents qui se sont passés tant en Russie qu'en Europe pendant ce temps là* (1744—1805). *Ark. Vor.* Vol. V. A memoir begun by Count Vorontsov, nephew of the Chancellor, in his 65th year and not intended for publication. It abounds with valuable details relating to the Court of Elizabeth and is, generally speaking, fair and just. It must always be a matter of the deepest regret that the History of Elizabeth by the same amiable author, frequently mentioned in these pages, has never yet been found.—(33) *Mémoires de l'Impératrice Catherine II.* Ed. Herzen. This enthralling book is too well known to be commented upon by me. Despite the strong under-current of self-glorification which pervades it, it is an edifying document, though not precisely in the sense intended by the illustrious author.

III.—MONOGRAPHS AND ESSAYS IN FRENCH AND GERMAN.

(34) Masslowski: *Der siebenjährige Krieg nach russischer Darstellung. Ed. Drygalski.* This work is, as its title specifies, a history of the Seven Years' War from the Russian standpoint, and as such most useful to military students. It is in three octavo volumes well provided with maps.—(35) Vondel: *Louis XV et Elizabeth.* A useful book, highly praised by no less an authority than the Duc de Broglie. It leans too much, however, on the all but worthless despatches of the Marquis L'Hôpital, and is now a trifle obsolete.

THE DAUGHTER OF PETER THE GREAT.

CHAPTER I.

INTRODUCTORY—PETER'S PUPILS.

DEATH of Peter the Great—Danger of a reaction—Peter's pupils—Menshikov, Tolstoi, Yaguzhinsky—Their promptness—Catherine I and her difficulties—The history of Russia during the eighteenth century the history of her foreign policy—Why this was so—Ostermann—The hostility of England brings about the Austro-Russian Alliance—Peter II—Anne of Courland—Brutality of her favourite, Biren—His character—The genius of Ostermann—Russia's triumphs abroad—Münnich and Lacy—Death of Anne—Merits and defects of her government.

WHEN Peter I expired, prematurely and somewhat suddenly, at the beginning of 1725, it was the confident expectation of the politicians of Europe that the work of the great Tsar would perish with him. During the last thirty years the terrorized nation had been compelled to break with the traditions of centuries and endure a whole series of social and political reforms which it secretly loathed as so many abominations; but now that the master mind, which, at so terrible a cost, had converted semi-Asiatic Muscovy into semi-European Russia, was withdrawn, a recoil in the direction of indolent, contented barbarism seemed inevitable, and, at least to the enemies of Russia, even desirable.

And but for the promptitude of the half-dozen of capable men, a motley but unanimous band, whom Peter, with

singular felicity, had gradually picked out and trained up
to assist him in his work, and to carry it on after his
death, a lapse into "the quagmire of Byzantinism," must
inevitably have taken place. The stern and ever increasing
severity of the late Emperor's system of government had
produced universal discontent, a discontent the more bitter
and intense because hitherto denied an outlet. The vast
majority of the clergy, at least half the Senate (though
that was a purely Petrine institution) and all the old boyar
nobility without exception, were ripe for revolt, and they
made no secret of their intentions of elevating to the throne
the son of the martyred Tsarevich Alexius, the Grand Duke
Peter, a child of eight. This faction of reactionaries represented more than half the wealth of Russia and nearly
all the influence that unofficial rank still retained in that
country; but it was much weakened by internal dissensions
and possessed no leader of sufficient force of character
to marshal its forces and lead it on to victory. On the
other hand, Peter's pupils, as we must call the opposite
party, were men of extraordinary energy, enlightened enough
to perfectly understand the real needs of their country,
and well aware that a moment's hesitation on their part
would mean the subversion of Peter's system and their own
ruin. Chief among them stood Alexander Danilovich Menshikov, whom Peter had literally plucked from the gutter
to set among princes. In his earlier years Menshikov had
plied the modest trade of an itinerant pieman in the streets
of Moscow, subsequently entering the service of François
Lefort, the young Tsar's early companion and mentor, at
whose house Peter first saw the lively young lacquey and
appropiated him. The intelligence with which Alexander
Danilovich grasped the leading ideas of the Tsar's reforms,
and the cheerful alacrity with which he was ready to break
with all the old Russian habits and customs, to please his

master, soon made him indispensable to Peter, and henceforth they became inseparable. Menshikov accompanied
the Tsar abroad, worked by his side in the dockyards of
Amsterdam, studied Dutch and German beneath his very
eyes, and plunged with equal enthusiasm into the multi-
tudinous labours and the monstrous orgies of the most
exacting of masters. Honours and riches were heaped upon
"little Alec" by "old Peter," and at the end of the Tsar's
reign Menshikov was that monarch's mightiest satrap, a
Prince of the Holy Roman as well as of the orthodox
Russian Empire, and indisputably one of the wealthiest
men in Europe. Menshikov's most energetic colleagues
were the already ageing ex-boyar, Count Peter Andryeevich
Tolstoi, the father of Russian diplomacy, notable for his
intellectual suppleness and extraordinary receptivity for new
ideas, and Paul Ivanovich Yaguzhinsky, the *enfant terrible*
of Peter the Great's "fledglings," a man of humble origin,
violent character, and unsurpassable courage who had ac-
quitted himself with distinction in affairs, and had exercised,
as Procureur-Général, a sort of supervision over the Senate
itself. These three men detested each other as rivals, but
common interests and a common danger now drew them
together, and they agreed that the only way to preserve
the new system established by Peter was to raise to Peter's
throne the extraordinary woman whom the Tsar had made his
consort, and intended for his successor, the widowed Tsaritsa
Catherine Aleksyeevna. There is no need to recount once
more the oft-told tale of the Swedish soldier's doxy, who was
brought half naked into the Russian camp as part of the spoils
of war, and passed on from possessor to possessor till she
finally fell into the hands of the autocrat whom she sub-
jugated as much by her sound sense and generous sympathy as by her flamboyant style of beauty. Suffice it to
say that, on the death of her imperial consort, Catherine

occupied an altogether unique position. She was, so to
speak, the incarnation of Peter's system in its extremest
form, a challenge to the conservative, a watchword for
the progressive faction. All the most cherished and inveterate traditions of old Muscovy stood in her way. She
was a woman, and women were regarded by the Russian
people at large as silly and dangerous creatures to be
rigorously kept under lock and key. She was a foreigner,
and the bare idea of a foreign domination was detestable
to every patriotic Muscovite. She had gone through the
form of marriage with a monarch whose first wife was still
living, and therefore in the eyes of every member of the
orthodox church, she was simply the late Tsar's concubine.
To place such a woman on the throne was, from the conservative point of view, an outrage; but to the pupils of
Peter it meant a final victory over ancient prejudices, a
triumphant vindication of the new ideas of progress which
Peter had been the first to formulate. Fortunately, too,
for them, the bulk of the army was on the side of Catherine. She had accompanied her husband through all his
later campaigns, she had shared the hardships and privations
of the common soldiers, and the sight of her imposing
masculine figure on horseback, in Amazonian costume, was
familiar to every man in the ranks. With the prompt
assistance then of such energetic supporters as Menshikov
and Tolstoi (she knew right well that for their own sakes
they *dare* not refuse to help her at this crisis) immediate
success seemed certain, and, clement and generous by
nature, she trusted to a wise policy of conciliation to
consolidate her position in the future. The hopes of the
Tsaritsa were realized with singular rapidity and complete-
ness. The energy and presence of mind of her partisans
overawed all opposition. Only a few moments after her
husband had breathed his last in her arms, a deputation

from the Senate, Army and Nobility petitioned her to
accept the vacant crown, and on the 11th February, 1725,
Catherine was solemnly proclaimed autocrat of all the
Russians.

The short reign of Catherine I (Feb. 1725—May 1727)
was chiefly remarkable for its humane and conciliatory
measures at home, and its cautious, pacific, but nevertheless
dignified, consistent and independent policy abroad. The
nation was still suffering intensely from the immediate
consequences of Peter the Great's hasty and violent reforms,
and something was done to mitigate this suffering. The
grinding poll-tax was reduced, a large part of the army
was disbanded, many of the vexatious restrictions on commerce imposed during the last reign were removed, and
attempts were even made to stimulate the copper, iron, and
other industries. But at home the government was able to
effect but little. Time alone could teach the nation at large
to gradually assimilate as much of western civilization as
was necessary for its welfare and development. The bulk
of the population was as sluggishly inert as ever, and so
it was to remain for another century. Indeed I may here
say, once for all, that, strictly speaking, that drowsy colossus,
the Russian people, has no history worth recording till the
great awakening which followed upon the disasters of the
Crimean War. *Till* then the history of Russia is mainly
the history of her diplomacy, and the wars resulting therefrom. She had to assert herself in Europe in order to
remain European; but, her position abroad once definitively
assured, she could then put her own house in order in her
own way, and at her own time. Thus Russia's foreign
conquests during the eighteenth century were, in a certain
sense, the necessary preliminaries of the domestic reforms
of the nineteenth century. Viewed from her own point of
view, all her aggressions and usurpations during this period,

were but the successive phases of a determined struggle to carry out the programme of Peter the Great in its entirety. The other great Powers would have confined this semi-Asiatic interloper within her native steppes; she herself, as represented by her ablest rulers, now saw in every fresh advance, westwards and southwards, an additional guarantee of her present stability and her future progress. From this point of view, the victories of Kunnersdorf and of Chesme were just as inevitable and as beneficial as the emancipation of the serfs.

And, fortunately for Russia, she possessed at this most critical period, in the person of Andrei Ivanovich Ostermann, a statesman of the first rank, who, for the next fifteen years, was to direct her foreign policy with the unerring instinct of genius. As his name suggests, Ostermann was of German extraction. He was born at Bochum in Westphalia, in 1686, of respectable and highly intelligent middle-class parents, and, after receiving an excellent education, made the grand tour, and, while in Holland, cultivated the acquaintance of the Dutch sailor, Cornelius Kruse, who had risen in the Russian service to the rank of Vice-Admiral, and had, besides, a standing commission from Peter the Great to pick up promising young men for him, wherever he could find them. Young Ostermann became Kruse's secretary, and accompanied him, in that capacity, to Russia. In 1717 the Tsar came on board Kruse's vessel, and enquired if he had any young man among his crew, capable of writing a good business letter. Kruse at once recommended Ostermann, who, by this time, had learnt Russian thoroughly, and Peter was so pleased with Ostermann's performance on this occasion, that, after submitting him to the searching test of a four hours' examination, he appointed him his private secretary. Quickly discovering that his new protégé understood German, Dutch, Italian,

French and Latin as well as Russian, the Tsar transferred
him to his Chancellery, as translator, where he speedily
became the right hand of the Vice-Chancellor Shafirov,
whom he materially assisted during the troublesome negotiations which terminated in the Peace of the Pruth. The
diplomatic talent Ostermann displayed on this occasion, as
well as on a subsequent mission to Berlin, to persuade
Prussia to take active measures against Sweden, so impressed
the Tsar, that he bound down the young diplomatist not
to quit the Russian service till the conclusion of a general
peace. Ostermann was one of the two commissioners sent
to treat with Sweden at the congress of Nystadt, in 1720,
and, for his services on this occasion, was created a Baron
and a Privy Councillor. Peter, moreover, provided him
with a bride in the person of the wealthy Martha Ivanovna Stoyeshosevaya, a connection which materially strengthened his position in Russia. Counting by years, Ostermann
was still a very young diplomatist, being scarcely three
and thirty; but, in truth, he was one of those men who
never can be said to have been young. Even in his teens
he had been remarkable for his precocious subtlety and a
cold passionless way of regarding life. The French Minister,
Campredon, was right in describing him as devoured by
ambition, and he had a perfect genius for attaining his
ends by circuitous methods, dextrously removing rivals out
of his way without seeming to move in the matter himself.
He was also afflicted with irritating fits of forgetfulness,
when he would, for the moment, lose all recollection of
certain languages which it did not suit him to remember,
and he used his very maladies (gout, for instance, from
which he suffered severely) as diplomatic subterfuges. Com-
pared, indeed, with the rough and brutal ways of the *canaille*
by which he was surrounded, Ostermann's methods seem
almost feline. He was a quiet, noiseless, seemingly inoffen-

sive man, who always guarded his tongue, and, as the Russian proverb has it, 'was a knife in nobody's eye.' But because he shrunk from violence and hated a fracas, he was no poltroon, as some have supposed, and, as we shall see, could face danger, and death itself, with imperturbable composure. The great blot on his career was the treacherous part he played in the plot to ruin his official chief, Shafirov, whom he supplanted as Vice-Chancellor towards the end of the reign of Peter the Great. But this is the only crime that can fairly be brought against him, and he possessed many virtues which were quite unintelligible to his contemporaries. Thus he was faithful in a faithless, clean-handed in a corrupt, and humane in a cruel age. His abilities, both as a statesman and a diplomatist, are beyond cavil or question, and his services to the country of his adoption were inestimable. He gave himself up, heart and soul, to the service of Russia, and was always ready to sacrifice his personal interests to her advantage. But, perhaps, the highest tribute to Ostermann's zeal and capacity is to be found in the eulogium pronounced upon him by his master, on an ever memorable occasion. 'Ostermann,' said Peter the Great to those gathered around his death-bed, 'Ostermann is indispensable to Russia. He best knows her needs, and he is the only one of us who has never made a diplomatic blunder.'

Menshikov, who became supreme in the latter days of Catherine I, had the wisdom to leave the control of foreign affairs entirely in the hands of the Vice-Chancellor. Continental diplomacy at this time was dominated by England, or, rather, by the foreign prince who sat upon the English throne, acting through an obsequious Whig ministry and Whig parliament, who secretly despised, yet could not dispense with, him. The anxiety of George I as to the safety of his Hanoverian Electorate, made it his main ob-

ject to form a league strong enough to maintain the existing
state of things in Europe against all possible disturbers of
the peace. This policy led him to draw near to France,
who, exhausted by the ruinous War of the Spanish Succession, was also pacifically disposed, and to regard Russia
with the utmost suspicion. The quarrel between England
and Russia had first begun when Peter the Great intervened
in German affairs after the overthrow of Charles XII.
Peter's high-handed procedure on that occasion had given
great offence to King George, and a rupture between the
two Powers was only with difficulty avoided. The protection accorded by Catherine to the young Duke of Holstein,
who had recently married (May 21st, 1725) the Tsaritsa's
eldest daughter Anne, still further alarmed the sensitive,
suspicious Elector, and, in the spring of 1726, an English
fleet was actually sent to Reval, under Admiral Wager,
who was also the bearer of a singularly insolent despatch
which categorically forbade the Russian fleet to put to sea,
until satisfactory explanations had been given of the state
of the Tsarita's armaments. The only result of this menace
was to throw Russia into the arms of England's enemies,
the Empress, by Ostermann's advice, at once acceding
(6th Aug. 1726) to the Austro-Spanish League, which had
been formed (30th April, 1725) to counterpoise the growing
Anglo-French influence on the continent. However, the
death of Catherine (16th May, 1727), the expulsion of
the Duke of Holstein from Russia by Menshikov in
August of the same year, and the general confusion and
disorganisation in Russia itself during the reign of Catherine's
successor, Peter II (May 1727—Jan. 1730), were so many
additional factors for the preservation of peace.

The short reign of Peter II is chiefly remarkable for the
rise to power of the national reactionary party, under the
leadership of the two great boyar families, the Golitsuins

and the Dolgorukis, who succeeded in overthrowing and exiling Menshikov (Menshikov himself had previously got rid of Tolstoi), but were obliged to tolerate Ostermann, partly because the young Tsar, whose governor he was, would not sacrifice him to their fanaticism, and partly, also, because the Vice-Chancellor had now become more indispensable than ever. But the domination of the old Russian Party speedily came to an end on the death of Peter II, and the elevation to the vacant throne of Anne, Duchess of Courland, the second daughter of Peter the Great's half-brother Ivan V. The oligarchs had incurred the implacable resentment of this masculine Princess by endeavouring, at the outset of her reign, to circumscribe her power within very narrow limits. The attempt was defeated, and "the Republican gentlemen," as the English Minister, Rondeau, calls them, were punished with a rigour, which seemed to aim not so much at the chastisement as at the extinction of the old aristocracy. The Russian gentry, indeed, had little cause to love the Empress Anne, yet they imputed their disasters, principally, to the jealousy and hatred of Anne's prime favourite, Ernst Johan Biren, or Bühren, whom she had brought along with her from Courland, and who brutally tyrannized the court and the nation during the whole course of her reign. The little we know of this sordid and sinister upstart is not very creditable to him. He was the grandson of a groom in the service of Duke James III of Courland, who bestowed upon him a small estate which Biren's father inherited, and where Biren himself was born on Dec. 1st, 1690. After an idle and vagabond youth, he gained a footing at the court of Mittau through the dishonour of his sister, attracted the attention of the Duchess by his handsome face and figure and bluff *bonhomie*, succeeded in supplanting her older paramour, Peter Bestuzhev, and, henceforth, exercised a paramount influence over her. Ambition and anxiety seem to have been the pivots on which this base adventurer's conduct constantly turned, the ambition of remaining the Empress's chief counsellor and an anxiety lest a turn of Fortune's wheel should cast him back into his original nothingness. During the latter years of Anne's reign, Biren increased so enormously in power and riches, that he must have been a marvel to himself as well as to others. His apartments in the Palace adjoined those of the Tsaritsa, and his liveries, furniture and equipages were scarcely less costly than hers. Half the bribes intended for the Russian court passed through his hands. He had estates in Livonia, Courland, Silesia and the Ukraine. His riding-school was one of the sights of the Russian capital. The massive magnificence of his silver plate astonished the French ambassador, and the diamonds of his Duchess [1] were the envy of Princes. The climax of this wonderful elevation was reached when, in the course of June, 1737, the Estates of Courland elected the son of the ostler of Mittau to be their reigning Duke, mainly through golden arguments. Henceforward his most Serene Highness received all the honours due to sovereign Princes.

The one thing that can be said in Biren's favour is that, at any rate during the reign of Anne, he had the good sense not to meddle with affairs of state, being well aware of his own deficiencies. The ostensible head of the Russian Cabinet was Prince Alexius Mikhailovich Cherkasky, an immensely wealthy nobleman, who had rendered signal political services to Anne on her accession, and had been rewarded with the Grand Chancellorship. As, however, Cherkasky was a man of very limited intellect who could

---

[1] She was formerly a Fraulein von Treiden, and bore him several children. It is very probable, however, that Biren's eldest son Peter, subsequently Duke of Courland, was really the son of the Empress Anne.

only converse with the foreign ministers through an interpreter, the conduct of affairs passed inevitably into the
hands of Vice-Chancellor Ostermann, whose position towards
the end of the reign became absolutely unique. At Court
he usually went by the name of "The Oracle," while the
foreign diplomatists, though they were constantly cursing
his devious ambiguous methods, admitted unanimously that
he was the one man in Russia who understood politics
thoroughly. The pivot of Ostermann's political system was
the Austrian Alliance, and he adroitly used it to increase
the influence of Russia in Europe. On the outbreak of the
War of the Polish Succession (1733—35), when France, on
the death of Augustus II, attempted to replace Stanislaus
Leszczynski on the throne of Poland, Russia not only
defeated the scheme by her vigorous intervention on
behalf of the Elector of Saxony, Augustus III, but was
even able (1735) to directly assist the Kaiser, by sending
an army of 20,000 men to the Rhine, under Peter Lacy,
a step which induced triumphant France to come to terms
with Austria more readily than she would otherwise have
done. It was the first time that a Russian army had ever
been seen in Central Europe, and the statesmen of France
and England were profoundly impressed by the sight of
these "well-disciplined barbarians." The Polish Succession
question was scarcely settled when the naturally pacific
Ostermann considered it necessary, again in alliance with
Austria, to embark in a struggle with the Porte, resulting
in a war which lasted four years, and cost Russia 100,000
men and millions of rubles. In return for these immense
sacrifices, she won but a single city, Azov, with a small
circumjacent district at the mouth of the Don, to contemporary observers a somewhat lame and impotent conclusion.
Yet, after all, more had been gained than was immediately
apparent. In the first place, this was the first war waged

against Turkey by Russia, in which the latter had been everywhere victorious. Only the utter collapse of the Austrians had prevented the Empress Anne on this occasion from anticipating and realizing the ambitious dreams of Catherine II, and, in any case, the ancient illusion of Ottoman invincibility was for ever dissipated. It was now clear to all the world that 10,000 janissaris and spahis were no match, in a fair field, for half that number of grenadiers and hussars. In the second place, Russia's signal and unexpected successes in the steppes had immensely increased her prestige in Europe. It was something strange and startling to see the Muscovite ambassador at Stambul competing with his French colleague there on equal terms, and at last both France and England grew equally apprehensive of the sudden rise of this new Power, which was beginning "to have a great deal to say in the affairs of Europe." [1] But perhaps the most striking tribute to the improved position of Russia during the war, was the anxiety displayed by Great Britain, towards the end of it, to enter into a diplomatic alliance with her. In 1734, when Ostermann himself had pressed for such a treaty, the English Cabinet had, with scant courtesy, declined to even entertain the idea of such a thing; in 1738, on the contrary, they offered their friendship with almost embarrassing insistence. But it was now the Russian Vice-Chancellor's turn to be diplomatically coy. His own eagerness for the alliance abated in proportion to the growing impatience of Rondeau to conclude it, and, while assuring the English Minister of the unalterable benevolence of the Tsaritsa towards the King of Great Britain, he dextrously eluded every attempt to extract from him a definitive treaty.

The plans of Ostermann had been materially assisted by

---

[1] Rondeau, the British Minister at St. Petersburg, to his Court.

the military genius of two soldiers, foreigners like himself, both of whom had identified themselves with the new Russia created by Peter the Great; I mean, of course, Burkhard Münnich and Peter Lacy.   Münnich (born 1683) sprang from a sturdy stock of Oldenburg squires, renowned for generations for their engineering talent, and had the privilege of learning the rudiments of the science of war under no less a captain than Prince Eugene.   After serving with distinction in the war of the Spanish Succession he was hesitating whether he should offer his sword to Charles XII or Peter I, when the sudden death of the Swedish hero determined him in favour of the Russian Tsar.   In 1721, he accepted the post of Lieutenant-General in the Russian service, and, for the next twelve years, devoted himself to the completion of the Ladoga Canal, Peter's gigantic scheme for making St. Petersburg the commercial as well as the political capital of his Empire.   For this standing monument of his engineering skill, Münnich was created by Anne, in rapid succession, War Minister, Field Marshal and Governor of St. Petersburg, while his brilliant services in the war of the Polish Succession and the Turkish War, were rewarded by vast estates.   Münnich was one of those men who make a better figure in adversity than in prosperity.   His most intimate friends used to protest that, from the moment that the Marshal's bâton was placed in his hands, his character materially deteriorated,   His latent but altogether extravagant vanity now began to assert itself, and, not content with his numerous offices and dignities, he began to meddle with the departments of finance and commerce, nay, at last, he even aspired to a place in the Cabinet, and aimed at ousting Ostermann from the control of foreign affairs. But the wily Vice-Chancellor was more than a match for this political tyro, and he contrived to keep Münnich in his proper place by hinting to Biren that the handsome,

elegant and graceful Field Marshal was bent upon supplanting him in the Empress's personal favour. The jealous
Courlander at once took the alarm, and henceforth was
careful to keep the insinuating soldier at a safe distance
from the Palace.

Unlike his meddlesome colleague, Peter Lacy had the
good sense to abstain altogether from political intrigues.
This gallant officer was born at Killedy, County Limerick,
in 1678, and adopted the military profession while still a
lad. His first taste of war was at the siege of Limerick,
and, on the capitulation of that town, he fled with Sars-
field to France. While Münnich had learnt the art of war
under Marlborough and Eugene, Lacy had had the equally
illustrious Catinat for his master, and, at the conclusion of
the War of the Spanish Succession, was introduced to Peter
the Great by the Duke du Croy, and took a conspicuous
part in the Great Northern War, emerging from the struggle
with the rank of a Lieutenant-General. He won his Marshal's *bâton* in the War of the Polish Succession, and was
Münnich's right hand in the Turkish War, but the supercilious Westphalian and the irascible Irishman could never
agree, and their want of harmony frequently endangered
the success of their strategy.

The last years of Anne were brightened by a domestic
event which promised to perpetuate the dynasty. In August
1740, the Empress had the satisfaction of holding in her
arms at the font, the long and eagerly expected heir to
the throne. The little Prince, Ivan VI of tragic memory,
(Anne, his sole sponsor, named him after her own father)
was the son of the Princess of Mecklenburg, the Empress's
niece, whom, on the death of the girl's mother (her own
favourite sister, Catherine Ivanovna), she had adopted,
and whom she loved like a daughter. The young lady
who, in 1733, was received into the Greek Church under

the name of Anne Leopoldovna, was anything but beautiful, and those who, like Lady Rondeau, only knew her in
her shy awkward girlhood, thought her stupid; but she was
a round-faced, pleasant-looking blonde, very easy-tempered
and good-natured, if somewhat indolent and lackadaisical,
and her aunt had intended, from the very first, that she
should be the mother of the future Tsar. When the girl
was still in her earlier teens, the Empress despatched Grand
Chamberlain Löwenwolde abroad, to select a husband for
her, and, by the advice of the Count of Vienna, he fixed
upon the youthful Prince Anthony Ulrik of Brunswick-Bevern,
who was sent to Russia forthwith, and also educated at the
Tsaritsa's expense. Thus the young couple grew up under
the very eyes of the Empress, but of anything like a
mutual inclination there was no trace. The Princess's visible
dislike of her fiancé suggested to the aspiring mind of the
Duke of Courland the audacious idea of marrying his own
son Peter to the Tsaritsa's niece, although he was only fifteen
years of age, and therefore five years the Princess's junior.
He durst not, indeed, propose such a thing to the Empress, but
he insinuated the idea to Anne Leopoldovna herself, through
one of the Tsaritsa's female buffoons, the Princess Shcherba-
tova. The rebuff he received, however, not only made
him abandon altogether his impudent project, but filled
him with an inextinguishable hatred of the Princess herself.
But he could not prevent the wedding, and, in July 1739,
the young people exchanged bridal rings in the church of
Our Lady of Kazan, and, ten months later, the Grand
Duchess, as they now called her, was brought to bed of
a fine boy whom the Empress at once appropriated, carrying him off to her own room, where his cradle was
henceforth placed and jealously guarded, nobody being
allowed to perform any service for the little gentleman
except in the presence of the Tsaritsa or the Duchess of

Courland. Six weeks later a still more momentous event brought home to the Duke of Courland the extreme instability of his power. On Sunday, 16th October, the Tsaritsa, while at table, was seized with a fit, and removed insensible to her bed, which she was never to leave again alive. Biren, horribly agitated, summoned Cherkasky and Alexius Bestuzhev (whom Biren had recently introduced into the Cabinet as a counterpoise to Ostermann) to the Palace, to advise him what to do; but they could only suggest that Ostermann should first be consulted, and both Ministers proceeded straightway to the Vice-Chancellor's residence, in the same carriage. Ostermann opined that the Grand Duke Ivan should at once be proclaimed successor to the throne, in conformity with the known wishes of the Tsaritsa, but declined to commit himself to any decision as to who should be Regent, well aware that Biren coveted that post for himself. On the return of the two Ministers to the Palace, where they now found Münnich and Löwenwolde closeted with the Duke of Courland, they delivered their message, Münnich stepping aside the while so as not to be obliged to speak prematurely; but Biren, determined that his rival should not escape responsibility, called to him: "Count, do you hear what the Cabinet Ministers say about the Government?"—"No, your Highness," replied Münnich, "I do not hear."—"They say," continued Biren, "that they don't want things here to be as they are in Poland where many rule instead of one."—This was an obvious hint to those present to declare themselves, and so Bestuzhev took it, for it was now that he pronounced the fateful words which were ultimately to prove the ruin of everyone present except himself: "I think," he exclaimed, "that nobody has a better right to be Regent than your Highness!"— "And yet," he added immediately afterwards, as if frightened at his own words, "and yet it will seem strange to

2

foreign Powers if we pass over the father and mother of the Emperor." Biren gloomily admitted as much, and fell a-musing, while Cherkasky whispered something in Löwen-wolde's ear. "Don't whisper, speak up!" cried the latter, and then Cherkasky said aloud that it was indispensable to elect the Duke of Courland, whereupon Münnich, not to be behindhand with the rest, also aquiesced: "I think myself," continued the Field Marshal boldly, "that it would be very deplorable if the Princess Anne had any share in the government. You know what a brute her father is, and if he came here, he would certainly wring all our necks. As for her husband—well, he has served under me for a couple of campaigns, and I don't know to this day whether he is fish or flesh."—This was encouraging for Biren, but as yet he durst not take any further step, and so nothing was decided that evening. A council of magnates, held next day, overawed by the chief dignitaries of the Empire, was easily brought to beg Biren to accept the regency in the name of the Russian nation, and he acceded to their lukewarm entreaties with an affectation of reluctance that deceived nobody. It now remained for him to obtain the sanction of the dying Empress to his appointment, but here he encountered unexpected difficulties. Anne, indeed, readily signed the ukaz appointing the infant Ivan her successor, and early in the morning of the 18th October, the guards, drawn up in front of the Palace, took the oath of allegiance to the new Sovereign, man by man, while the Tsarevna Elisabeth, the Princess Anne, her husband Prince Anthony, and all the Ministers, Generals, Senators and Prelates did the same in the Chapel of the Winter Palace. But when it came to appointing her favourite Regent, the Tsaritsa hesitated, not from any diminution of affection, but from a true regard for his future safety. Her clear common-sense told her that the only

possible way for the man she loved to disarm the resentment
of his innumerable enemies, who were only awaiting her
death to fall upon him, was to descend from his already
untenable position as speedily and as gracefully as possible.
But the infatuated adventurer, blinded by ambition, could
not see the abyss already yawning at his feet, imagining
that he had only to continue his authority in order to
maintain it. Again and again the Empress tried to save him
from himself. When he handed her the petition for the
Regency, she thrust it impatiently beneath her pillow.
"Duke, duke!" she cried piteously, "my heart is sad for
thee, for thou art compassing thine own ruin!" Immediately
afterwards she sent for Ostermann, who, this time really
crippled by gout, was conveyed to the Palace in a sedan
chair, to the infinite chagrin of Biren who had surrounded
the Tsaritsa with his creatures, and suffered nobody, not
even her own family, to approach her without his permission. The unwonted spectacle of the Vice-Chancellor
out of doors (he had not quitted his own house for five
years) was the first intimation the public had of the dangerous condition of the Tsaritsa, for her illness had hitherto
been kept a profound secret, and the mere allusion to the
possibility of her decease was treated as a capital offence.
What passed between Anne and Ostermann is not known;
but the Vice-Chancellor must have confirmed the Empress in
her resolution, for she kept all the petitions and other
documents presented to her and made no sign. Five
anxious days elapsed. At first Anne rallied, and it was
hoped that the skill of her Portuguese physician, Sanchez,
might prolong her life for some months, though, from the
nature of her malady, a permanent cure was well-nigh
impossible. On the 22nd she was so much better that
there was some talk of a complete recovery, but on the
26th the Tsaritsa had a relapse which left no doubt as

to her approaching end. Ostermann and Biren were summoned in haste to her bedside, and, in their presence, she signed her will, leaving the throne to her grand-nephew, Ivan Antonovich, and a so-called "positive declaration," drawn up by Bestuzhev, in favour of Biren's Regency, and signed by 194 dignitaries in the name of the Russian people. The tears and entreaties of her favourite had prevailed at last against her own better judgment. Two days later (Oct. 28th) Anne Ivanovna expired between 9 and 10 o'clock in the evening. Her life, as a whole, had not been a happy one, but few Sovereigns have been so uniformly successful.

The government of Anne was, on the whole, most beneficial. Under Catherine I and Peter II, Russia had stood still, as it were; but under Anne, her advance in every direction was unmistakable. Vigorous measures were taken to arrest the decay and repair the damage done to the State during the haphazard sway of the reactionary party under Peter II, and beneath the watchful eyes of Ostermann and Münnich both the army and the fleet recovered more than their old efficiency. But, on the other hand, the government was needlessly severe, and it showed an unjust partiality for foreigners which the nation could not forgive. Peter the Great, even in the hottest fervour of his reforming zeal, had been very jealous of the national honour. He had employed intelligent foreigners freely, but he had never entrusted to them the foremost places in the realm, which, he maintained, belonged of right to natives alone. Even on his death-bed, he had confided the destiny of Russia to the care of Russians. Unfortunately, when the all-controlling hand of the master had been withdrawn, his pupils began to quarrel among themselves, and their mutual jealousies and hatreds had, as we have seen, ended in the extermination of the Russian Party. Menshikov had ruined

Tolstoi, the Dolgorukis and the Golitsuins had ruined Menshikov, Cherkasky had ruined the Dolgorukis and the Golitsuins. At the death of Anne, the Government was entirely in the hands of foreigners, for the Grand Chancellor, Cherkasky, was a mere cipher. Such a state of things was far too anomalous to last, even under the most favourable conditions. A revolution in favour of the national party had become inevitable, and it was to be accelerated by the suicidal dissensions of the foreigners actually in power. The history of this revolution and its remoter consequences will be set forth in the following pages.

CHAPTER II.

IVAN VI.

Oct. 1740—Dec. 1741.

BIREN Regent—Public humiliation of the new Tsar's father—Biren's measures—
His unpopularity—Discontent of the Princess Anne and of Münnich—
Plot against Biren—Münnich's midnight coup-d'état—Fall of Biren—
Princess Anne proclaimed Regent—Ambition and arrogance of Münnich—Foreign affairs—Death of the Emperor Charles VI—Cynical
behaviour of Frederick of Prussia—Outbreak of the First Silesian War—
Tergiversation of France—Convention of Nymphenburg—Treaty of
Breslau—Münnich's incompetence—His resignation—Foreign policy
of Ostermann—His difficulties—Hostility of France to Russia—Sweden
declares war against Russia—Battle of Vilmanstrand—The Regent's
fondness for Fräulein Mengden—Her liaison with Count Lynar—Dangers of the situation—Alarm of Ostermann—Character of the Marquis
de la Chetardie—A ceremonial squabble—Chetardie's plot in favour
of Elizabeth Petrovna—Popularity of the Tsarevna—Her hatred of
Ostermann—His difficult position—And growing weariness of office.

ON the morning of Oct. 29th, 1740, the day after the
death of the Empress Anne, the dignitaries of the Empire
assembled in the great hall of the Summer Palace (Biren's
usual residence), and Vice-Chancellor Ostermann, after formally
announcing the demise of the Crown, called upon the Procurator-General, Prince Trubetskoi, to read aloud her late
Majesty's last will and testament, appointing her great-
nephew, the Grand Duke Ivan, her successor, and his Serene
Highness the Duke of Courland, Regent, till the little Prince,

FIELD-MARSHAL COUNT MIENNICH.

who was then but five months old, had completed his seventeenth year. The oath of allegiance to Ivan VI was then administered to all who were present, as well as to the regiments of infantry and cavalry drawn up in the front of the Hall, and thus, despite many dismal forebodings, the succession and regency were established as easily and tranquilly as if her late Majesty had simply removed from the Winter Palace where she had died, to the Summer Palace where her favourite now was enthroned.   Nay, so strong did Biren feel already, that on the second day of his regency he proceeded to humiliate the father of the new Sovereign in the most outrageously public manner conceivable.   Prince Anthony, not unnaturally, felt aggrieved at being set aside in favour of a vulgar upstart like Biren. He considered that the ties of blood gave him a natural right to rule in the name of his son, and he freely gave vent to his spleen in the presence of several of the officers of the Semenovsky Guard, of which he was lieutenant-colonel, even going so far as to insinuate that her late Majesty's last will was not a genuine document.   A wise man, in Biren's position, would have winked at a little harmless grumbling under the circumstances ; but his Serene Highness, professing to regard this ebullition of temper as high treason at the very least, resolved to make an example of the offender.   Accordingly, Prince Anthony, was summoned to appear before a general assembly of the Cabinet, the Senate and the Nobility, when the Regent, in his most authoritative manner, asked him for an explanation of his disloyal conduct.   The Prince, instead of asserting himself like a man, had the weakness to burst into tears and confess to a conspiracy, whereupon he was severely lectured by General Ushakov, the director of the terrible Secret Chancellery, who remarked, with a sneer, that if the Prince had been of riper years and of a genius capable of con-

ducting such a design at all, he, Ushakov, should have
considered it his duty to proceed against him for lèse-
majesté.   Thereupon the Regent, with an adroit affectation
of modesty, offered to resign his office in favour of Prince
Anthony, if the assembly thought the latter better fitted
for the post, with the natural result that he was clamorously
petitioned graciously to continue to give Russia the benefit
of his august administration.   The document appointing
him Regent was then read a second time, and signed and
sealed by all present, including Prince Anthony, who was
forthwith deprived of all his offices and charges, and practically banished to the apartments of his consort, whence
he did not venture to emerge till after the fall of his
persecutor.   The minor offenders in the Semenovsky
Guards were subsequently knouted and degraded to the
ranks.[1]

In the opinion of his friends,[2] Biren's position was now
fairly secure, and he even condescended to make a few
bids for popularity.   Thus, he ordered that all the sentinels
on duty should be provided with furs, to protect them from
the severity of the night frosts;[3] he assured an obsequious
meeting of his adherents, whom he addressed in Russian,[4]
that he meant to have no favourites, but would distribute
his graces by order of merit alone; he also addressed himself
to business with commendable diligence; introduced several
wise economies, and issued a new sumptuary law restricting
the use of gold and silver on wearing apparel, to the great
relief of the poorer gentry who had been unable to keep
pace with the late Empress's magnificence.   But it was

---

[1] The best account of this scene will be found in *Finch's Despatches*, Vol. 85
of *Sb. of Imp. Rus. Hist. Soc.*; compare also *Chetardie's Despatches* and
Manstein's Memoirs.

[2] *Finch*, for instance, who applauds his firmness and prophesied his stability.

[3] *Solovev.*   [4] *Chetardie Despatches.*

contrary to the nature of the man to be consistently conciliatory, and the very sight of the tyrant who had trampled
upon them, so long and so cruelly, was odious to all patriotic
Russians. It had been hard to endure Biren the favourite,
even when he shone with a reflected lustre; but Biren the
omnipotent Regent was an abomination. It was monstrous,
people whispered, that this ignorant and supercilious
foreign heretic should sit in the seat of Peter the Great,
simply because he had been the late Empress's paramour!
And to think that the Russian nation was to be saddled
with this interloper for seventeen long years! If, it was
argued, an alien Regent were neçessary at all, who had a
better right to that dignity than the Emperor's own father?
And again, why should the last survivors of Peter's race,
the Tsarevna Elisabeth and her nephew the Duke of Holstein, be passed over? But all this murmuring might have
remained ineffectual if Biren had not hastened to alienate
his most obvious ally, the Tsar's mother, Anne Leopoldovna, and his most useful colleague, Marshal Münnich.
The Princess had never liked Biren, and she had less
reason than ever to like him now. He had usurped the
dignity of Regent, which she considered hers by right of
blood; he had publicly insulted her husband, and he even
bullied her when she protested against the indignities to
which the Prince and herself were subjected. Warm alter-
cations occurred between them every day, for the Princess,
though lazy and good-natured, did not want for spirit when
fairly roused, and it is said that on one occasion the
Regent went so far as to threaten to pack the father and
the mother of his Sovereign off to Germany.[1] Such was
the position of affairs when on Saturday, Nov. 19th, Münnich waited upon the Princess in order to present some cadets

[1] Finch.

for her Highness's choice of pages, and, on being left alone
with him, she, at Ostermann's instigation as many suppose,
complained with tears that, ever since her late Majesty's death,
she herself and the Prince, her husband, had been continually
exposed to the greatest affronts, indeed they were living in such
constant apprehension of the Regent's violence that they
seemed to have no other choice left them than to leave
the country.   She then begged Münnich to use his credit
with the Duke that they might take their child with them.
"Madam," said the Marshal, "have you told this to anyone else?"   The Princess assured him that she had not,
whereupon the Marshal asked her whether she would
honour him with her entire confidence, and, receiving
a satisfactory reply, declared that his duty to his
Sovereign and his abhorrence of the Regent's iniquitous
conduct determined him to risk his life in her Highness's
service, if only he might deliver Russia from this fatal
and tyrannous regency.   In reality Münnich's motives were
by no means so pure as he represented them to be.
Jealousy and wounded vanity were at the bottom of his
conduct.   He had been mainly instrumental in the elevation
of Biren; he had even secretly, and very disreputably,
assisted him in getting rid of Prince Anthony; but Biren,
so far from rewarding his deserts with the coveted dignity
of Generalissimo, had shown little disposition to make an
already dangerous rival still more dangerous.   Münnich,
therefore, resolved to speculate on the gratitude of the
Princess Anne and her husband, and gratify his vengeance
and his ambition at the same time by wiping out Biren altogether.   And now the opportunity had actually arrived,
and he seized it with characteristic promptness.   As the
Preobrazhensky regiment, whose lieutenant-colonel he was,
happened to be on guard next day, the 20th, for the last
time, and its turn would not come again for a week, he

resolved to strike the blow at once, and, quitting the Princess, made all the necessary arrangements for a *coup d'état*. Then, with a singular mixture of audacity and treachery, he went to dine with the Regent and his family, and a few mutual friends. That day Biren was not himself. He told Münnich that he had been much struck during the morning by the dejected gloomy air of the people he had met in the streets, and it seemed to him to bode no good. Münnich airily laughed the matter off, but the usually bluff and boisterous Regent continued silent and pensive throughout the meal. Dinner over, Münnich went back to the Princess and asked her if she had any final orders to give, as all his plans were laid, and he meant to execute his project that very night. The Princess, startled at the suddenness of the affair, asked him what means he meant to employ. "Your Highness must excuse me from telling you," replied Münnich, "but do not be alarmed if I arouse you about 3 o'clock in the morning," and, with these words, he left her, and returned to the Summer Palace, to sup for the last time with the man he was conspiring to destroy. He found the Duke more pensive than ever, and complaining of a lowness of spirits the like of which he had never felt before. All the evening he was but a poor host, and said hardly a word to keep up the conversation. So the Marshal, for the amusement of the other guests, began to talk over his battles, and all the actions he had been in during his forty years of service. Suddenly one of the other guests, Count Loewenwolde, quite innocently, asked Münnich whether he had ever been in any action at night. The oddness of such an ill-timed question, just at that juncture, struck the Field Marshal, especially when he observed the Duke, at the same time, lean forward and anxiously support his head in his hands; but, keeping a good countenance, he replied with seeming indifference, that to be sure he must have been in some action or other at all hours of the twenty-four, since, after all, the precise time of fighting depended so much on the enemy. At 10 o'clock they all retired, and at two the next morning Münnich rose, sent for his adjutant, General Manstein, communicated his plan to him, and bade him go on before, prepare the officers of the Preobrazhensky Guard, and join him with them at the Winter Palace immediately. On arriving there himself, a few moments later, Münnich found the officers all ready, and introduced them into the apartments of the Princess, who, primed beforehand, informed them that the Marshal was acting by her orders, and they were to obey him implicitly. When they had retired to make a draught of the best grenadiers of the regiment, Münnich pressed the Princess to get into her coach and follow under his escort, in order to animate the detachment by her presence; but Anne Leopoldovna's courage failing her at the critical moment, the Marshal, prudently minimizing his risks, did not insist upon the co-operation of so doubtful a coadjutor, but took his leave, and, placing himself at the head of his party, eighty strong, proceeded on foot in full regimentals, to the Summer Palace. On reaching it, Manstein was detached to tell the sentinels that the Field Marshal had been ordered to escort the Princess Anne, who was following in her coach, to communicate to the Regent matters of the utmost consequence. Now there was a picket of an officer and forty men in the gardens, under the very windows of the Duke, and sentinels placed all round the house: if a single man had done his duty, Münnich's enterprise must have failed miserably. No resistance was offered, however, and Manstein, who had orders from Münnich to enter the Palace with twenty fusiliers, arrest the Duke, and, in case of resistance, cut him down without mercy, proceeded up the grand staircase with his men, to the Regent's bedchamber. So secure had Biren felt, that he had not even taken the precaution of locking his doors, and he was sleeping tranquilly by the side of his Duchess, when Manstein awoke him with the intelligence that he was his prisoner, and must follow him to the Winter Palace. Biren, who was no coward, at once leaped from his bed and called for help; but after a desperate struggle, for he kicked and bit to the last, he was bound fast with soldiers' scarves for lack of cords, gagged with a handkerchief, and flung, with nothing but a quilt round him, into Münnich's coach. The Duchess was served the same way, and, her curiosity getting the better of her alarm, she asked who was in command of the expedition. On learning that it was Münnich, her husband's guest of the evening before, she uttered the remarkable words: "Well, I would sooner have believed that God in Heaven could die than that the Field Marshal could have played us this trick!" Before day-break, all Biren's partisans, including his two brothers and his ablest supporter, Count Alexius Bestuzhev, were also arrested, and at nine o'clock the same morning, the Princess Anne, with the title of Grand Duchess, was proclaimed Regent during the minority of her son. That afternoon the whole Courland family was sent off to the fortress of Schlüsselburg; all the acts of Biren's regency were can-celled and their record expunged from the public archives, and a solemn Te Deum was sung in honour of the "happy event." [1] Thus, after a short three weeks, ended the Regency of Biren.

As for the fallen Satrap himself, it must be confessed

---

[1] By far the best account of this smart little revolution is to be found in the Despatches of *Finch* (*Sb. of Imp. Russ. Hist. Soc.*, Vol. 85.), who had all the particulars from Münnich's own mouth. Compare *Manstein Memoirs*; *Chetardie Despatches*, and *Solovev*.

that, considering his numerous atrocities, his punishment
rather erred on the side of leniency than of severity. He
was kept for some weeks in rigorous confinement at Schlüsselburg, and was subjected to many petty indignities and
a searching examination, though, strange to say, without
torture. Finally, the commission appointed to try his case,
condemned him (11th April, 1741) to death by quartering,
but this horrible sentence was commuted, by the clemency
of the kind-hearted Regent (25th April), to banishment for
life to Pelin in Siberia, the house in which he was to
reside being built after a plan actually sketched by his
rival Münnich, who possessed considerable artistic talent.
All Biren's vast property was of course confiscated, including his diamonds valued at 3,000,000 rubles. Henceforth, for two-and-twenty years, the ex-Regent disappears
from the high places of history; but we catch a glimpse
of him, now and then, as a humble suppliant for, or as a
grateful recipient of, small favours. Yet he was to live to
rule his Duchy once more, and to die not unregretted by
the Courlanders.

By this revolution Russia had after all only exchanged
the rule of one rapacious foreigner for another, for Münnich
was fully determined to suck all the advantage possible
out of his signal service. He could not indeed prevent
the Princess, the moment she heard of the success of
the *coup d'état*, from sending for Vice-Chancellor Ostermann, the "oracle" who always had to be consulted before
anything was done; but he was quite determined to occupy
the first place himself in any readjustment of affairs, and
to keep his colleagues as much in the background as possible. His vanity was so enormous that he placed no
bounds to his self-sufficiency, and he complacently flattered
himself that his position was practically unassailable. The
new Regent being an indolent, timid young woman of

twenty-two, infinitely good-natured and incredibly stupid, he argued that from her he had nothing to fear, and, besides, was she not under the deepest of obligations to him? The Regent's husband was so insignificant that even his colourless consort seemed a woman of character by contrast. Münnich could therefore venture to disregard him altogether. The Vice-Chancellor was still a power in the state, but he was growing old and infirm, and, apparently, stood absolutely alone. So Münnich, who, for the moment, was as much in the favour of the Regent as ever the Duchess of Marlborough was in the favour of Queen Anne, readily persuaded her to consent to a distribution of offices whereby he became everything, and everyone else nothing. The two nominally highest dignities in the Empire, the Grand Chancellorship and the Vice-Chancellorship, were entrusted respectively to two Russian noblemen of tried incapacity, Prince Alexius Cherkasky and Count Michael Golovkin. Prince Anthony was, as a matter of form, appointed Generalissimo, while Ostermann was relegated to the harmless office of Grand Admiral! For himself Münnich invented a new office unknown in Russia before and since. He called himself "Premier-Minister," with the supreme control of foreign affairs, and as, moreover, he was already War Minister, Lieutenant-Colonel of the Preobrazhensky Guards, President of the School of Cadets, Chief of the Militia of the Ukraine, Director of the Ladoga Canal, and Colonel of half-a-dozen regiments of the line, his patronage was enormous and his authority almost unlimited.

The new Government had scarce been constituted when it was confronted by a political event of the last importance, which was to exercise the minds of statesmen and disturb the equilibrium of Europe for more than a generation; I mean, of course, the outbreak of the War, or rather, Wars of the Austrian Succession.

On Oct. 20th, 1740, died the Kaiser Charles VI, leaving all his hereditary dominions to his youthful daughter Maria Theresa, by virtue of a Pragmatic Sanction, to which, after infinite trouble and many sacrifices, her father had secured the solemn adhesion of all the European Powers except Bavaria. The claims of Augustus of Saxony, such as they were, [1] had been abandoned on consideration of the Kaiser procuring the election of that Prince to the throne of Poland ; France and Spain had been pacified by an ingenious system of exchanges, whereby the former obtained Lorraine for next to nothing, and the latter was allowed the benefit of an advantageous readjustment of her possessions in Italy. Nevertheless the event proved that the aged Prince Eugene had been right, and that the only way of absolutely guaranteeing the stability of the Pragmatic Sanction, was for the Court of Vienna to have kept on foot an army of 180,000 men. Charles VI had hardly been laid in his coffin when Charles Albert, Elector of Bavaria, openly laid claim [2] to all the hereditary possessions of Maria Theresa. His pretensions, however, would have remained pretensions but for the simultaneous action of the King of Prussia. That young Prince had inherited from his father, who hoarded troops as a miser hoards money, a superb army of 76,000 men, a treasure of 8,700,000 thalers, and not a penny of debt, and he had secretly determined not to let this immense political capital lie idle, but invest it in the acquisition of fresh territory. The defenceless condition of Maria Theresa was his

---

[1] Augustus claimed a portion of the inheritance in the name of his wife, who was the eldest daughter of Kaiser Joseph I, although the Grand Duchess, on her marriage, had solemnly renounced all her putative rights.

[2] The Elector of Bavaria claimed the whole of the Austrian hereditary estates as the descendant of Anne, the eldest daughter of Kaiser Ferdinand I, on the baseless assumption that Ferdinand had settled the succession upon the children of this Princess, in case of the extinction of male heirs, in the Archduchy of Austria and the Kingdom of Bohemia.

opportunity, and he proceeded to make the most of it, with a cynical disregard of political morality which has rarely been equalled and never surpassed. At first, indeed, his movements were so mysterious that they excited the suspicion even of his sworn allies. "The conduct and the language of the King of Prussia," wrote Amelot, the French Minister of Foreign Affairs, to La Chetardie, the French Ambassador in Russia, in the course of December 1740, "are at present an inexplicable mystery. He has recognised the archduchess as Queen of Bohemia and Hungary, and universal heiress of the late Emperor; he has given both to Holland and England assurances that he will faithfully maintain the engagements he has entered into for the guarantee of the Pragmatic Sanction, and, at the same time, he has marched off 25,000 men in the direction of Silesia, which they say he means to seize." Nay, more, on the very eve of his departure for the front, the King of Prussia gave General Botta, the Austrian Ambassador at Vienna, the strongest assurances that he meditated no design which would not be *for the service and advantage of the Queen of Hungary*.[1] A few days later, 16 Dec. 1740, Frederick, in the spirit of a magnanimous highwayman, after offering Maria Theresa his alliance and 2,000,000 thalers, on condition that she instantly ceded Lower Silesia to him forthwith, an offer which the high-spirited Princess naturally rejected with scorn, crossed the frontier, and, by the end of January 1741, had occupied the whole province with the exception of the fortresses of Glogau, Brieg and Neisse, in which the surprised and outnumbered Austrians took refuge.

The prompt success of the First Silesian War, as Frederick II's act of brigandage is generally called, encouraged all the

---

[1] Amelot to Chetardie, Dec. 1740. "Ce prince, depuis qu'il est sur le trône," he adds significantly, "n'a pris conseil que de lui-même, et personne ne peut pénétrer ses vues." *Sb. of Imp. Russ. Hist. Soc.*, Vol. 92.

other enemies of the Queen of Hungary to throw off the
mask.   The most powerful and dangerous of these enemies
was France, who, after an eclipse of a quarter of a century,
had become, once again, the paramount Power of Europe.
The cardinal motive of her policy for generations had been
the depression of the House of Hapsburg; but in return for
Lorraine, she had so solemnly pledged herself to the late
Kaiser to guarantee the Pragmatic Sanction, that at first
Ostermann felt justified in relieving the fears of England
on this head. Very shortly, however, alarming news reached
St. Petersburg from Paris. When Prince Cantemir, the
Russian Ambassador there, formally invited Cardinal Fleury
to support the Queen of Hungary, the aged prelate evasively
replied that that was the business of the Powers which had
guaranteed the Pragmatic Sanction, which France had not.
Upon Cantemir expressing his surprise and disgust at such
an answer, "when the ink of the treaty signed between
France and the late Emperor was scarcely dry," the Cardinal floundered into such absurd contradictions, that Cantemir, for very shame, refrained from reporting them. [1]   As
a matter of fact, Fleury still desired peace, but the war
party, headed by the brilliant Marshal de Bellisle, was too
strong for him, and the old statesman was obliged to give
way. Events now moved forward rapidly. By the Convention of Nymphenburg (May 28, 1741) a triple alliance
to despoil Maria Theresa of her hereditary possessions, was
contracted between France, Spain, and the Elector of Bavaria,
the two former Powers engaging, moreover, to guarantee the
imperial crown to the Elector, and on June 5th France and
Prussia concluded a defensive alliance at Breslau, in the
same sense, to which Augustus of Saxony speedily acceded.
   The case of the Queen of Hungary now seemed so de-

---

[1] Cantemir to Ostermann, in *Solovev*. *Ist. Ros* XXI.

sperate, that all her friends urged her to come to terms
with her numerous enemies, and sacrifice a part to save
the bulk of her domains, this she refused to do and applied
to her allies for help. Unfortunately for her, Russia, the
ally on whom she mainly depended for active assistance,
was swayed at that moment by Münnich, the one Russian
minister who was unfavourably disposed towards the Court
of Vienna, and therefore inclined to listen to her adversaries,
especially when they came to him as they did with bribes
and cajoleries. Frederick of Prussia, always well informed,
had lost no time in gratifying Münnich's avarice and flattering his vanity at the same time, by sending him his
portrait in brilliants and a ring from his finger accompanied
by an enormous gratuity, receiving in return a renewal of
an old defensive treaty between Prussia and Russia, sufficiently explicit to bind the hands of the latter for a time.
This, however, was the last piece of mischief which Münnich
was destined to accomplish. His boundless rapacity (he
had harvested more in two months than Biren had done in
his first seven years) and his outrageous insolence had
become too much at last even for the long-suffering Regent,
who began to feel that even gratitude had its limits, and
readily listened to Ostermann when he represented to her
that the Premier-Minister's ignorance of affairs was damaging
Russia, both at home and abroad, and that a reconstruction
of the Cabinet was therefore indispensably necessary. The
immediate effect of this representation was the Ukaz of
28 Jan./8 Febr. 1741, whereby Ostermann was reinstated
in the direction of foreign affairs, domestic affairs being
entrusted to Cherkasky and Golovkin, while Münnich's
jurisdiction was limited to the army and the Ladoga Canal.
Enraged at a repartition of offices in which he had not
even been consulted, Münnich, believing himself to be indispensable, sent in his resignation (March 14) and was

inexpressibly mortified to find it accepted with alacrity, though he professed to receive it as "the greatest favour which the Regent could bestow upon him." A Ukaz, published the same afternoon, set forth that in view of the age of the Premier Minister (he was only fifty-six) and of his desire to be relieved of all his employments, his Majesty had seen fit to grant his request, and, as if to complete the Marshal's humiliation, his dismissal was ordered to be proclaimed by roll of drum, a ceremony constantly practised whenever anyone had been disgraced and consequently exiled to Siberia. In Münnich's case, this was simply an inadvertence, there being absolutely no precedent for such a gracious dismissal as his. His wounded feelings were soothed, however, by a public apology from the Senate and a pension of 15,000 rubles (£3,000).

And now Ostermann, the sagacious Palinurus who, for the last five and twenty years, had steered the ship of state through so many storms, returned to the helm once more, and during the next nine months, amidst ever in-creasing difficulties, both at home and abroad, which finally overwhelmed him, he was to justify the expectations of his admiring friends and the fears of his bitterest enemies. For the first time in his life his abilities had absolutely full play. Hitherto they had always been subordinated to circumstances or the will of reigning favourites, but now, for the moment, he stood alone, without rival or equal. "Count Ostermann," wrote the French Ambassador, La Chetardie, to his Court, "has never been so great and powerful as he is now, it is not too much to say that he is Tsar of all Russia. He has to do with a Prince and Princess who, owing to their age and the way they have been brought up, can have neither wisdom nor experience, and their youth will always render them sensible to the representations which Count Ostermann will always be able knowingly to insinuate while he himself exercises sovereign authority." [1] In this there is much exaggeration. Ostermann's position, as we shall see, was never so stable as it appeared; but it may safely be said that during the remainder of 1741, he practically ruled the Empire.

Ostermann's policy, as I have already explained, was based upon the Austrian Alliance. He had therefore guaranteed the Pragmatic Sanction with the deliberate intention of defending it, and had carefully laid his plans for eternalising his name and serving Russia at the same time. [2] The sudden irruption of the King of Prussia into Silesia, the defection of France and the treachery of Saxony had, however, annihilated his project. Old in statecraft as he was, he had not calculated upon such a cynical disregard of solemn treaties. He stigmatized the invasion of Silesia as "an ugly business," and when, after Frederick's first successes, the confederates showed their hands still more plainly, and the Prussian Minister, Mardefeldt, officially informed Ostermann of the partition treaty between Saxony, Prussia and Bavaria, whereby the Elector of Saxony was to receive Upper Silesia, Lower Austria and Moravia, with the title of king formerly attaching to the latter province; Prussia, all Lower Silesia; and Bavaria, Bohemia, Upper Austria and the Tyrol, the Russian Foreign Minister burst into sharp and bitter reproaches, and sarcastically enquired whether this was the way in which Saxony meant to manifest the devotion she had always expressed for the House of Austria? What especially alarmed Ostermann was the design of re-establishing a kingdom of Moravia in perpetuity for Saxony, as he shrewdly guessed that such an arrangement must inevitably be accompanied by a surrender of the Crown of Poland to Stanislaus Leszczynski, the French King's

[1] Chetardie to Amelot.
[2] Do. do. 25th April, 1741.

father-in-law, whom he (Ostermann) had succeeded in excluding, only five years before, at the War of the Polish Succession, [1] in which case Russia would be directly threatened. He had already sent a strong note of remonstrance to the King of Prussia, and had assured the Courts of the Hague and St. James's of his readiness to concur in any just measures for preserving the indivisibility of the Austrian domains; but before he had time to send an army into Prussia, as the English ministers earnestly pressed him to do (they themselves, by the way, despite his urgent demands for co-operation, moving not a finger), [2] France had already saddled him with a war close at home, which effectually prevented him from sending any active assistance to the hard-pressed Queen of Hungary.

Russia, as the natural ally of Austria, was very obnoxious to France, indeed it was only the accident of the Russian alliance which now seemed to stand between Austria and ruin. To sever that alliance, and, if possible, to drive Russia back into the semi-barbarism from which she had scarcely emerged, was the object that French statesmen constantly set before them. "Russia, in respect to the equilibrium of the north," wrote Cardinal Fleury to Chetardie, the French minister at St. Petersburg, [3] "has mounted to too high a degree of power, its union with the House of Austria is extremely dangerous." The most obvious method of rendering the Russian alliance unserviceable to the Queen

---

[1] See Bain: *Pupils of Peter the Great.* Chap. VI.

[2] Harrington to Finch, 14 Feb. 1741, and Finch to Harrington, March 11. Ostermann's plan was for two Dutch-Hessian-Hanoverian Army Corps to coöperate, by way of Magdeburg and Bremen respectively, with a Russian army advancing through Pomerania. The English Ministry, however, alarmed at the formidable nature of the league against the Queen of Hungary, considered it more prudent to bring about an accommodation between her and the King of Prussia.

[3] See the secret instructions of Fleury to Chetardie in *Sb. of Imp. Ist. Rus. Ob.* Tome XCII.

of Hungary was by implicating Russia in hostilities with some other State in the North, whose friendship, might be regarded by the French as useful and permanent. Such a State was Sweden. Sweden, though she had descended from her ancient rank of a first-class Power, was still a considerable State whose alliance had a marketable value. The possession of Finland placed her within a day's march of the Russian capital, the possession of Pomerania gave her an entry into the very heart of the moribund *Reich*, and the nimbus of her former military glories added not a little to her prestige. Moreover, ever since the Thirty Years' War, a community of interests had closely united France and Sweden, and though Charles XII, from personal ill-will, and his successor Chancellor Horn, from political consider-ations, had reversed the traditional policy of Sweden, there had always been a strong French party in the country, and, in 1738, this French Party, known in history as the *Hats*, came to the front. Glory and honour were its watchwords, it aimed at nothing less than recovering the lost Baltic Provinces, and, from the first, it assumed a menacing and irritating attitude towards Russia. Instigated by France whose ample subsidies, paid three years in advance, had replenished their empty coffers, and encouraged by the assurances of La Chetardie that a simultaneous rising in Russia itself in favour of the Tsarevna Elizabeth, would paralyze the Muscovite resistance, the Swedish Government, on the most frivolous pretexts, formally declared war against Russia in the beginning of August, 1741.

Ostermann, however, had been apprised, months before-hand, of what was coming, and the Swedish declaration found him quite prepared for every eventuality. More than one hundred thousand of the best Russian troops were already under arms in Finland, and, on the last day of August, Marshal Lacy, who had been appointed Commander-in-Chief, departed for the front. Three days after taking the field, the gallant Irishman utterly defeated the Swedish General, Wrangel, under the very walls of the frontier fortress of Vilmanstrand, which was carried by assault two hours later after a gallant resistance. The total Swedish loss amounted to 5,500 men with all their artillery and stores, indeed only a fragment of the army escaped, and Wrangel and his staff were among the prisoners. On arriving at the capital to report his success, Lacy was presented to the Regent, who did him the honour to kiss him on both cheeks, and conferred upon him an estate of the value of £10,000. The same evening all the Foreign Ministers were invited to court to present their congratulations, and the British Minister, Finch, who was present, and keenly enjoyed the discomfiture of his diplomatic rivals, tells us that Herr von Mardefeldt, the Prussian Envoy, made but a sorry appearance on the occasion, and was awkward enough in wishing joy, while Mons. de la Chetardie was obliged to stand and hear more about the great victory than was quite to his liking.

The rout of Vilmanstrand had relieved Ostermann of all fears from without, and apparently he was now more secure than he had ever been; but, at this very time, a domestic incident occurred, which struck at the very foundation of his influence.

Some years before her marriage, Anne Leopoldovna had been suspected of entertaining a dangerous tenderness for the Saxon Minister, Lynar, "an uncommonly pretty fellow", as the then English Minister, Rondeau, had called him, of whose company she was very fond. Before she had time to compromise herself, however, her aunt, the rigorous and circumspect Empress Anne, induced Lynar to return to Saxony for the benefit of his health, and hastily wedded her niece to Prince Anthony of Brunswick, whom the Princess secretly despised as a milksop. The union was harmonious enough during the Empress's lifetime and the Biren regency, (the instinct of self-preservation naturally drawing the consorts more closely together for a time,) but when Anne herself became Regent, she bestowed all the affection of which she was capable upon a country-woman of about her own age, Fräulein Julia Mengden, who occupied apartments adjacent to her own, in which the Regent, very much *en déshabillé*, and with her head tied up in a striped cotton handkerchief, used to spend most of her time, surrounded by the German lady's relations, talking and playing cards in an atmosphere like that of a hot-house. " I should give "your lordship but a faint idea of the great affection that "the Grand Duchess has for Mdlle. Mengden," wrote Finch to Lord Harrington, " by adding that the passion of a lover "for a new mistress is a jest to it. By good luck, she (Miss "Mengden) has no great share of parts, nor, as they say, "of malice, so that it is to be hoped that she will neither "have the power, nor the inclination, to do much harm." The brother, mother and a few sisters of Fräulein Mengden were also invited to Russia and loaded with gifts. One sister, Bina, was attached to the person of the little Emperor, who, Finch tells us, was a remarkably fine child for his age; another had married Münnich's son, [1] and all of them were making immense fortunes rapidly. But they were not ungrateful. When, in the beginning of 1741, Count Lynar returned to St. Petersburg as representative of Saxony, and it was evident to Fräulein Mengden that the partiality of the Regent for that gentleman was stronger than ever, this complaisant bosom-friend, in order to mask her mistress's *liaison*, allowed herself to be married to Lynar, and the intrigue between the Grand Duchess and the ambassador was secretly carried on in

---

[1] This proved fortunate for Münnich, as, but for the intercession of Julia Mengden, he would in all probability have been sent to Siberia. *Solovev.*

Miss Mengden's apartments, only nine days after the birth of Anne Leopoldovna's second child Catherine. [1] Nay, more, Fräulein Mengden is said to have mounted guard at the door of the Regent's bedchamber, and denied Prince Anthony access to his own wife. [2]

This disreputable *ménage à trois*, if so I may call it, had important political consequences, for it brought about a coldness between the Regent and Ostermann, the old Minister deeply detesting the interloping favourite, but being much attached to the injured husband, who confided in him implicitly, and habitually alluded to him as "my mentor." Moreover, Ostermann was not blind to the serious effect which the Regent's scandalous conduct was having upon public opinion. Many began to fear that, in the person of Lynar, Russia was about to be threatened with another favorite, a second Biren. Another disquieting feature of an awkward situation was the utterly trivial character of the Regent herself. A bold and brutal Princess like the Empress Anne may do as she will and frown down all opposition; a bold and brilliant Princess like Catherine II may dazzle the popular imagination by the very splendour of her vices; but, excepting her natural mildness, Anne Leopoldovna had not a single quality which could by any possibility command respect or admiration. Even Finch, who thought much better of her than she deserved, is bound to admit that she was "of too retired a temper;" it is certain that she suffered so much at public functions that she avoided them as much as possible. [3] Ostermann, who had had considerable experience of the ways

---

[1] Compare *Solovev* and *Chetardie* Despatches. Finch, indeed, says nothing about the intrigue, but then he meant to present the Regent in the best light possible.

[2] Chetardie to Amelot.

[3] Even her rare out-of-door excursions were taken at night when there was a moon.

of Sovereign Princesses, and had contrived to influence natures so widely different as Catherine I, the Grand Duchess Natalia and the Empress Anne, could make nothing at all of the dull and sullen inertia of Anne Leopoldovna. Such a state of things would have been bad enough even if the Grand Duchess had had nobody to fear, but unfortunately for her, she possessed in her cousin, the "exceedingly obliging and affable"[1] Tsarevna Elizabeth a possible rival whose popularity was increasing every day. Here, indeed, lay the real danger of the Government, for a revolution in favour of the daughter of Peter the Great was the second trump-card which the French Minister, La Chetardie, was holding in reserve, and he hoped thereby to win the game of intrigue which he had been playing against the Russian Government even since the death of the late Empress.

Joachim Jacques Trotti, Marquis de la Chetardie, who had been especially charged by Cardinal Fleury to plot clandestinely against the court to which he had been accredited, was not the right man for such a delicate operation. The noble presence, easy gallantry, and sprightly wit of this brilliant patrician, made him the model and the mirror of every society which he honoured with his presence, and he scattered his *louis d'or* and his *bon mots* with equal grace and *grandeza:* but an inordinate vanity, which sacrificed realities to appearances, and a childish punctiliousness in regard to the prerogatives of his rank and station, invariably led him to view mere trifles as very serious matters, and very serious matters as mere trifles. He was not without courage and address, but his whole cast of mind was so frivolous and adventurous, that he lightly plunged into the most foolhardy enterprises without ever

---

[1] Finch, whose testimony is all the more convincing as it is that of a partisan of the opposite side.

calculating their consequences beforehand. His diplomatic mission was an uninterrupted series of blunders, and his singular lack of judgment repeatedly misled his government. It may, indeed, be said for him, that, in most instances, he only followed his instructions; but, on the other hand, it is equally true that a wise servant often serves a foolish master best by disobeying him.

La Chetardie's first blunder was to implicate himself in an absurd ceremonial squabble as to the proper way of presenting his credentials, he insisting upon delivering his letters of credit to the baby Tsar personally instead of to the Tsar's mother, although she, as Regent, directly represented the Sovereign. That La Chetardie deliberately meant thereby to gratuitously insult the Princess was obvious enough; but Ostermann, who did not wish to break with the Court of Versailles just then, because peace with France meant peace with the Porte also, after amicably arguing the point with La Chetardie for some months, consented at last to a compromise. The French Minister *did* present his credentials to Ivan VI personally; but the Regent, who stood beside the nurse, received them on behalf of her son, and replied to the Ambassador in the Tsar's name instead of in her own. This trumpery triumph was dearly bought by a corresponding loss of usefulness, for henceforward the Russian Court naturally regarded La Chetardie as an enemy to be avoided. All the great houses were therefore closed against him; all the ambassadors, except the Prussian and Swedish Ministers, sedulously held aloof from him; he could only despatch couriers by round-about routes; Ostermann's secret spies dogged his footsteps, and he was cut off from all official sources of information, to the no small detriment of his Government.

The strict surveillance under which La Chetardie now lived had the additional inconvenience of seriously impeding his political intrigues with the Tsarevna Elizabeth, whom the French Government had resolved to raise to the Russian throne. This resolution was prompted, not by any benevolent intentions towards the Princess herself, but by the hope of thereby plunging Russia back again into her original semi-barbarism. La Chetardie expressed himself morally convinced (and his Court believed him) that, when once Elizabeth was on the throne, she would banish all foreigners, however able, give her entire confidence to necessarily ignorant Russians, retire to her well-beloved Moscow, let the fleet rot, and utterly neglect St. Petersburg and the "conquered provinces," as the Baltic seaboard was still called. La Chetardie's original plan was a rising in the capital simultaneously with the invasion of Russian Finland by the Swedes. The Swedes were to take the field as the avowed champions of Elizabeth, and, to stimulate their efforts on her behalf, she was to give La Chetardie's active coadjutor, Nolcken, the Swedish Minister at St. Petersburg, a solemn undertaking to cede part of Finland to Sweden as a reward for that country's intervention. This, however, Elizabeth patriotically refused to do. She was quite willing, she said, to subsidize the Swedes during the war and contract a perpetual alliance with them afterwards, but never would she, the daughter of Peter the Great, relinquish an inch of the territory won by the sword of her father and the blood of her countrymen. In vain did both Le Chetardie and Nolcken overwhelm her with their arguments and reduce her to silence with their sophisms; on this point she was immovable. The sudden and unexpected collapse of the Swedes, showed what a broken reed the Tsarevna would have leant upon had she trusted to them. She was now driven to depend entirely upon her own resources, and these were limited enough. Moreover, she had to proceed with the utmost caution, for a careful watch was kept upon all her movements; but she contrived to communicate with La Chetardie and Nolcken through her physician, a Frenchman, Lestocq by name, who conveyed money and letters to and fro between them, and when La Chetardie, for prudence' sake, hired a country villa on the Neva during the summer, Elizabeth would frequently ply her gondola up and down the stream, close by his landing-stage, or land in the adjacent woods and meet him "accidentally" that way.

The Tsarevna herself, all this while, was vacillating perpetually between the two opposite poles of extreme terror and extreme temerity. Sometimes a strong sense of her loneliness and helplessness, and the dread of being shorn of her hair and buried for the rest of her days in a convent, paralyzed all her energy, while at other times the irrepressible enthusiasm of the soldiers of the Guard, who frequently visited her at her little house, the Smolyani Dvor, or Pitch Court, near the barracks, [1] inspired her with the most absolute self-confidence. She did her best to disarm suspicion by maintaining the most friendly relations with the Regent, appearing most dutifully at Court on all public occasions, and even standing sponsor to the Tsar's newly-born sister, who was christened Catherine, [2] and showed in general a commendable humility of demeanour. Only once was she hurried by anger into an outburst of violence. Of all the members of the Government, there was none

[1] Elizabeth, whose good nature was illimitable, had for some years been in the habit of standing sponsor to the children of the soldiers of the Guard, who had always been devoted to her, as they had been to her mother before her. The relations between her and them were therefore of a strictly sociable, I might even say, matriarchal character. When objections were raised to the visits of the soldiers, Elizabeth could always plead that the parents of her numerous god-children had a right to visit her whenever they felt so disposed.

[2] On this occasion Elizabeth presented her god-child with a pair of earrings worth 7,500 livres, and, at the same time, gave the Regent a cup and saucer of the gold of Siberia, resplendent with brilliants and sapphires of great beauty.

whom she so thoroughly detested as Ostermann, not only because he was the ablest, and therefore the most dangerous, of her enemies, but also and chiefly because he who owed everything to her father and mother, had set her aside in favour of aliens and foreigners. La Chetardie, who also feared and hated Ostermann, was always harping upon the gross ingratitude of the old statesman to the daughter of his benefactor, and Elizabeth frequently declared that she would one day teach this "petty little secretary" his proper place. In the course of the summer, Nadir Shah sent an Ambassador to the Russian Court, laden with rich gifts for all the high personages there, including Elizabeth. He was not permitted, however, to have an audience of the Tsarevna at all, and the gifts he had intended to present to her personally, were conveyed to her by Count Apraksin instead. This slight was too much for the equanimity of Elizabeth. Turning to Apraksin, she exclaimed: "Tell Count Ostermann from me that he thinks he can deceive all the world, but I am well aware that he tries to humiliate me on every occasion, and, by his advice, measures are being taken against me which the Regent is too good-hearted to think of. He forgets what he was and what I am, he forgets how much he owes to my father who found him a mere clerk and made him what he is now." [1] "The wrath and spite with which she spoke on this occasion," remarks Finch, "struck and surprised everyone." But, indeed, this outburst against the old statesman was perfectly safe, for at that very time Ostermann was engaged in a struggle for very existence against those who should have been his most loyal supporters. The incredibly narrow and sordid Michael Vasilivich Golovkin, [2] who owed

---

[1] *Solovev: Istoria Rossyi.* Tome XXXI.

[2] *Finch,* who gives innumerable instances of his greed and stupidity, calls him a conjunction of pride, egotism and self-sufficiency, and a perfect misanthrope.

everything to Ostermann, had declared openly against his benefactor, in order to curry favour with the Regent and Lynar,[1] and, in conjunction with the Austrian Minister, Botta, who was growing impatient of Ostermann's procrastinations, had induced the Regent to recall to Court Alexius Bestuzhev who had been implicated in Biren's fall and banished to his estate, but was now brought forward again by Ostermann's enemies as the one man capable of supplanting him. No wonder, then, if the veteran statesman reserved all his efforts for the struggle against his more pressing foes, and left the Tsarevna, whose character he despised and whose ability he vastly underrated, very much to her own devices. Besides, he was well aware that not a single notability was on her side, and that she could not look for wise counsels from any of the motley crew that paid its court to her. He therefore concluded that he had nothing to fear from the unaided efforts of a Princess whose whole career had hitherto been a tissue of frivolity, especially now that her Swedish friends had failed her. It must be borne in mind, too, that Ostermann had all his life-long been averse to violent expedients. He was, as his friend Finch well remarks, "a fair-weather pilot who in storms keeps under hatches, and how well soever he may serve this Government when settled, he will always lie by when it is not so." And indications are not wanting that, at last, the old statesman, who had always clung so strenuously to power, was really growing weary of the burden of office. On the conclusion of a new and more definitive defensive treaty with England, Nov. 18, 1741, his last official act, when, with characteristic contempt for mere money, he absolutely refused to receive the very considerable gratification (more than double the usual allowance)

---

[1] Lynar, however, quitted Muscovy in the autumn of 1741 with half a million rubles in his pockets.

offered to him, he told Finch, to whom in his hours of chagrin he frequently unbosomed himself, that he had procured a consultation from four of the best physicians, recommending him to use the waters of Spa, and that possibly he might proceed to pay Finch a visit in England, and pass the remainder of his days there in philosophical contentment. But—alas! for these good resolutions too long postponed!—Ostermann's Nemesis was already upon him. Ten days after this conversation, he was arrested in his bed, and, before the year was out, he found himself on his way, not to the peaceful shores of England, but to the desolate *tundras* of Siberia.

CHAPTER III.

THE MIDNIGHT COUP D'ÉTAT.

Dec. 6th, 1741.

IMMEDIATE causes of the Revolution of Dec. 6th, 1741—La Chetardie's mis-
givings—Self-confidence of the Tsarevna Elizabeth—Scene in the
Winter Palace between her and the Regent—Extreme peril of Elizabeth—
Conference of the Conspirators at Elizabeth's house—The appeal to
the Grenadiers—The midnight drive to the Preobrazhensky Barracks—
Elizabeth wins over the soldiers—The march to the Winter Palace—
The Regent seized in bed—Arrest of the Ministers—Elizabeth proclaimed Empress—Enthusiasm of the people—Largesses of the new
Empress—The trial of Ostermann and Münnich —Their dignified
conduct—Tragic scene on the place of execution—The capital sentences
remitted—The fate of Ostermann, Münnich, and their associates.

ON December 6th, 1741, La Chetardie, the French Ambassador at St. Petersburg, wrote as follows to Amelot, the
French Minister of Foreign Affairs, as to the prospects of
a *coup d'état* in favour of the Tsarevna Elizabeth: "An
outbreak, the success of which can never be morally certain,
especially now that the Swedes are not in a position to
lend a hand, would, prudently considered, be very difficult
to bring about, unless it could be substantially backed up." [1]
That very same evening, Elizabeth, without any help from
without, overthrew the existing government in a couple of
hours, a circumstance carefully to be borne in mind, as many

---

[1] Chetardie to Amelot. *Sb. of Imp. Rus. Hist. Soc.* Vol. 96.

historians, rashly relying on certain ex-post-facto statements by La Chetardie, have credited that diplomatist with a leading part in the revolution which placed the daughter of Peter the Great on the Russian throne. As a matter of fact La Chetardie, beyond lending the Tsarevna 2,000 ducats instead of the 15,000 she demanded of him, took no part whatever in the actual *coup d'état*, which was as great a surprise to him as it was to everyone else. The merit and glory of that singular affair belong to Elizabeth alone.

It must also be observed that, from the first, Elizabeth had taken a much saner view of the situation than any of her foreign advisers, and all along, despite much fear and faltering, she seems to have never been without the comforting persuasion that her courage would rise to the level of her necessities. Thus, when the Swedish Minister, Nolcken, suggested that she should rally all her partisans and arrange everything beforehand, even to the choosing of a leader for the enterprise, she objected, very pertinently, that the inveterate distrust with which every Russian regarded every other Russian, rendered any such combination impossible. To even attempt it would be sufficient to ruin everything. It were far better, she said, to win over her partisans one by one, and make each of them believe that he was contributing equally to the glory of the enterprise. To prevent any jealousy, moreover, she meant to head the Guards herself when the moment for action arrived. "I know very well," she concluded, "that you suspect me of weakness, but I will not be false to my blood, I will show myself worthy to be the daughter of Peter the Great."[1] Yet nearly twelve months had elapsed since these brave words were spoken, and still nothing had been done. Elizabeth's

---

[1] Chetardie to Amelot. *Sb. of Imp. Rus. Hist. Soc.* Vol. 96.

vacillation was intelligible enough, it is true. The least evil which she knew would befall her in case of failure, was life-long seclusion in a monastery, and this to a Princess "who," to use Mr. Finch's elegant expression, "had not an ounce of nun's flesh about her," was the most terrible prospect in the world. She was ready to endure much before risking such a contingency, but a point was reached at last beyond which even her endurance refused to go.

On Dec. 4th, the Tsarevna and most of the Foreign Ministers attended a crowded reception at the Winter Palace. The Regent, who appeared to be unusually perturbed that evening, withdrew early into an inner chamber, and shortly afterwards Elizabeth was summoned to her presence. No sooner did the Grand Duchess perceive her cousin than she exclaimed: "Matushka! [1] what is this I hear of you? They tell me that you are in correspondence with the enemies of our country, and that your doctor is intriguing with the French Minister."—Elizabeth protested, with well-feigned astonishment, that this was the first she had heard of it, adding that she knew her duty better than to break the oath she had sworn to the young Emperor. But the Regent was not so easily mollified, "Madam," said she, adopting a harder tone, "I am about to request the King of France to recall M. de la Chetardie, and I must therefore request you never again to receive him at your house."—"Never again!" exclaimed Elizabeth, piqued in her turn. "I might refuse to see him once or twice perhaps, but to promise never to see him again is impossible."—"But I insist upon it!" cried Anne.—"My cousin," retorted Elizabeth, "you are Regent, and have but to command to be obeyed. Surely it would be much simpler if you were to order Count Ostermann to tell La Chetardie

---

[1] Lit. "little mother," a familiar endearment among relations.

expressly not to visit me any more."—By this time both Princesses were growing warm, and had raised their voices, and while the Regent had recourse to threats, Elizabeth took refuge in tears. At the sight of her cousin's distress, the Regent was herself visibly affected, and the agitated ladies finally composed their quarrel in each other's arms, Elizabeth swearing eternal fidelity, and the Regent professing implicit faith in her loyalty. Nevertheless this scene seems to have at last opened the eyes of the Tsarevna to the imminence of her danger. She knew very well that the indolent and foolishly good-natured Regent would never have taken such a high hand with her unless prompted to do so, and she rightly suspected the hand of Ostermann in the affair. She was confirmed in her suspicions next day by another still more significant event. On the morning of Dec. 5th, the Government issued orders to all the regiments of the Guards in the capital to hold themselves in readiness to march to the seat of war within four-and-twenty hours, as the Swedish general, Levenhaupt, was reported to be advancing rapidly towards Viborg. This, however, was a mere pretext. Ostermann was well aware that Levenhaupt was still in his cantonments at the other end of Finland; the manœuvre was simply intended to render Elizabeth defenceless, and there can be little doubt that the astute old Minister intended to arrest the Tsarevna as soon as the Guards were gone.

That same night, at about 10 o'clock, a hurried and anxious conference was held at the Tsarevna's house,[1]

---

[1] There are six distinct accounts of this strange *coup d'état*, i. e. (1) Solovev: *Istoria Rossy.* Vol. XXXI; (2) La Chetardie's official report to Louis XV in *Sb. of Imp. Russ. Ist. Ob.* Vol. 96; (3) an anonymous: "*Relation de la Révolution arrivée en Russie le 6 Dec.* 1741," in the same volume; (4) Narration of Finch in *Sb. of Imp. Russ. Ist. Ob.* Vol. 85; (5) Manstein's account: *Mémoires* etc.; (6) Kostomarov: *Russkaya Istoria.* Of these Solovev's is the most correct, Chetardie's the most circumstantial, and Manstein's the least

after Lestocq, her surgeon, had reconnoitred the town and
made certain that all the lights in the Winter Palace and in
Ostermann's house had been extinguished. The only persons present besides Lestocq, were the Princess's Kammerherr, Michael Ilarionovich Vorontsov; her old music-master,
Herr Schwarz; her favourite, and future husband, Alexius
Razumovsky, and Alexander and Peter Shuvalov, two of
the gentlemen of her household. No monarch ever had
more devoted servants than these men were to prove to
Elizabeth; but they were, all of them, subaltern spirits who
looked to their mistress to take the initiative, and now, at
the supreme moment, it seemed as if she were about to
yield to a sudden fit of panic, for she began to expatiate
on the dangers they were likely to run. "Truly, Madam,"
replied Vorontsov, "the affair demands no little daring,
but where shall we look for it if we cannot find it in the
blood of Peter the Great?" At these words the Tsarevna
recovered her sangfroid, and, turning to Lestocq, ordered
him to send at once for the twenty most resolute grenadiers
of the Guard, whom he had already bought with the ducats
of the French Ambassador, [1] and, upon their arrival between
eleven and twelve, they were admitted into the presence
of the Tsarevna, and she asked them point-blank if she
could absolutely rely upon their fidelity. "Yes, Matushka!
we are ready to die for you," they exclaimed, whereupon
she bade them withdraw for a moment, and, flinging herself
down before an ikon of the Saviour, made a solemn vow

reliable, though written by a contemporary. Kostomarov's account too contains
a few apocryphal details. La Chetardie's account is somewhat vitiated by
the author's impudent assumption of omniscience, but in the main it is accurate,
but the anonymous "Relation", though shorter, is much more reliable. I have
constructed my account, after a very careful comparison between these six
sources. For confirmatory details, compare also the Letter of La Chetardie's
maître d'hôtel to his daughter, and Vasilchikov: *Semeistvo Razumovskikh.*

[1] La Chetardie had placed 2,000 ducats at Lestocq's disposal.

to God that if her enterprise succeeded, she would never sign a death-warrant as long as she lived. Then rising from her knees and taking a cross in her hand, she went out to the soldiers and said: "If God be merciful to us and to Russia, I will never forget your devotion. Go now to the barracks, assemble your comrades with all speed and secrecy, and await my arrival, I will be with you immediately." When they had gone she returned to her oratory, and remained on her knees in silent prayer for nearly an hour, till Lestocq, growing anxious, reminded her of the danger of further delay, and handed her the insignia of the order of St. Catherine (a decoration cherished by her as having been instituted in honour of her beloved mother), which she put on forthwith, and a silver cross, which she concealed about her person. He also persuaded her to wear a mail cuirass beneath her clothes, escorted her to a sledge which was already waiting at the door, and took his seat himself by her side, while Vorontsov and one of the Shuvalovs mounted up behind, and Razumovsky remained in the house to keep order. [1] It was close upon two o'clock in the morning when they set off on their adventurous drive through the silent snow-covered streets of the city to the Preobrazhensky Barracks, where nearly two hundred of the Guards were already awaiting them. Immediately on dismounting, Elizabeth snatched a spontoon from one of the soldiers, and led the way into the mess-room, ordering first of all, however, that all the drums in the barracks should be slit up, so that nobody could give the alarm. The men crowded after her, and when they were all assembled,

---

[1] According to Count A. R. Vorontsov (*Notes sur ma Vie*), his uncle M. I. Vorontsov alone accompanied the Princess, Lestocq having been detached elsewhere. According to other accounts, not Shuvalov but Schmidt was one of three companions of the Princess. I have adjusted these discrepancies as best I could.

she exclaimed: " My children, you know whose daughter I am ! It is my resolve this night to deliver you and all Russia from our German tormentors. Will you follow me ? "— " Matushka ! " they cried enthusiastically, " we will follow thee to the death, and as for the *nyemtsui*, [1] we will cut them all to pieces ! "—" Nay, my children," replied Elizabeth, " if you hurt a hair of their heads, I will not go one step with you. There must be no bloodshed. What we are going to do we do simply for the benefit of our country."— Having thus restrained their savage zeal within due limits, she knelt down, all present following her example, and producing her silver cross, held it aloft and exclaimed: " I swear before Heaven to die for you, will you swear to die for me ? "—" We swear ! " thundered the Grenadiers.—" Then let us go ! " cried the Tsarevna, rising, " and remember, my children, whatever befall, no bloodshed ! "—By this time her escort of grenadiers had swelled to nearly 400, all of them with bayonets screwed on and grenades in their pockets. Her first care was to despatch well-mounted messengers to the barracks of the Semenovsky and Ismailovsky Guards, bidding the soldiers assemble before her house as speedily as possible, and there await further orders; then, at the head of the Preobrazhensky Regiment, she proceeded on her way to the Winter Palace where the Regent was reposing in absolute security. As she passed through the grand avenue of the Nevsky Prospect on her way thither, she had the persons of the Vice-Chancellor, Count Golovkin and Baron Mengden, who resided there, secured in their beds, and, on arriving at the end of the avenue leading to the Admiralty, she sent three separate detachments of grenadiers to arrest Count Ostermann, his three brothers-in-law the Streshnevs, all of whom were generals, and Field Marshal

---

[1] Germans.

Münnich who lived at the other end of the city. At this point, moreover, in order to stimulate the zeal of her men, she descended from her sledge, and walked on foot in their midst, but the grenadiers soon perceiving that their "Matushka" had much difficulty in keeping pace with them, lifted the by no means ethereal form [1] of their little mother on to their shoulders and so carried her the remainder of the distance, to the gates of the Winter Palace.

The guards in the barracks of the Winter Palace were surprised in their slumbers, and Elizabeth did not allow them a moment's time for reflection. "Wake up, my children!" she cried, "and listen to me. You know who I am, and that the crown belongs to me of right. Will you follow me?"—Most of the men responded with shouts of devotion, but four subaltern-officers and one private hesitated, and she ordered them to be arrested on the spot. Her command was not only instantly obeyed, but was even in danger of being exceeded, for the loyal grenadiers in their fiery zeal would have bayoneted their lukewarm comrades there and then, had not the Princess struck up their weapons with her pike. The backsliders having been safely secured, Elizabeth proceeded, like a prudent general, to marshal and distribute her forces for the final assault. Despatching numerous small detachments of her grenadiers to guard all the staircases and other exits, she ascended the grand staircase at the head of the remainder of the party, after once more solemnly adjuring them to use no violence. The guards in front of the Grand Duchess's apartments made no resistance, and Elizabeth entering the bedroom, found Anne Leopoldovna asleep in bed with Julia Mengden

[1] Elizabeth's fine figure had by this time assumed very ample proportions. A few months before, Finch, writing to Harrington, says: "We may say of her [Elizabeth] as Shakespeare makes Julius Cæsar say (of one of his opponents), that her Highness is too fat to be in a plot."

by her side. "Awake, my sister!" cried Elizabeth, gently shaking the slumbering ex-Regent, who started up exclaiming: "What is it you, Sudaruinya?"[1] Then perceiving the helmets of the grenadiers behind the Princess, she guessed the truth and quietly submitted, merely begging that no harm should be done to her children, and that she should not be separated from her friend Julia. Elizabeth assured her cousin that neither she nor her children had anything to fear, and she bade the grenadiers convey the Grand Duchess to her own litter. The persons of the infant Tsar and his lately born sister, Catherine, were then secured, and they were both brought in to Elizabeth. Taking them in her arms, she kissed them both, exclaiming: "Poor children, it is not you, but your parents, who are to blame." They were then placed, with their nurses, in a second sledge and driven to Elizabeth's own palace, she following closely behind them in her own sledge with Anna Leopoldovna and Julia Mengden. The seizure and abduction of the ex-Regent and her children had been effected in less than half an hour, indeed so smoothly, swiftly and noiselessly had the whole revolution proceeded, that, as late as eight o'clock the next morning, very few people in the city, except the confederates, were aware that Elizabeth Petrovna had, during the previous night, been raised to the throne of her father, on the shoulders of the Preobrazhensky Grenadiers.

On regaining her mansion, Elizabeth despatched Lestocq, Vorontsov and Schwarz to all parts of the city, to summon the notables, civil and ecclesiastical, to her presence. The Commander-in-Chief, Field Marshal Lacy, was one of the first to be advertised of the change. "To which party do you belong?" enquired the emissaries of the Tsaritsa. "To the party in power," responded the prudent old Irishman,

---

[1] Madame.

without the slightest hesitation, and he immediately hastened to Elizabeth's mansion in order to place his services at the disposal of the new Empress. He found her surrounded by the chief dignitaries of the realm, holding her first council, the immediate results of which were a new oath of allegiance and a skilfully worded manifesto, the joint production of the lately recalled ex-Minister, Alexius Bestuzhev, and Count Brevern, Ostermann's private secretary, who had already deserted his life-long benefactor, to the effect that her Majesty, moved by the prayers of her faithful subjects, had accepted the throne in order to put an end to the prevalent confusion caused by the late government. At eight o'clock the oath and manifesto were ready, the Council rose, and the Empress, after declaring herself Colonel of the three regiments of the Guards, and investing herself with the insignia of St. Andrew, appeared in the midst of the distinguished mob which was already thronging her ante-chambers, and received the congratulations of the nobility, gentry and high officials with a gracious *bonhomie* which won every heart. Then, despite the Arctic severity of the weather, she ordered the windows to be thrown open, stepped out on the balcony, and showed herself to the people who crowded the square below. She was received with a loud burst of enthusiasm, the like of which had not been heard in St Petersburg since the death of Peter the Great.

After sufficiently gratifying the curiosity of the populace, Elizabeth retired to rest for a short time, and then proceeded in state to the Winter Palace, which had, in the meantime, been prepared for her reception. The din of salvoes from the Citadel, and the still louder roar of the joyous multitude that thronged the line of route, marked her triumphal progress. Indeed so dense was the throng that the Court dignitaries had to leave their carriages and fight their way into the Palace, on foot. After hearing a

Te Deum at the Imperial chapel, in the midst of her grenadiers, whose captain, at their urgent petition, she had
consented to become, the Empress held a reception. The
new oath was then administered to the Guards and to all
the civil, military and ecclesiastical functionaries, and couriers were despatched to all parts of the realm announcing
her Majesty's happy accession. [1]

The confederates and adherents of the new sovereign were
rewarded with a promptness and a liberality only to be
expected of the most bountiful of Princesses; the favourites,
Peter and Alexander Shuvalov, were made Generals and
Colonels in the Guards; Alexius Razumvosky became a
Lieutenant-Colonel and a Kammerherr, and Lestocq was
made the Empress's first body-physician, a Privy Councillor
and Director of the College of Medicine, with a salary of
7,000 rubles. [2] He also received her Majesty's portrait set
in brilliants worth 20,000 rubles. Twelve thousand rubles
were distributed among the soldiers of the Preobrazhensky
Regiment, which received at the same time the title of
the Imperial Body Guard, with a new uniform; and nine
thousand rubles were distributed among the soldiers of the
Semenovsky and the Izmailovsky Regiments respectively.
All the officers of these regiments were raised in rank, the
very corporals becoming captains, while each private was
made a lieutenant, ennobled and gratified with a small
estate. All persons proscribed for political offences during
the last two reigns were recalled to Court and restored to
favour. Conspicuous among them was the aged Field
Marshal Vasily Vladimirovich Dolgoruki, one of the victims

---

[1] By a subsequent manifesto, dated Nov. 28/Dec. 9, Elizabeth based her
right to the succession on the will of Catherine I, which, although giving
precedence to the male descendants of Peter I, expressly excluded the un-
orthodox. The will of Anne was set aside as being extorted from her, in
her agony, by Biren, Münnich and Ostermann.

[2] £1,750 in those days.

of Anne's cruelty, who was released from his dungeon at Narva, where he had languished for ten years, to preside over the War Office. Moreover, he and his family had their estate restored to them, and their wives and daughters were appointed to considerable posts near the Empress's person, along with the female relations of their old rivals, the Golitsuins. Biren also was released, but, by the advice of La Chetardie, he was forbidden the Court and ordered to live quietly on an estate which was bestowed upon him, with an honourable maintenance.

Yet this bloodless revolution, this pleasing picture of a liberated nation rejoicing around the idolized monarch of its choice, was not without its sinister touch of tragedy, and chief among its victims was the man to whom, next after Peter the Great, belongs the honour of having laid the foundations of modern Russia. Ostermann could indeed expect little mercy from a Princess whom all his life long he had consistently neglected and despised. Perhaps Elizabeth's good nature might ultimately have got the better of her resentment, but La Chetardie was constantly at her elbow to keep alive her wrath against the most formidable enemy of the French system in Russia, and so the illustrious statesman was sacrificed. At first he so far abased himself as to address a couple of appealing letters to the Empress, which were treated as "very mean and paltry perform-ances;"[1] but during the subsequent farcical proceedings, dignified with the name of a trial, before a tribunal presided over by the personal enemies of the accused, he comported himself with a quiet resignation not without dignity. Accused, among other things, of contributing to the elevation of the Empress Anne by his cabals, and of suppressing the will of Catherine I in favour of her daughter Elizabeth (both

[1] Finch.

charges equally false and frivolous), he declared, simply, that all he had ever done was for the good of the State, finally throwing himself on the clemency of the Tsaritsa. His principal fellow-victim, Münnich, on the other hand, confronted the court with the nonchalant audacity of a brave soldier, who, with nothing more to hope from life, has resolved to die like a man. The chief witnesses against him were suborned from among the common soldiers, but their evidence was so confused and contradictory that the Marshal sarcastically observed that, in order to simplify matters, it would perhaps, be better if the court were to dictate beforehand what answers he, the Marshal, was expected to make. When he was accused of wasting his men during his Crimean campaigns, he referred to his despatches in justification of his conduct, and declared aloud that the only thing in the past he really regretted was having neglected to hang the President of the Tribunal, Prince Trubetskoi, for malversation of funds while serving under him as Chief of the Commissariat. The result of such a trial was a forgone conclusion, yet everyone was struck by the extreme savagery of the sentences. Ostermann was condemned to be first broken on the wheel and then beheaded; Münnich to lose his hands first and then his head; Count Golovkin, Count Löwenwolde, Baron Mengden, Secretary Temiryazev and the rest to simple decapitation. The estates and property of the convicts were confiscated as a matter of course. [1]

Early in the morning of the 29th January, [2] 1742, large crowds began to assemble in the great square on the Vasilovsky island, close to the spot where the University

---

[1] It was mainly out of the proceeds of the confiscations that Elizabeth dispensed her *largesse* to her adherents.

[2] The Empress had departed for the country to avoid hearing or seeing anything of this tragedy.

now stands, round a tall scaffold surmounted by two blocks
with axes on them, closely guarded by 6,000 soldiers of
the Guard and of the Astrachan regiment of the line. At
the stroke of ten a gun was fired, and the dismal procession
of the condemned (ten in all) was seen wending its way
from the Citadel to the scaffold, each convict walking
between two soldiers with fixed bayonets, except Ostermann,
who was so gouty that he had to be conveyed to the
place of execution in a rough peasant's sledge drawn by
a single hack. He wore a short, old, fox-skin jacket which
he had been wont to work in for years, and a short peruke
surmounted by a black velvet forage cap, beneath which
his grey hair straggled wildly. Münnich, jaunty to the last,
had taken care to be well shaved and powdered, and a
fine mantle floated over his handsome new uniform. Count
Löwenwolde, haggard, ragged, sordid and unkempt, looked
like a mechanic out of work. On reaching the scaffold,
the condemned were placed in a circle, side by side,
(except Ostermann who was suffered to remain in his sledge)
(and there, in the intense cold, they were forced to
listen bare-headed, while the Secretary of the Senate
recited the charges against them, which covered five folio
pages. [1] It was observed by an eye-witness that Ostermann
listened to the charge and sentence with the utmost composure, and with that rapt attention which was peculiar to
him whenever he gave his mind to business. Even at that
awful moment the sardonic humour of the old diplomatist did
not desert him, and he silently commented on the paragraphs
he liked the least by softly shaking his head and raising
his eyes in amazed deprecation to Heaven. [2] The sentence
read, he was lifted from his sledge by four soldiers, and
carried to the scaffold, where his head was laid on the block,

---

[1] Finch.
[2] Despatches of Saxon Minister, Pezold. *Sb. of Imp. Rus. Ist. Ob.* Tome VI.

one soldier baring his neck and raising his long grey locks,
while another took the axe out of its bag. The same instant the Secretary of the Senate again came forward, and
exclaimed aloud: "God and her Majesty give thee back
thy life!" Whereupon the soldiers raised Ostermann up
again and carried him back to his sledge, where he remained
till the sentences of the other convicts had been read to
them in turn. He spoke but once during this terrible ordeal,
and that was when he was replaced in his sledge, when
he said: "Pray give me my wig and cap again!" and the
only sign of emotion he betrayed was a slight trembling
of the hands as he slowly readjusted his head-gear and
re-buttoned the collar of his ragged shirt. The other prisoners were spared the agony and humiliation of mounting
the scaffold. Münnich listened to his sentence "with as erect,
intrepid and unmoved a countenance as if he had been at
the head of an army or a review." [1]   When it was all over,
he gave the soldiers who conducted him a purse full of
ducats, and jested gaily with them all the way back to
the fortress. The other prisoners, with the exception of
Golovkin who broke down miserably, showed equal calmness
and dignity. "If," comments Mr. Finch on this sad scene,
"if leading a wretched life in perpetual banishment in the
remotest parts of Siberia may appear to any of these unhappy persons a more eligible fate than a speedier end to
their misery, it is entirely owing to her Majesty, for those
who sat on their trials would no doubt have pursued them
to the death." It was indeed a dismal mockery of clemency. Ostermann's sentence was mitigated to banishment
to Berezov, where Menshikov had languished before him,
and there he died six years later, in the arms of his devoted
consort. Münnich was sent to Pelim, to reside in the very

---

[1] Finch.

house which he himself had designed for the reception of Biren, whom, by a singular irony of fate, he chanced to encounter in the midst of the frozen wilderness, at the extremity of European Russia, posting hopefully back to all that his rival, Münnich, was leaving behind him. As the sledges swiftly passed each other, the eyes of the two men met for a single instant in an intent look of wonder and hatred, but not a word was spoken on either side. The fellow-prisoners of Ostermann and Münnich were equally fortunate in escaping the block in order to languish slowly among the Siberian snows.

CHAPTER IV.

A CROSS-FIRE OF INTRIGUE.

1741—1743.

INFANCY of Elizabeth—Project of wedding her to a French Prince—Early years—Abilities—Unsettled state of Russia—Mr. Finch's view of the situation—Who is to succeed Ostermann?—The new Ministers—Alexius Cherkasky—Nikita Yurevitch Trubetskoi—Armand Lestocq—Michael Vorontsov—Michael Bestuzhev—Alexius Bestuzhev—His early career and character—The Swedish difficulty—La Chetardie as mediator—His effrontery—Dignified firmness of the Empress—Peace of Abo—The treacherous despatch—Departure of La Chetardie—The policy of the Bestuzhevs—Their immense difficulties—Elizabeth's antipathies—Plot to ruin the Bestuzhevs—Arrest of Natalia Lopukhina—Her character—And accomplices—The trial—The sentence—Horrible scenes on the scaffold—Estrangement between Austria and Russia—The Court moves to Moscow.

ELIZABETH PETROVNA was born on December 18th,[1] 1709, at the vast old wooden palace of Kolmenskoe,[2] near Moscow, which Peter the Great, always so lavish to those he loved, had bestowed upon her mother, Martha Skovronskaya, the mistress of his choice, whom, three years later, defying the prescriptions of ages, he was to raise, not merely to his nuptial couch, but to his imperial throne. The child could not have come into the world at a more auspicious moment. On the very day of her birth the

---

[1] 5th Sept., the date given in Münnich's *Zapiski*, is incorrect.
[2] It had 270 rooms and 3,000 windows.

THE GRAND DUKE PETER.

Ætat. 16.

mighty Tsar made his triumphal entry into Moscow, drag-
ging after him a captive band of statesmen and soldiers,
the spoils of Pultawa, and the visible tokens of the ruin
of the Swedish Empire which had overshadowed Muscovy
for more than a century. It was Peter's intention to have
celebrated his crowning victory by an elaborate religious
ceremony; but on being informed of the birth of another
daughter, he contented himself with a hasty Te Deum at
the Uspensky cathedral, and posted off to Kolmenskoe, to
fête the mother and babe in his usual boisterous and bar-
baric fashion. From her earliest years the child delighted
everyone by her extraordinary beauty [1] and vivacity.
Attired in rich variegated Spanish costume, or in gold
and silver brocade, she figured conspicuously at the rough-
and-tumble assemblies which Peter had introduced for the
purpose of breaking down the stiff exclusive etiquette of
the old court life, and the grace with which the little
marvel (she was only nine) danced the quadrilles and
menuets then in vogue, and the ingenuity with which she
devised fresh figures for the cotillons, filled everybody with
admiration. Her parts were evidently good, if not brilliant; but unfortunately her education was both imperfect
and desultory. Her father had no leisure to devote to her
training, her mother was too illiterate to superintend her
studies. The earliest instructors of herself and her sister
Anne (they were educated together) were a Russian nurse,
Ilin'ichnaya by name, and a Finn woman from Carelia,
Elizabeth Andreevna. After the death of Peter, the mother
of the girls provided them with a French governess, Mdlle.
Lenoir, but she did not reside at the palace and only saw
her pupils at lesson-time. The Minister of Police, Devier,

---

[1] "At twelve, when I saw her first, she already had a beautiful figure and
was full of grace, though inclined, even then, to corpulence, and bursting
with health and vivacity." *Münnich, Zapiski.*

was their governor till banished by Menshikov. At a later day Elizabeth picked up some knowledge of Italian, German and Swedish, and could converse in these languages with more fluency than accuracy.

It was Peter's intention to have married his second daughter to the young French king, Louis XV, who was of the same age. The idea first occurred to him during his visit to France in 1717, and was subsequently communicated to the French Court through Chateaneuve, the French Minister at the Hague; but the Regent d'Orleans declined to entertain the matter, ostensibly for fear of offending England, who dreaded a Franco-Russian alliance above all things. Nevertheless the idea was not abandoned by Russia, and, after Peter's death, Catherine I and Menshikov laboured hard to bring about a family union between the two crowns, nor would it have been the first time that they had been so united, Henry I of France having wedded the daughter of Jaroslav of Kiev, seven centuries before. Moreover, the sudden rupture of the negotiations for the marriage of Louis XV to a Spanish Infanta, had somewhat revived the hopes of the Russian Court. It was also well-known there that a band of adroit and discreet emissaries, armed with mysterious instructions, were being despatched on a mission of enquiry to all the Courts of Europe possessing marriageable Princesses, and, although they did not proceed as far as Russia, we are told that the name of the Tsarevna Elizabeth came *second* on the list of the eighteen eligible beauties finally submitted to the French Minister of Foreign Affairs as worthy of the attention of His Most Christian Majesty. Catherine, too, was prepared to bid high for the privilege of placing her daughter on the French throne. She offered, in case of success, to place all her forces at the disposal of France, and proposed that the King's uncle, the Duke of Bourbon, should marry the daughter of Stanislaus Leszczynski, promising, in such case, to get him elected King of Poland on the first vacancy. But the pride of the French Court rebelled against the idea of a union between the grandson of the Grand Monarch and the daughter of a base-born *parvenue*. It is even more than doubtful whether the Russian proposals were ever actually submitted to the French Council of State, and an end was put to the matter by the marriage of the young French King (16 Aug. 1725) to Mary Leszczynska, whose homely virtues and unambitious character marked her out as the most befitting consort for a slow-witted Prince whom his Ministers meant to still keep under tutelage. Elizabeth was then offered to the Duke of Bourbon, who refused her without giving any reason for his refusal, after which double rejection a coldness arose between the two Courts, which, under the circumstances, was not perhaps unnatural. Other connubial speculations foundered on the personal dislike of the Princess for the various suitors[1] proposed to her, so that on the death of her mother (May, 1727) and the departure from Russia, three months later, of her beloved sister Anne, her only remaining near relation, the Princess found herself at the age of eighteen practically her own mistress. So long as Menshikov remained in power, she was treated with liberality and distinction by the Government of Peter II; but the orthodox and conservative Dolgorukis, who supplanted Menshikov and hated Peter the Great and all his ways, meanly persecuted[2] Peter's daughter and thus obliged her to spend most of her time far away from Court, in the charming environs of Moscow. Like most of the Princesses of the House of Romanov, she preferred a country to a town life, and, robust and athletic as she was,

---

[1] *E. g.* Maurice of Saxony and Ferdinand of Courland.
[2] For particulars, see Nisbet Bain: "Pupils of Peter the Great," Chap. IV.

delighted in all sports requiring the exercise of strength and skill. She hunted wolves and hyenas at Kurghanika, went hawking with a bevy of young hoydens as unruly as herself at Aleksandrovskoe, and laid out gardens and built churches and mansions at Ismailovoe. The remainder of her time was spent in boating, riding, sledging and skating, according to the time of year. She loved above all things to collect together the peasant girls from the surrounding villages and make them sing their songs and dance their picturesque dances for the entertainment of herself and her little Court, regaling them afterwards with fruits and sweetmeats. Unfortunately, however, the pastimes of this most charming of Princesses were not always of such idyllic innocence. She had inherited more than was good for her of her father's sensual temperament, and, being free from all control, frequently abandoned herself to her animal appetites without the slightest reserve. While still in her teens, she made a lover of Aleksius Nikiforovitch Shubin, a sergeant in the Semenovsky Guards, and when he was removed from her and sent to Kamschatka, minus his tongue, by order of Empress Anne, Elizabeth, after a few months of passionate grief, consoled herself in the arms of another Aleksius, a handsome young Cossack, who chanced to be a chorister in the Court Chapel, and first won her heart by the exquisite melody of his voice. Shortly after becoming Empress, she married her Cossack lad secretly, and, altogether, this second connexion was more honourable to both parties than might have been expected from the circumstances.[1] During the reign of her cousin Anne, Elizabeth effaced herself as much as possible. She was well aware that the Empress, whose severe stateliness suffered by contrast with the Tsarevna's radiant

[1] For fuller details, as well as for other particulars regarding Elizabeth's private life and character, see Chapter VI.

beauty, and who, moreover, regarded her as a possible supplanter, could not endure the sight of the frivolous *belle*, and she very adroitly avoided giving that grim virago the slightest cause of offence, content with her own ever increasing popularity. It is said that so much beloved was she by all classes of the population, that the very shop-keepers frequently refused to take money from her when she bought their wares, and the mere fact of the Revolution is the best possible proof that the common soldiers were ready to risk their heads for her sake.

And now, at the age of three-and-thirty, this naturally indolent and self-indulgent woman with little knowledge (ten years of neglect had not only caused her to forget nearly all she had ever known, but had bred within her a positive dislike of letters) and no previous training or experience of affairs, was suddenly placed at the head of a great empire, for whose honour and safety she was primarily responsible, at one of the most critical periods of its existence. Fortunately for herself and for Russia, Elizabeth Petrovna, with all her defects and shortcomings, was no ordinary woman—indeed in more respects than one she was her illustrious father's own daughter. Her amiability, good nature and common sense, she no doubt owed in great measure to her mother; but her very considerable knowledge of human nature, her unusually sound and keen judgment, and her diplomatic tact again and again recall Peter the Great. What in her seemed irresolution and indolence to her impatient contemporaries was, most often, the result of careful deliberation and a wise suspense of judgment under exceptionally difficult circumstances. Add to this that the welfare of her beloved fatherland lay nearest of all to her heart, and that she was ever ready to sacrifice the prejudices of the woman to the interests of the sovereign, and we shall recognise at once that Russia did well at this crisis to place her destinies into the hands of Elizabeth Petrovna.

Yet, in 1741, most of the statesmen and diplomatists of Europe thought differently. Both friends and foes alike regarded the speedy disintegration of Russia under Elizabeth as inevitable and irremediable. They thought, and said, that the green young Empire was about to fall back into its original condition of a semi-barbarous state, belonging rather to Asia than to Europe, and, according to their political sympathies, they deplored or rejoiced over the coming collapse. Thus, in a letter written by Amelot, the French Minister of Foreign Affairs, to Mons. de Castellane, the French Ambassador at the Porte, early in 1742, the former represented that the accession of Elizabeth must be taken as marking the term of the greatness of Russia, inasmuch as the Princess was bound, by natural inclination, to entrust the chief offices of state to native Russians, and, as there was no native talent at hand to fill these charges, Russia, abandoned to herself, could not fail to instantly relapse into her former insignificance.[1] Still more remarkable were the words written just *before* the Revolution by the English Minister, Mr. Finch, and, be it remembered, we are now listening not to an enemy of Russia, but to a friend: "After all the pains which have been taken, for the last forty years, to bring this country out of its ancient state, it is only violence and superior force which prevent it falling back into it immediately, as it will do one day or other, sooner or later, for there is not one of them here who would not wish St. Petersburg at the bottom of the sea and all the conquered provinces[2] at the Devil, so they could but return to Moscow, where, being in the

---

[1] *Sb. of Imp. Russ. Hist. Soc.* Vol. I. Despatches of the French Ministers at St. Petersburg.

[2] *I. e.* the Baltic Provinces.

neighbourhood of their estates, they could all live with greater splendour and with less expense. Besides, they are all persuaded that it would be much better for Russia in general, to have nothing more to do with the affairs of Europe than it formerly had.... After all the pains which have been taken to bring their country into its present state, I must confess that I can see it in no other light than a rough model of something meant to be perfected hereafter, in which the several parts neither fit nor join, nor are well glued together, but has only been kept so, first by one great peg, and now by another, driven through the whole, which peg pulled out, the whole machine would fall to pieces. The first peg was Peter the Great, the present one is Count Ostermann. Let him drop, whose age and infirmities cannot set it at a great distance, and what will follow must soon be seen." [1] And now the dreaded contingency was an accomplished fact. That great sustaining "peg," Count Ostermann, *had* dropped, dropped altogether out of sight. Who was there left to take his place? Mr. Finch looks round upon Ostermann's supplanters, and can only shake his head. "The new councillors," he writes, [2] "even though united, would be unequal to their posts, and besides, they are already quarrelling together, and forming into different parties. Her Majesty certainly has a mean opinion of their heads, and a still worse of their hearts." [3] And who then were these new councillors who, to use the words of the Saxon Minister, Pezold, also an anxious observer, were at this time waging a "bellum omnium adversus

---

[1] *Sb. of Imp. Russ. Hist. Soc.*, Vol. 91.

[2] Jan. 6th, 1742.

[3] It should of course be borne in mind that Finch at this time was suffering from a severe fit of spleen, in consequence of the Revolution, which was a great blow to him. He had so identified himself with the cause of the late Regent, that the new Empress and her Ministers naturally regarded him with dislike, and he returned the compliment.

omnes?" Chief amongst them was the Grand Chancellor, Prince Alexius Mikhailovich Cherkasky, a dull, unwieldy, narrow-minded old epicure, who could only converse with the foreign ministers through an interpreter, and shamelessly made use of his official position to add to his already enormous wealth.   As a politician, Cherkasky was the mere mouthpiece of his son-in-law, Prince Nikita Trubetskoi, Pro-curator-General of the Empire and President of the re-habilitated Senate.   Trubetskoi, also a Russian of the ultra-conservative school, was every whit as mercenary as the Grand Chancellor, and infinitely more dangerous.   He had won his way into the favour of the Empress by an affectation of zeal and *bonhomie*, and could be amiable and plausible enough to gain his ends; but he was naturally imperious and vindictive, and the very soul of malice and chicanery.   None was ever so treacherous a friend, so implacable a foe; and he had an impartial, ineradicable, hatred of all foreigners, which almost amounted to mono-mania.   Nevertheless he was not without administrative ability, being adroit, alert and infinitely industrious.   Trubetskoi's special bugbear was the Empress's surgeon, Armand Les-tocq, whom the latest turn of Fortune's wheel had elevated to a position ludicrously out of keeping with his character and abilities.   He was the son of a Huguenot physician who had settled at Hanover after the Revocation of the Edict of Nantes.   Armand adopted his father's profession, and in 1713 went to Russia to seek his fortune.   Peter the Great, always on the look-out for intelligent foreigners able and willing to lick his subjects into shape, received the bright young fellow with open arms, and appointed him his *Leib-medicus*.   It was not very long, however, before Lestocq got into serious trouble.   A *bon vivant* of the first order and always frivolous and flighty when in his cups, he frequently allowed his tongue to wag too freely.   What his particular offence was,[1] we know not; but it must have been something out of the way, for Peter, generally so tolerant of moral lapses, in 1718 banished him to Kasan. On Peter's death, Lestocq returned from his seven years' exile, and Catherine I attached him to the Court of her daughter Elizabeth as medical adviser. His merry, jovial humour recommended him to the Tsarevna at once, and to do him justice, he was always devoted to her interests, and frequently risked his life in her service, for he had all the spirit and *élan* of the true adventurer. But though he made a brave enough show, he altogether lacked those solid qualities which make for greatness. The extravagant rewards bestowed upon him by the Empress for his services during the Revolution, completely turned his head; he imagined that intrigue and effrontery were the sole requisites for playing a leading part in the world, and plunged recklessly into politics, partly from love of excitement, partly to replenish a purse that leaked like a sieve. Had Elizabeth been less wise and wary, this dissolute feather-brain might have wrought much mischief, for in his professional capacity he had access to her at all times of the day or night; but the Empress thoroughly understood the character of the man whose lively sallies amused her leisure, and his political influence was never half so considerable as his contemporaries supposed.[2]

Lestocq and Trubetskoi were such bitter haters that they frequently insulted each other before the whole Court.

---

[1] Solovev attributes it to a liaison with a court lady, but Peter, would never have punished a moral lapse of that sort so severely.—We know indeed very little of Lestocq's life. Helbig's account of him (*Russische Günstlinge*) is, as usual with this author, very unreliable. Compare Kostomarov and scattered notices in the despatches of the Foreign Ministers.

[2] Both Manstein (*Mémoires*) and Helbig (*Russische Günstlinge*) are far too favourable to Lestocq. Most of the anecdotes told of him by the former are apocryphal, and the latter's brief notice of him bristles with inaccuracies.

The Procurator-General would have crushed the *Leibmedi-cus* had he dared; but Lestocq, independently of the active and potent support of La Chetardie, had behind him a strong party at Court, the principal members of which were Count Rumyantsev, recently returned from Constantinople; General Buturlin, a former favourite of the Empress; Prince Ushakov, the terrible chief of the Secret Chancellery; and Michael Larionovich Vorontsov, the Empress's chamberlain, who was married to her favourite cousin and crony, Anna Karlovna Skovronskaya. This Vorontsov was one of the few honourable and upright men at the Russian Court; but unfortunately his abilities were mediocre, and he was cursed with a constitutional timidity.

But there was a third party at Court, more or less opposed to the other two, and gradually gaining ground upon them. The leader of this third party was Count Michael Bestuzhev, who had recently returned to Russia from Stockholm, and had been made Grand Marshal of the Imperial Household. No other Russian diplomatist had had such a long and wide experience as Michael Bestuzhev. Born on the 7th September, 1688, and educated abroad, he had begun his diplomatic career at Copenhagen when only eighteen, and had since then successively represented Russia at London, the Hague, Hamburg, Hanover, Berlin [1] and Stockholm, returning to his native land on the accession of Elizabeth after an absence of nearly forty years. His knowledge of foreign affairs was therefore immense, and a long residence at half the Courts of Europe had given him an unusual air of distinction, which his noble figure and fine presence set off to the best advantage. The chief members of Michael Bestuzhev's party were Admiral Golov-

---

[1] It was while he was Russian Minister at Berlin that he succeeded in reconciling King Frederick William I with his son, the Crown Prince Frederick, afterwards Frederick the Great.

kin, Prince Kurakin, Prince Golitsuin, and his own younger
brother Alexius. The latter, who, at the beginning of the new
reign, was quite overshadowed by the more imposing personality of his elder brother, was in reality, the one capable
statesman whom Elizabeth as yet possessed, and, much
as she disliked him personally, she had already resolved
to employ and promote him. In this the Empress showed
great wisdom, for the younger Bestuzhev was no ordinary
man, and his peculiar talents were, just then, absolutely
indispensable to Russia.

Alexius Petrovich Bestuzhev Ryumin,[1] to give him his
full title, was born on May 2nd, 1693. It is interesting
to note, by the way, that the one Russian Minister who
loved England to his own hurt and harm, was himself of
English origin. A fairly reliable tradition informs us that
the progenitor of the Bestuzhev family was a Kentish
yoeman named Gabriel Best, who emigrated to Russia in
1403. Gabriel's son Jacob received the rank of boyar and
the town of Serpaisk from one of the Grand Dukes of
Muscovy. Alexius's father, Peter Mikhailovich, won the
favour of Peter the Great by his zeal and fidelity, and the
favour of Peter's niece, Anne of Courland, by his handsome person; but was supplemented in the lady's affections
by one of his own *protégés*, the insinuating Carl Johan
Biren, who sent her former benefactor into exile.[2] Young
Alexius was educated with his elder brother Michael at
Copenhagen and Berlin, distinguishing himself greatly as a
linguist, and also showing a considerable aptitude for science.
He adopted the career of diplomacy, and, at the early

[1] Bestuzhev himself succeeded so effectually in destroying his own traces
that less perhaps is known of him than of any other statesman of equal rank.
It is only with the greatest difficulty that I have succeeded in finding out
anything about him, and I know of no biography.
[2] See Nisbet Bain: "Pupils of Peter the Great," Chap. V.

age of nineteen, was sent to the great Congress of Utrecht, to
assist the father of Russian diplomacy, Prince Ivan Ivanovich Kurakin.   While staying at Hanover, he attracted the
attention of the Elector George, who, with the consent of Peter,
gave the young man a place at his Court with 1,000 thalers
a year, and from 1717 to 1720, he, Alexius Bestuzhev,
a native Russian, occupied the honourable but peculiar
position of Hanoverian Minister *to* Russia.   In 1720, he was
appointed Russian envoy at Copenhagen, and, in 1721,
completely gained the favour of his master, by giving a magnificent banquet to all the foreign diplomatists at the
Danish Capital, in commemoration of the lately concluded
Peace of Nystad.   At this banquet the image of Peter the
Great was represented in the centre of a splendid transparency, as the second Hercules, whose labours had healed
the wounds of exhausted and languishing Europe; for which
compliment the Tsar sent Bestuzhev his portrait garnished
with brilliants, all the way from the Persian frontier.   During
the subsequent fifteen years, for some mysterious reason,
Bestuzhev remained under a cloud, and had to be content
with the comparatively humble post of resident at Hamburg,
while his elder brother shone as Ambassador Extraordinary
at Stockholm.   Towards the end of the reign of Anne, however, Biren recalled him to Russia, to counterpoise the
influence of Ostermann; but he fell with his patron, and
only re-emerged from the obscurity of disgrace shortly
before the accession of Elizabeth.   He was employed to
draw up the new Empress's first Ukaz, and made Vice-
Chancellor at the end of the year; but so insecure did he
feel, that shortly afterwards (Feb. 1742) he employed the
good offices of the Saxon Minister, Pezold, to bring about
a good understanding between himself and the reigning
favourite, Lestocq, whom, at the bottom of his heart, he
thoroughly despised.   It is a very difficult task to diagnose

the character of this sinister and elusive statesman who took such infinite pains to obliterate all his traces. Indeed there is no other statesman of equal eminence of whom so little is known. He seems to have been moody, taciturn and somewhat melancholy, with a hypochondriac's anxiety about his health, full of wiles and ruses, passionate when provoked, but preferring to work silently and subterraneously, and only coming to the surface to strike sudden and crushing blows. Most of his spare time was devoted to chemical and physical research, and he concocted a nerve tincture[1] which was long regarded as a sovereign specific at the Russian Court. Of this invention he was prouder than of his most brilliant political triumphs. He was happily married to a German lady, Anna Boettiger by name, and for her sake protected the Lutherans, though himself severely orthodox. In his old age he had a strong religious turn, and published devotional works of a hortatory character. Inordinate love of power was certainly his ruling passion, but he had to wait for his first great chance till he was nearly fifty. Then, however, he seized it instantly and made the most of it. Personal considerations had no weight with him whatever when his ambition was concerned. He was a man who remorselessly crushed his innumerable enemies, one after the other, and never would allow himself the luxury of a single friend. Yet, to do him justice, it must be added that most of his enemies were also the enemies of his country; that his implacability was actuated as much by patriotic as by personal motives; that he would never accept gratuities either from the friends or from the enemies of Russia, and that no power on earth could turn him one hair's-breadth from the policy which he considered to be best suited to the interests of his country. And this

---

[1] Tinctura tonica nervina Bestuscheffi.

true policy he alone, for a long time, of all his contemporaries had the wisdom to discern and the courage to pursue.

The first care of the new Empress after abolishing the cabinet-council system, which had been in favour during the rule of the two Annes, and reconstituting the Administrative Senate as it had been under Peter the Great,[1] with the chiefs of the great Departments of State, all of them now Russians again, as *ex officio* members under the presidency of the sovereign,[2]—the first care of the Empress was to compose her quarrel with Sweden, not merely because the Finnish War was a drain upon her resources, but also because the general political situation required her attention more urgently elsewhere. Now, as we have already seen, Sweden had been induced by French intrigues to attack Russia, so as to prevent her from lending aid to the hardly pressed Queen of Hungary, who was consequently compelled to rid herself of her most dangerous enemy, Frederick of Prussia, by formally ceding to him the provinces he had ravished from her during the First Silesian War. It was with tears in her eyes and bitterness in her heart that Maria Theresa had signed the preliminary treaty of Breslau (June 11th, 1742).[3] "Silesia is the best jewel in the Queen's crown," said the Austrian Chancellor to the Russian Ambassador, Lanczynski, after the treaty had been signed, "and we cannot even hope for a durable peace as we may be attacked again at any moment. But what are we to do? England has put the knife to our throats and we have no

---

[1] Ukaz of 12/23 Dec. 1741.

[2] From the end of 1741 to the end of 1742 Elizabeth presided seven times in the Senate, generally remaining two hours there.

[3] Thereby ceding to Prussia all Silesia up to the Oppa, exclusive of the duchies of Troppau, Teschen and Jägerndorff, together with the county of Glatz, representing 38,000 square German miles and 1,400,000 inhabitants, the lowest price at which Frederick would sell his neutrality.

money wherewith to carry on the contest." [1] So far, then, the intrigues of France had been successful, but the unexpected collapse of Sweden had come as a disagreeable surprise, and it now became the chief object of France in the North to baulk Russia of the fruits of her triumph, and obtain the best possible terms for discomfited Sweden. La Chetardie was accordingly instructed to offer the mediation of France between the belligerents, and to use all his endeavours to cajole the Empress into an abandonment of the rights of conquest. Never for an instant did he doubt of success. For the first three months after the Revolution, he was undoubtedly the most popular man in Russia. "The first bow here is to her Majesty," observes Finch shortly after that event, "but the second is to Mons. de la Chetardie." The officers of the Guard kissed his hand, the Ministers cringed before him, the Empress was closeted with him for hours, and he was the only foreign envoy who enjoyed the privilege of accompanying her Majesty on her frequent religious pilgrimages. For the moment he seemed omnipotent, yet, as a matter of fact, he never possessed any real influence. The merry and vivacious Elizabeth had a very natural penchant for the witty and brilliant Frenchman, delighted in his conversation, and even ridiculed the peculiarities of her own ministers and servants to amuse him; but he was very soon to discover that in affairs of state she had a will of her own. Early in February, 1742, in pursuance of his instructions, La Chetardie had a long private interview with the Empress; Lestocq, already in the pay of France, alone being present to interpret whatever her Majesty did not perfectly comprehend. At this interview [2] the French Minister had the effrontery to formally propose

---

[1] Lanczynski's Despatches cited by Solovev.

[2] *Sb. of Imp. Russ. Hist. Soc.* Vol. I. Despatches of La Chetardie. Compare *Solovev: "Istorya Rossy."*

that the victorious Russians should sacrifice something for the benefit of the vanquished Swedes, in order to satisfy the honour of France, who, said he, could not abandon her most ancient ally. The Empress very pertinently enquired what opinion her own subjects would be likely to have of her if she, the daughter of Peter the Great, so little regarded the interests of her country, and the glorious memory of her illustrious father, as to cede provinces which he had won at the cost of so much Russian blood and treasure?—"But, Madam," mendaciously persisted La Chetardie, "consider the situation of the King my master, a situation into which only the desire to see you on the throne has plunged him, and I am sure you will do all in your power to help him out of it by providing him with the means to hasten on the conclusion of peace."—"I hope, Sir," replied Elizabeth, with dignity, "that the King will not disapprove of my sentiments. I feel sure that he would be the first to set me the example of obedience, if he had, like me, to carry out the wishes of a father."— La Chetardie was equally unsuccessful with Vice-Chancellor Bestuzhev whom he next approached on the subject, and whom the FrenchChargé d'Affaires, D'Allion, had vainly attempted to bribe beforehand. Bestuzhev roundly declared that no negotiations with Sweden could be thought of except on a *uti posseditis* basis. "I should deserve to lose my head on the block," he concluded, "if I counselled her Imperial Majesty to cede a single inch of territory."—And the deeds of the Russian Court were as good as its words. At a Council, over which the Empress presided, it was resolved to refuse the mediation of France and prosecute hostilities with the utmost vigour. There is no need to follow the course of the war. The Swedish army was, by this time, so demoralized that it fled panic-stricken at the very rumour of the enemy's approach, while the Swedish fleet, from which so much had been expected, became, owing to a criminal neglect of the most ordinary sanitary precautions, little better than a floating hospital. The Russian advance, under Lacy and Keith, was a triumphal progress. On August 26th, 1742, the whole of the Swedish forces, 17,000 strong, capitulated at Helsingfors, and were allowed to cross over to Sweden after surrendering their artillery. By the end of the year all Finland was in the hands of the Russians. On January 23rd, 1743, direct negotiations between the two Powers were opened at Abo, and, a month later, the Empress held another council at St. Petersburg, to consider the conditions of peace. The majority of the Ministers, including Trubetskoi and both the Bestuzhevs,[1] wished to retain the whole of Finland, but the Empress, who was very desirous of peace and dreaded the active intervention of France and perhaps of Prussia also, was in favour of a compromise. It was advisable, she opined, to surrender the greater part of Finland, which was more necessary to Sweden than to Russia, and would serve besides as a barrier between the two countries, " as, if our possessions extended to the coast, we should be more liable than ever to attack in the future." The Council thereupon unanimously thanked her Majesty for her "frankness", and endorsed her opinion. One condition, however, Elizabeth previously imposed upon the Swedish Estates. They were to elect as heir to the Swedish throne her cousin, Adolphus Frederick of Holstein Gottorp, Prince Bishop of Lübeck, and this request of the Tsaritsa the dominant Hat party in Sweden carried through the Riksdag with obsequious alacrity. Nothing now prevented the conclusion of peace. On August 7th, 1743, by the Treaty of

---

[1] Alexius Bestuzhev, in particular, vehemently urged the Empress to keep all her conquests, and called the Russian Commissioners poltroons and traitors for counselling otherwise; but he was overruled.

Abo, Sweden ceded to Russia all the southern part of Finland east of the river Kymenne, which thus became the boundary between the two States, including the fortresses of Vilmanstrand and Fredrikshamn. Thus the war with which France had saddled Russia, with the benevolent intention of crippling her permanently, resulted in her territorial aggrandizement, and the temporary establishment of her diplomatic supremacy in Sweden itself.

The Peace of Abo was a great blow to France, but it was not the only one. More than a twelvemonth before this treaty was signed, another event had occurred which rendered La Chetardie's presence at St. Petersburg superfluous. The Vice-Chancellor, privately informed by Prince Cantemir, the Russian Ambassador at Paris, of the double dealing of the Court of Versailles, and well aware, from the same source, that Russia had nothing to fear from the impotent malevolence of France, had secretly warned the Empress against lending an ear to the suggestions of La Chetardie, and chance now threw in his way a weapon which enabled him to complete the discomfiture of the French Minister. This weapon was no less than the secret despatch, already alluded to, of Amelot, the French Minister of Foreign Affairs, to Mons. de Castellane, the French Envoy at the Porte, which was intercepted by the Austrian Government on its passage across the frontier, and placed at the disposal of the Russian Ministers by the Austrian Envoy at St. Petersburg, the Marquis de Botta. In this document the accession of Elizabeth was represented as marking the decline of Russian greatness, and the Porte was urged to unite forthwith with the Swedes, in order to disembarrass itself, once for all, of its troublesome northern neighbour. [1]

---

[1] *Sb. of Imp. Russ. Hist. Soc.* Tome I. *Despatches of Chetardie.* Compare Solovev. Amelot attempted to brazen the matter out by pretending that the document in question was a Vienna forgery. "Toute réflection faite," he

We can quite understand that Elizabeth was "much upset" [1] when this precious despatch was laid before her. Only a few months before, she had been shown another despatch in which Louis XV had unctuously expressed the opinion that Providence had recompensed his sister's virtues by bestowing upon her a crown. And now the servants of her most christian brother were secretly endeavouring to tarnish this Heaven-sent diadem! No wonder if, after this, La Chetardie, who in the meantime had been raised to the rank of Ambassador Extraordinary, found innumerable difficulties thrown in the way of his presenting his new credentials, whilst his proffered advice on the Swedish question was absolutely ignored. It became evident at last, both to himself and his employers, that he was no longer of any use at St. Petersburg, and, at the end of July, 1742, he presented his letters of recall and quitted Russia, [2] leaving Mons. D'Allion behind him as Chargé d'Affaires.

La Chetardie rightly imputed his defeat to the machinations of the Bestuzhevs, especially of the Vice-Chancellor, and his defeat was none the less mortifying because he had always affected to regard the latter gentleman as more fool than knave. Again and again he had represented to his court that Alexius Bestuzhev was an imbecile, a poltroon, who could not take a single step without first consulting his brother Michael. Yet now this poltroon, this imbecile, had not only compelled him to ignominiously quit Russia, but had added the final insult of overwhelming him with

cynically observes, "il vaut mieux ne jamais convenir de cette lettre, la cour de Vienne a inventé tant de faussetés sur notre compte, qu'on peut bien encore mettre cette invention sur son compte."

[1] Solovev.

[2] Nevertheless, personally, he still retained the Empress's good-will, and he departed laden with gifts, Elizabeth bestowing upon him in addition to the usual parting gratuity of 12,000 rubles (£4,000), the order of St. Andrew, with her portrait set in brilliants, and a large diamond ring, worth together 100,000 rubles. *Record Office MSS. Russia. Despatches of Sir Cyril Wych.*

ironical compliments on his departure. The French Government, too, had now learnt, by bitter experience, that
it had nothing to hope from Russia so long as the Bestuzhevs took any part in the direction of affairs. Henceforth,
therefore, it became the prime object of the Court of Versailles to overthrow them as speedily as possible, especially as it shrewdly suspected them of a secret desire to
aid the Queen of Hungary. This, indeed, was actually
the intention of the Bestuzhevs. They were as well aware
as Ostermann had been before them, that France was the
natural enemy of Russia. The interests of the two States
in Turkey, Poland and Sweden were diametrically opposite,
and Russia could never hope to be safe from the intrigues
of France in these three border lands. Hostility to France
being thus, so to speak, the norm of Russia's true policy,
all the enemies of France were necessarily the friends of
Russia, and all the friends of France were necessarily her
enemies. Consequently Great Britain, and, still more,
Austria, as being a nearer neighbour and more directly
threatened by France, were Russia's natural allies; while
the aggressive and energetic King of Prussia, who had the
disquieting ambition of aggrandizing himself at the expense
of all his neighbours, of whom Russia was the chief, was
also a danger to be guarded against. It was the policy
therefore of the Bestuzhevs to bring about a quadruple
alliance between Russia, Austria, Great Britain and Saxony, in
other words, an alliance strong enough to counterpoise the
strength of France and Prussia combined; but here, unfortunately, they were on dangerously slippery ground, where a single
stumble meant irretrievable ruin. For the representatives of
the three Russophil Powers above mentioned, had all been
active and ardent supporters of the dethroned Brunswickers. Finch, the English Minister, had warned Ostermann
against the intrigues of Elizabeth; the Austrian Minister,

the Marquis de Botta, had advised her arrest; while the late Saxon Minister, Lynar, had gone still further and suggested that she should be immured in a convent. The Empress's antipathies, therefore, were very naturally directed against the ambassadors who had been her persecutors while she was only Tsarevna,[1] and these antipathies were of course reflected, at first, in her foreign policy. And then, personally too, she preferred France to England.[2] Nor was she much more pleased with Austria. The Court of Vienna had hesitated at first to concede to her the Imperial title, and Elizabeth retaliated by contemptuously alluding to the despoiled Maria Theresa as "the naked Queen". She also suspected Botta of attempting to bribe her Ministers, and would not listen to his insinuations against La Chetardie. It therefore required no small courage on the part of the Bestuzhevs to defend a policy which was abhorrent to their Sovereign; but they resolutely persevered, and gradually began to gain ground, especially when, in the course of 1742, Sir Cyril Wych superseded the obnoxious Mr. Finch, and the offensive Botta was transferred to Berlin and succeeded in St. Petersburg by a more acceptable envoy. They also enjoyed the support of the Grand Chancellor, Cherkasky, who had two things in common with the Bestuzhevs, a steady friendship for England, and

---

[1] Nevertheless she rendered them all justice. Thus she sent a massage to Finch to the effect that she could not blame him nor suppose that he acted contrary to the "principles of a man of honour," but "she supposed me too reasonable to expect a return of thanks for the pains I gave myself on that occasion" (*i. e.* the pains he took to warn her enemies of the impending revolution). *Sb. of Imp. Rus. Hist. Soc.*, Tom. 91. *Despatches of Mr. Finch.*

[2] "They pretend to know in France, that the Czarina herself is extremely averse to England, and they give as one instance of it, that having dined lately with Princess Kurakin, and having there very much admired a portrait of the Tsar Peter, as soon as she was told it had been drawn in England, she turned another way and declared before all the company that she could not bear anything that came "from there." *Record Office. Russia.* Carteret to Wych. Nov. 30, 1742.

a frantic hatred of the meddlesome Lestocq.   On the other hand, he was jealous of their ability and stupidly obstructive, so that it was a distinct relief to the brothers when the old gourmand died suddenly of apoplexy at the end of 1742. Cautiously feeling their way, they contrived to gradually reconcile the Empress with the idea of an English alliance; but they could not prevent her from signing (March 27th, 1743) a renewal of the long-standing defensive alliance[1] with the King of Prussia, whose persistent fear of Russia was already notorious.   But in truth the brothers were in imminent peril, for a combination of all their enemies was already conspiring their ruin.   Chief among these enemies was Lestocq, now a Count and a Privy Councillor (the Empress had ennobled her surgeon at her coronation), who could not forgive the Bestuzhevs for disowning their obligations to him and acting independently.   This extravagant adventurer was now at the height of his power, and England, France, Prussia and Poland competed eagerly for his support.   He unblushingly took retaining fees from all four, but it was the dirty work of France which he did by preference, and that, too, without the slightest regard for the interests of his adopted country.   Thus he accepted a pension of £600 a year from England, a still larger sum from France, and a portrait of the King of Poland richly embellished with diamonds, besides making the acquaintance of the elusive ducats of the King of Prussia.   Poor Wych, who had a slender purse and a weak stomach, seriously imperilled both by sitting up whole nights at a time, gambling and drinking with this mighty toper.   Lestocq was vigorously supported by the

---

[1] This treaty was regarded by Frederick himself as a mere blind. He calls it: "Un assemblage des mots sans âme qui promettent et ne roulent sur rien." It was only intended to impose upon Europe, and make him appear more formidable than he really was. *Pol. Corr.* Vol. II.

French Chargé d'Affaires, D'Allion, a far cooler and craftier rogue than La Chetardie, who was prepared, if necessary, to forge compromising documents wholesale;[1] and by Herr von Brummer, the Holstein Minister, an equally unscrupulous intriguer, and a man of large experience, who hoped to get Alexius Bestuzhev's place,[2] and was perhaps the most dangerous member of the Triumvirate. Frederick of Prussia seems to have known of the conspiracy. Anyhow, so confident was he of the impending downfall of the Bestuzhevs, that he ostentatiously sent the order of the Black Eagle to Count Michael Vorontsov, the Empress's chamberlain, whom he regarded as the coming man in Russia. The Bestuzhevs, thanks to the friendly warnings of Sir Cyril Wych, knew of the existence of this hostile cabal, but they had taken their precautions, and trusted to their own astuteness to parry every attack. Nevertheless the expected blow, when it actually fell, was so sudden and so terrible that they reeled beneath it.

On the 21 July / 1 Aug. 1743, a rumour spread through the capital, that a dangerous conspiracy[3] against the Empress and for the restoration of Prince Ivan (who, since the Revolution, had been detained provisionally with his parents at the fortress of Dunamunde near Riga) had been miraculously discovered, and, the same day, Lestocq, hastening from the country château of Petershof to St. Petersburg, startled Elizabeth with the intelligence, and implored her, as she valued her life, not to quit her Capital till full

---

[1] Wych says he actually did obtain such documents from Sweden.

[2] Lestocq proposed to recommend for the vacant post of Grand Chancellor, Aleksander Ivanovich Rumyantsev, an experienced diplomatist, and tolerably pliable.

[3] My chief authorities for this mysterious affair are two Russian documents: (1) *Pisma kasayushch'sya zagovora Markiza Bottiya.* (2) *Natalia Fedorovna Lopukhina.* Compare *Despatches of Wych, Pezold* and *D'Allion;* also *Kostomarov* and *Solovev.*

investigation had been made. A guard was at once placed round the palace, troops, fully armed, patrolled the streets —and four days of intense anxiety ensued. At last on July 25th/Aug. 5th, at five o'clock in the afternoon, Lieut.-Col. Ivan Lopukhin was arrested, and examined by a Special Commission consisting of Prince Trubetskoi, General Usha-kov and Lestocq. Lopukhin belonged to a family which the Empress already regarded with suspicion and dislike. He was the son of General Stephen Lopukhin, who had been the *protégé* of Anne of Brunswick's friend, Count Loewen-wolde; while his mother, Natalia Fedorovna Lopukhina, was notoriously the personal enemy of Elizabeth. The feud between the two women was of long standing. Natalia Lopukhina was a relation of the disreputable German adventurers, the Monses,[1] who had been the cause of the brief but bitter estrangement between Catharine I and Peter the Great in the Tsar's later years, and Elizabeth, whose domestic affections were very strong, had never forgotten that unhappy episode. Moreover, Natalia, who was one of the loveliest women in Russia and also one of the most vicious (she was the mistress of her husband's patron, Count Loewenwolde), had, during the last reign, gone out of her way to insult and humiliate the Tsarevna, who was the only other beauty whose charms competed with her own. Elizabeth had silently endured this contumely, and, being naturally magnanimous, had, on her accession, not only allowed Natalia to retain her post of Lady in Waiting, but had even presented her with her own portrait set in brilliants, an extraordinary distinction. But Natalia's jealousy of her rival was stronger than her gratitude to her Sovereign, and on the occasion of a state ball she had the temerity to appear in a pink dress with

---

[1] See R. Nisbet Bain: "Pupils of Peter the Great," Chap II.

pink roses in her hair, though she well knew that this was the Empress's favourite colour, and that the ladies of the Court were expressly forbidden to appear in pink for that very reason. The consequence was, that when Elizabeth entered the ball-room and observed this grave breach of etiquette, she was unable to control herself. Summoning Natalia to her side, she sent there and then for a pair of scissors, and, after snipping off the provocative roses, soundly boxed the ears of the rebellious beauty with her own imperial hands, in the presence of the whole court. Naturally enough Natalia did not love the Empress any the more for this, and lost no opportunity of traducing her in her own private circle. She appears to have been particularly free-spoken to her bosom friend, the Countess Anna Gavrilovna Bestuzheva (the widow of Peter the Great's Procurator-General, the famous Yaguzhinsky), who, a few weeks before, had married Count Michal Bestuzhev, against the wishes of Elizabeth, who disliked Anna Bestuzheva almost as much as Natalia Lopukhina. Both these ladies, it may be added, were intimate personal friends of the late Austrian Minister, the Marquis de Botta, and they used to hold indignation meetings at each other's houses, where the personal failings of the Empress and the faults of her government were discussed with more vivacity than charity. Moreover, Lopukhina was in constant, though irregular communication with her old lover, Count Loewenwolde, who had been implicated in Ostermann's fall, and was kept under guard at Solikamsk in the distant Uralian province of Perm. Here then was Lestocq's opportunity. Two spiteful matrons of indifferent character, hating, and hated by, the Empress, both of them friends of the late Austrian Minister, both of them secretly attached to the dethroned dynasty, one of them in direct communication with a state prisoner, and actually *the wife* of the

Grand Marshal Bestuzhev—here, surely, was material enough for malevolent ingenuity to spring a bogus conspiracy upon the terrified Empress, to damage the Austrian government and ruin the Bestuzhevs at the same time. The ground was prepared by the French Chargé d'Affaires [1] obtaining from the Marquis de Valori, the French Ambassador at Berlin, some documents of a very compromising nature (if genuine) relating to Botta, skilfully manipulated extracts whereof Lestocq undertook to lay before the Empress. Meanwhile the indefatigable surgeon had suborned Lieut. Berger, who had the custody of Count Loewenwolde at Solikamsk, but was a friend of the Lopukhins and during his periodical visits to St. Petersburg had served as the intermediary between Natalia Lopukhina and her lover,—Lestocq, I say, suborned this man to ply foolish and garrulous young Ivan Lopukhin with liquor at a tavern which they both frequented, in order to worm something compromising out of him. The traitor succeeded only too well, and the idle gabble of a besotted lad was the slender foundation on which this diabolical plot was reared. In consequence of the "admission" of the accused, his father, General Stephen Vasilevich Lopukhin; his mother, Natalia Lopukhina; the Countess Anna Bestuzheva; her youthful daughter by her first marriage, Nastasia Pavlovna Yaguzhinskaya; her step-daughter the Princess Gagarina; Kammerherr Lilienfeld, and eighteen other persons were successively arrested and brought before the Special Commission, of which Lestocq himself was the ruling spirit! At the same time the Grand Marshal Michael Bestuzhev was put under arrest at his own country

---

[1] In June, 1743, D'Allion wrote to Lanmary at Stockholm: "As, humanly speaking, so long as the Bestuzhevs rule the court, we shall never do any good here, you may be sure I shall leave nothing in the world untried to pull them down from the height of their greatness." *Pisma kasayushch'sya zagovora M. Bottiya.*

house, and all his papers were sealed. The true conspirators, Lestocq and Company, were jubilant. Nevertheless
the prosecution did not proceed as smoothly as was anticipated. The most minute examination of the correspondence of Stephen Lopukhin failed to elicit anything criminal.
Ivan Lopukhin, indeed, confessed, under torture, all sorts
of absurdities, but his father, the General, was dumb;
while Anna Bestuzheva and Natalia Lopukhina defended
themselves with infinite spirit and address. The former
steadily denied everything; while Natalia Lopukhina, in
order to save her friends and her family, very adroitly
implicated the Marquis de Botta as much as possible—
a perfectly safe course to pursue, as Botta was now at
Berlin, and consequently beyond the reach of the tribunal.
Baffled and furious, the Commission, which, to use the
expressive words of a Russian writer, was determined to
"squeeze and wring out a conspiracy somehow,"[1] ordered
the wretched women to be tied to the whipping-block; but,
though they were tortured till their joints cracked and they
became hysterical, no confession of a conspiracy could be
extorted from them. Thus, after a most rigid inquisition
extending over twenty-five days, during which every variety
of moral and physical torture was unscrupulously employed
against the accused, the terrible plot was found to be little
more than "the ill-considered discourses of a couple of
spiteful passionate women, and two or three young de-
bauchees."[2] Nevertheless, the report of the Commission,
coloured as darkly as possible, was duly submitted to the
Senate on August 19/30, 1743, and, after a session lasting
from 8 o'clock in the evening till 4 o'clock in the morning,

---

[1] "*Dopuitat'sya do otkruitie zagovora.*"—Alluding to these tortures, the
French Chargé d'Affaires cynically reports that the two ladies had been put
into a place "whence nobody ever emerges whole."

[2] *Despatch of Sir Cyril Wych*, 5 Aug. 1743. (*Record Office.—Russia.*)

all the accused were sentenced to death as political offenders. Stephen and Ivan Lopukhin, Natalia Lopukhina and Anna Bestuzheva were further condemned to lose their tongues and be broken on the wheel before being beheaded. For ten days the sentence remained in Elizabeth's hands unsigned. At last an imperial rescript was issued, mitigating the capital sentences to perpetual banishment. The three Lopukhins and Madame Bestuzheva, however, were first to be knouted and have their tongues cut out, while the remaining twenty-one prisoners were to be simply whipped. The execution took place on Sept. 11th, 1743, in front of the public offices, in the presence of an enormous crowd; the Empress had previously left town to avoid the horrible spectacle. The first to suffer was Natalia Lopukhina. Still handsome and stately, despite her cruel sufferings and her three-and-forty years, she ascended the scaffold with a firm step, followed by her companions in misfortune, while the sentence was being read aloud, amidst the deepest silence, by the Secretary of the Senate; but when the executioners roughly laid their hands upon her and tore her dress from her shoulders, she could contain herself no longer, and fought furiously with them in an agony of terror. At length, still struggling, she was hoisted on to the shoulders of the hangman's assistant, who held her hands fast, the knout hissed through the air, and, in a few moments, the body of the unhappy creature, whose screams were heard all through the square, was seamed with bloody furrows. Sick with pain, she was then thrown to the ground, and the executioner, pressing her throat till the tongue lolled out, seized it with his fingers and cut off half of it. Moaning piteously and spluttering blood, she was then flung into a cart and removed, while the hangman held up the severed tongue, and cried with true gallows humour: "Who wants a tongue? It is going cheap." The turn of Anna Bestuzheva came next, but even at that awful moment the Countess's presence of mind did not forsake her. As her dress was slipped down, she contrived to put into the executioner's hand a gold cross studded with gems. The man took the hint, and, while making a fierce display with his scourge, punished his second victim but lightly and only cut off the extreme tip of her tongue. When all had been punished, they were removed in common carts to the fortress, to say farewell to their kinsfolk before departing into perpetual exile.

Thus all the Russians who had presumed to find fault with, and speak ill of, the Empress had been savagely punished; but what of the Marquis de Botta, the Queen of Hungary's Minister, who was alleged to have set them on. Lanczynski, the Russian Minister at Vienna, was instructed to demand Botta's condign punishment, in a special audience; but Maria Theresa declared, with her usual spirit, that she never would admit the validity of extorted evidence, and proceeded to issue a manifesto to all the Great Powers, defending Botta and accusing the Russian Court of gross injustice. This drew forth an indignant letter from Elizabeth to Lanczynski, demanding instant satisfaction, and at last, after much hesitation, Maria Theresa promised that Botta should be put upon his defence before a special tribunal.

Thus Lestocq and his accomplices had at last succeeded in estranging the Courts of St. Petersburg and Vienna, and the result of the trial was naturally hailed at Paris as a great diplomatic victory. But, on the other hand, they had failed to bring the Bestuzhevs to the block, or even to drive them into "some obscure hole in the country," as D'Allion had confidently predicted. At the very crisis of their peril, the Empress, always equitable when not frightened into ferocity, had privately assured the Vice-Chancellor that her confidence in him was unabated, and that not a hair of his head should be touched. She knew that he had always opposed his brother's union with the Countess Yaguzhinskaya, and this was a strong mark in his favour. Furthermore, it had come out at the trial, that this unlucky marriage, though it was only five months old, had been the reverse of happy, and that the consorts were scarcely on speaking terms. Indeed, the Countess Bestuzheva had expressly declared that she had never opened her mind on the subject of Elizabeth to her husband. Both the brothers, therefore, could breath freely once more. Shortly afterwards, Michael Bestuzhev was appointed Ambassador at Berlin in place of the too pliable Chernuishev—an honourable exile, removing him out of harm's way. Meanwhile Alexius accompanied the Court to Moscow, resolved to resist his enemies to the last. He knew that a still fiercer storm was about to burst upon him. His old adversary, La Chetardie, was already travelling post-haste to Moscow, to complete his ruin, and a still more formidable opponent, Frederick of Prussia, had now thrown the full weight of his unscrupulous energy and his immense influence into the scales against the still tottering statesman. All the Chancelleries of Europe, with their eyes fixed upon Moscow, now anxiously awaited the issue of the apparently unequal contest.

THE GRAND CHANCELLOR, COUNT ALEXIS BESTUZHEV-RYMIUM.

CHAPTER V.

THE TRIUMPH OF BESTUZHEV.

1744—1748.

CARL Peter Ulric—His early career—Arrival in Russia—Made Grand Duke
and heir to the throne—Arrival of the Princesses of Zerbst—Serious
illness of the bride elect—Sophia Augusta becomes Catherine
Aleksyevna—The betrothal—The wedding—European Politics—Fre-
derick's dread of Russia—His intrigues against Bestuzhev—Beginning
of the Second Silesian War—La Chetardie expelled from Russia—
Bestuzhev made Grand Chancellor—Reconciliation of Austria and
Russia—Reverses of Frederick II—Frederick declares war against
Saxony—Warning protest of Elizabeth—End of the Second Silesian
War—Expulsion of "Madame Zerbst" from Russia—Quarrel between
Bestuzhev and Vorontsov—Dismissal of Mardefeld—Death of Anne
Leopoldovna—Negotiations with England—The Anglo-Russian Alli-
ance—March of the Russian troops to the Rhine—Signal triumph and
commanding position of the Grand Chancellor—Disgrace of Lestocq.

IN transferring the court, for a time, from the marshes of
St. Petersburg to the groves of Moscow, Elizabeth was chiefly
preoccupied with the thought of securing the imperial
succession by marrying her nephew, the youthful Grand
Duke Peter, as soon as possible to a suitable Princess. The
young gentleman in question, the only son of Elizabeth's
elder sister, Anne, Duchess of Holstein, was born at Kiel,
on January 29th, 1738, and christened Carl Peter Ulric. His
mother died a week after his birth, and, for the first twelve
years of his life, the unfortunate had, who was at best a

7

poor creature physically and mentally, seems to have been abandoned to the tender mercies of ignorant and brutal tutors and guardians. [1] No doubt, like most semi-idiots, he was naturally obstinate and intractable; yet there could be no excuse for half starving him, while to tie him to a stone column or a table, and belabour him with heavy riding-whips, was certainly excessive chastisement for merely childish faults. Nor was it discreet to plant the young Duke, dunce though he was, in a doorway, with a rod in his hand and the effigy of an ass round his neck, full in view of the table where his own gentlemen sat dining. It must therefore have been like exchanging purgatory for paradise when the little Duke, at the invitation of his imperial aunt, settled permanently in Russia, in February 1742. He was received with open arms and over-whelmed with benefits and blessings. Elizabeth's do-mestic affections were very lively and constant. The mere mention of her mother's name was sufficient to bring the tears to her eyes; she venerated the memory of her il-lustrious father, and cherished the most tender recollec-tions of her sister Anne. With the exception of a few female cousins, her nephew was now her sole surviving relative, and the love she henceforth bestowed upon him was utterly inexplicable to the world of diplomacy which refers everything to self-interest, and takes no count of natural affection. At this time, too, Carl Peter Ulric, though frail and puny, was not ill favoured, and even prepossess-ing. [2] The very day of his arrival, the Empress decorated

---

[1] See (in Solovev) an anonymous document sent by Korff, the Russian Minister at Kiel, to Bestuzhev. As this document was apparently procured for the purpose of injuring Brummer, Bestuzhev's enemy, it is naturally ex-aggerated, but many of the statements therein are confirmed by other sources.

[2] His Highness is possessed of many good qualities, which, being invested in a very agreeable person, make him every way recommendable. *Despatch.* 8 Nov. 1742. *Wych to Carteret. Record Office. Russia.*

him with the order St. Andrew in brilliants, and assigned
him and his suite sumptuous apartments in the Palace
of the ex-Duke of Courland. The regiment of the Brunswick Cuirassiers was re-naméd the Holstein-Gottorp Regiment in his honour, and he was appointed its first commander. His birthday, which fell a few days later, was celebrated with great magnificence, and when, shortly after his
arrival, a deputation came to St. Petersburg from the Swedish
Riksdag, announcing that the young Prince had been elected
successor to the Swedish crown, [1] the Empress drily told
the deputation that they had come a trifle too late, as she
did not mean to part with her nephew. He now, too,
received proper instructors, special care being taken to teach
him the truths of the orthodox religion, which the Empress
was determined he should profess as soon as possible. On
the 18th November, 1742, he was formally received into the
Russian Church, at the Court Chapel, under the name of
Peter Theodorovich, and thereupon proclaimed Grand Duke
and heir to the Russian throne. So secretly was the whole
affair conducted that, to the very last moment, nobody,
except Lestocq and Brummer, the Prince's Governor, knew
anything about it; even Bestuzhev and the Senate were
left in the dark.

The Empress's next care was to provide her nephew
with a suitable wife, but here diplomacy had a word to
say in the matter. Bestuzhev was in favour of Mary, the
daughter of Augustus of Saxony. It was part of the Vice-
Chancellor's political system to unite Russia closely with
Saxony and the Maritime Powers, by way of counterpoise
to France and Prussia, and a family alliance between the
Courts of Dresden and St. Petersburg would have been a

---

[1] His right to the Swedish throne was indisputable, for he was the
great-nephew of Charles XII, and the great-grandson of Charles XI of
Sweden.

good step forward in that direction. Lestocq, however, supported, if not actually prompted, by Frederick of Prussia, proposed Sophia Augusta Frederica of Anhalt Zerbst, the daughter of Elizabeth of Holstein, who was the sister of Adolphus Frederick, Prince Bishop of Lubeck, recently elected hereditary prince of Sweden in lieu of the Duke of Holstein. Lestocq adroitly represented to Elizabeth that the daughter of a petty German family would be far more manageable than a Princess taken from a great sovereign house like Saxony, and also—a delicate point with Elizabeth —that a protestant lady like the little Princess of Zerbst, would be far less dangerous to orthodoxy than a bigoted catholic like the Saxon Princess. These considerations decided the Empress. At the end of December, 1743, the Princess of Zerbst and her daughter were invited to St. Petersburg, a draft for 10,000 rubles to cover their expenses (they were known to be very poor) accompanied the Empress's invitation." [1]

On the 3/14 February, 1744, mother and daughter arrived at St. Petersburg. The elder Princess was surprised at, nay, almost overcome by the unwonted magnificence of their reception. [2] It was the first time in her life she had ever been treated as a person of supreme distinction, and her natural vanity expanded luxuriously in the light and warmth of the imperial favour. Elizabeth was awaiting them at Moscow, but the authorities at St. Petersburg, acting under orders, fired salvos, gave receptions and banquets, and did their utmost to entertain the newly arrived guests whom the Empress delighted to honour. "I am treated like

---

[1] The affair was kept very secret. The ostensible cause of the coming of the Princess of Zerbst was to thank the Empress for her kindness to the House of Holstein.

[2] See the *Relation* of the Princess Elizabeth of Zerbst. *Sb. of the Imp. Rus. Hist. Soc.* Vol. VII.

a Queen," cries the Princess of Zerbst rapturously, "and I must say, to the glory of the Russians, that they are all of them *gens d'esprit!*" In a bed-like sledge, well lined with rich soft furs and covered with scarlet cloth laced with silver, a sledge as comfortable as it was sumptuous, the Princesses sped onwards to Moscow at the rate of ten German miles every day, relays of sixteen fresh horses awaiting them at every stage. The guests, on their arrival, were at once conducted to the bed-chamber of the curious and impatient Empress, who embraced them with effusion. Next day mother and daughter were decorated with the order of St. Catherine, and lodged magnificently in one of the palaces of the Kremlin. The bride-elect, a shrewd, piquant, observant, preternaturally precocious little creature of fourteen, who had already made it *" a rule of conduct"* to please everyone worth pleasing, easily won the heart of the good-natured Empress who was very fond of young people. Great pains were taken with her education, especially with the religious side of it. Vasily Adadurov was appointed her instructor in Russian, and the Archimandrite, Simeon Theodorsky, expounded to her the dogmas of the orthodox faith. Sophia Augusta astonished everybody by the keenness of her intelligence and the ardour of her application. In ten days she had learnt enough Russian to converse with her spiritual father in that language. Then she gave the whole court a great scare. In order to master the difficult idioms of the Slavonic tongue as rapidly as possible, the little Princess used to get up in the middle of the night to study her tasks for the following day, and as her rooms were kept at a very high temperature, she would frequently kick off her slippers and walk about barefoot for hours, repeating her exercises aloud. The consequence was she contracted a violent cold which turned to pleurisy, and for a month the girl's life

hung upon a thread. [1]   The Empress was away at the time
on a pilgrimage to the Troitsa Monastery, and during her
absence the doctors disputed over the patient without
daring to stir a finger to aid her, while her own mother
refused to have her daughter blooded as the physicians
recommended.   On the fifth day of Sophia's illness, the
Empress, apprised of the news, flew back to Moscow and
instantly ordered a consultation, to which Lestocq was also
summoned.   The doctors unanimously advised blooding,
and Elizabeth herself held the unconscious little maid fast
embraced while the operation was performed.   On coming
to herself Sophia found herself in the Empress's arms, and
for the next three weeks, during which she hovered between
life and death and was blooded sixteen times, Elizabeth
scarcely quitted her bedside.   Finally a tumour broke out
in her side, and she began to recover.   Yet even in the
throes of what might have been a mortal illness, the tact
and common-sense of the little Princess did not desert her.
During an interval of ease, her mother, whose conduct
throughout seems to have been anything but maternal, [2]
suggested to her that she should see a Lutheran pastor.
"No," replied the girl, "I should prefer a talk with my
confessor, Simeon Theodorsky."   These words were of
course reported to the Empress, as Sophia meant they
should be, and won her the favour of the whole Court.
At last on April 21st, 1744, her fifteenth birthday, the little
Princess, "long and lean, as thin as a skeleton, deadly pale,
and minus a good deal of my hair," [3] was able to appear in

---

[1] It is somewhat odd that the little Princess's mother absolutely ignores
this illness in her *Relation*. Catherine's own account of it in her *Mémoires*
is full of bitterness against her mother.

[2] It is true we have only the testimony of Catherine herself, and it is certain
that Catherine did not love her mother, and loses no opportunity of disparaging her.   On the other hand the mother seems to have been exacting
and tyrannical.   [3] *Catherine II, Mémoires.*

public again with the assistance of a rouge-pot privately conveyed to her by the anxious Empress.

On Sophia's complete recovery, the Empress took her and the Grand Duke on a pilgrimage to the Troitsa Monastery, and for the next two months she was occupied, almost incessantly, with religious exercises in preparation for her anointing and reception into the Russian Church. That function took place, with great pomp and ceremony on June 28/July 8, 1744. The Princess repeated her confession of faith, on her knees, in Russian, clearly and distinctly, with a faultless pronunciation, and comported herself throughout with so much dignity, and with such devout attention to every ceremonial detail, that all the old men present sobbed aloud, and the Empress was dissolved in tears. [1] The anointing accomplished, and the benediction pronounced, the Empress led her by the hand to the altar, where she was communicated, and then a prayer was recited for Catherine Aleksyevna, under which name Sophia Augusta was formally received into the Orthodox Church. After the ceremony, the Empress presented the girl with a diamond agraffe worth 100,000 rubles. [2] On the following day Peter and Catherine exchanged rings [3] of betrothal in the Cathedral of the Kremlin, and a Ukaz was read, in which Catherine was, for the first time, given the title of orthodox Grand Duchess of all the Russias. The ceremony lasted four hours, and, at the moment when the rings were actually exchanged, all the bells of the city pealed forth, and all the guns of the citadels fired salvos. Banquets, balls and illuminations followed hard upon the glad event, and, by the end of the day, the Princess Mother had a red spot, the size of a German florin, on the

---

[1] A very interesting account of the ceremony, in which a full description of the upholstery is not forgotten, will be found in the *Relation* of Catherine's mother. [2] £25,000. [3] Each ring was worth 50,000 *écus*.

palm of her right hand, due to the congratulatory kisses imprinted thereupon. From the 26th July to the 1st October, the Court resided at Kiev, then the ecclesiastical metropolis of Russia, where the Empress received the most flattering ovation from her Cossack and Ruthenian subjects, whom she edified by the austerity of her devotions, and enchanted by the magnificence of her hospitality. During the course of this pilgrimage, the Grand Duke, who had been suffering from fainting-fits all the summer, was attacked by smallpox, and his life was for a time in danger. The Empress, despite the warnings of the doctors, persisted in nursing her nephew herself, and her prayers and tears were at length rewarded by his recovery. But he was now feebler than ever, and so hideously pockmarked that his *fiancée*, who had always secretly despised him, could scarce endure the sight of him. [1] No sooner, however, was the Grand Duke fairly on his legs again, than the Empress hastened on the wedding, and the ceremony took place at St. Petersburg, on August 21st, 1745. Early in the morning, the bride, in a *déshabillé* of white and gold, was escorted to the parade chamber of the Empress, who warmly embraced her, and helped to attire her in a brilliant, richly embroidered costume of cloth of silver. Her Majesty then added all imaginable embellishments in the shape of priceless jewels, with just a touch of rouge to show off the girl's fine complexion; but the young lady was allowed to wear her beautiful lustrous dark-brown hair without powder, and many considered this her chiefest ornament. Then the Empress, having first arrayed herself in chestnut-coloured robes of unexampled splendour, proceeded to the cathedral in an immense carriage, a veritable castle in size, drawn by eight horses, with the young people by her side. The

---

[1] "He had become frightful," says Catherine in her *Mémoires*. Catherine was fifteen at this time and the Grand Duke a year older.

Archbishop of Novgorod and the attendant prelates received
the Empress at the door of the cathedral, and escorted
her up the nave, her train being sustained by the Grand
Master of her household and four chamberlains.   When
she had been enthroned, the betrothed couple took their
seats on two tribunes a little below her.   After Mass had
been recited, the officiating Archbishop approached the
throne, and, making a low obeisance, asked for the Ukaz
permitting the marriage, which having received, he returned to the sanctuary, followed by the Empress holding
the bridegroom by one hand and the bride by the other.
On reaching the altar, Elizabeth placed the Grand Duke
on the right hand and the Grand Duchess on the left, and
fell back a step behind the former.   Then the Archbishop,
assisted by two other prelates, emerged from behind the
curtain, carrying little golden crowns which were placed
on the heads of the young couple.   The Gospels having
been read, the Archbishop exchanged and blessed the
wedding-rings, whereupon the Empress also blessed them
and passed them on to the spouses.   When the ceremony
was over, the young people threw themselves at the feet of
the Empress, who instantly raised and embraced them with
transport.   The marriage was followed by a grand banquet at
Court, and a state ball which lasted for an hour and a half,
after which there was a procession to the nuptial chamber, the
Empress bringing up the rear.   Elizabeth's appearance in the
nuptial chamber was the signal for the gentlemen to withdraw, and on their departure the doors were closed, and the
ladies of the Court proceeded to disrobe the bride, the Empress giving the signal by taking off the Grand Duchess's
crown, which she had worn ever since the marriage. [1]

---

[1] There seems to have been some dispute between the bride's mother and
the Princess of Hesse–Homburg as to which of them should have the honour
of putting on the young lady's *robe-de-nuit.*

Catherine was then arrayed in "the most magnificent *déshabillé* conceivable," while the impatient Empress hastened into the ante-chamber to look after her nephew who was there preparing for his nuptial couch with the help of the Grand Equerry, Count Cyril Razumovsky. Her Majesty speedily brought the young gentleman back with her, and the blushing spouses, having received her Majesty's benediction on their knees, were tenderly embraced by her, whereupon she also departed, leaving the Princess Mother, the Princess of Hesse-Homburg and the Countess Razumovsky to put the spouses safely between the sheets in a huge and sumptuous state bed, under a canopy of poppy-coloured velvet hung with garlands and adorned with hymeneal emblems. Early on the following morning, the Empress sent for the Grand Duke, and gave him, for his bride, two superb toilet-sets, one in emeralds and the other in sapphires, besides other costly gifts, and a prayer-book printed in very large type. [1] A crowded reception followed at eleven o'clock, and the following ten days were given up to festivities of all sorts, not even the common people being forgotten, for oxen stuffed with game were roasted in all the public squares for their entertainment, and all the fountains ran with wine at the expense of the Empress's privy purse, so that everybody so minded could get drunk gratis.

This unnatural union, so prolific of mischief, so miserable in its immediate consequences, so tragical in its *dénoûment*, was, as we have already seen, born of political intrigue, and during all these domestic rejoicings, sincere, at any rate, on the part of the Empress; during all these nuptial festitivities, a struggle, all the fiercer because of its secrecy and silence, was uninterruptedly proceeding between Alexius Bestuzhev,

---

[1] "To save your eyes, my dear," as the Empress afterwards explained.

as the representative of Russia's true interests, and Frederick of Prussia, Russia's most insidious enemy, in which struggle all the principal parties to the marriage, except the bride and bridegroom themselves, were more or less directly concerned.

From the very beginning of his reign, Frederick II had rightly regarded Russia as his most formidable neighbour. Her interests in moribund Poland, at whose expense he proposed at some future day to expand his domains, were antagonistic to his own, and she was also the natural ally of his inveterate enemy, the Queen of Hungary. Semibarbarous and comparatively poor as Russia was, the King of Prussia never shut his eyes to the fact of her immense if latent resources, while her very vastness made her practically invulnerable. Frederick therefore had a wholesome fear of Russia, and was always on his guard against her. On June 1st, 1743, he wrote to Mardefelt, his Minister at St. Petersburg:[1] "I should never think of lightly provoking Russia, on the contrary there is nothing in the world I would not do in order to always live on good terms with that Empire." These words were written during the short interval of peace between the First and Second Silesian Wars, when Frederick was resting securely on the spoils he had wrested from Maria Theresa by the treaties of Breslau and Berlin. A few months later, the friendship, or at least the neutrality, of Russia, had become of vital importance to him. Alarmed for the ultimate safety of Silesia[2] by the victories of Austria and her allies over the French and the Bavarians in the course of 1743, and especially disturbed by the Compact of Worms (13 Sept., 1743) when England and Sardinia seemed to renew the guarantee of the

---

[1] *Pol. Corr.* Vol. II.

[2] His most lucrative province. It had cost him nothing, and brought him in 3,000,000 thalers per annum.

Pragmatic Sanction in its entirety, Frederick resolved to make sure of his newly won possessions by attacking the Queen of Hungary a second time, before she had time to attack him. But how would Russia take this fresh and unprovoked act of aggression? That was the question upon which everything else depended. Fortunately the so-called Botta Conspiracy provided him with an opportunity of ingratiating himself with the Tsaritsa, and he took advantage of it with his usual promptitude and astuteness. He wrote a holograph letter to Elizabeth, expressing his horror at the plot against her sacred person, and ostentatiously, not to say officiously, demanded of the Court of Vienna that Botta, who had been transferred from St. Petersburg to Berlin, should be instantly recalled. Elizabeth was charmed by this chivalrous attention. She declared aloud, at a public banquet, that the King of Prussia was "the most perfect monarch in the world," and the Prussian Minister, Mardefelt, was petted and fêted in his master's honour. Yet, despite these friendly demonstrations, Frederick was still anything but easy. He had no very high opinion of the constancy of women, and he knew that by the side of the Tsaritsa stood Alexius Bestuzhev, the one Russian statesman who, from purely political reasons, was his most determined opponent. From the first he regarded Bestuzhev as the one great obstacle in his path, to be removed at any cost. "I can never repeat to you often enough," he wrote to Mardefelt on Jan. 25th, 1744,[1] "that until this man has been rendered harmless... I can never reckon upon the friendship ... of the Empress, and I am impatiently waiting to learn from you the real cause of the extraordinary independence the Empress permits this Minister to have, though he generally acts against her interests." A month later

[1] *Pol. Corr.* Vol. III.

(29th Feb.) he writes again: "It is absolutely necessary to oust the Vice-Chancellor ... So long as he is in office, he will never cease to cause me a thousand chagrins." And not content with warnings and menaces, Frederick did not consider it beneath his dignity to lend a hand himself to overthrow his enemy. The elder Princess of Zerbst came to Russia, not merely as the mother of the future Grand Duchess, but also as a Prussian spy and political agent, and she received her instructions from Frederick personally before she started. She was to act in concert with Lestocq, Mardefelt, La Chetardie and Bestuzhev's other enemies, on every occasion; she was to neglect no opportunity of insinuating to the good-natured Tsaritsa that the Vice-Chancellor was deceiving her; and, if possible, she was to show Elizabeth a private letter from the King of Prussia, warning her, as a friend, against the machinations of this dangerous Counsellor. "Having regard to the way in which you have concerted measures with the Princess of Zerbst," wrote Frederick to Mardefelt, in February 1744, "I don't see how the blow can possibly fail." Yet fail it did, and the Vice-Chancellor not only manfully parried the thrusts of his numerous opponents, but riposted with telling effect. Nor was he as isolated as was commonly supposed. The Empress still believed in him, and the English Minister, Lord Tyrawley, supported him. [1] He had also wormed himself into the confidence of the Tsaritsa's confessor, and was on the best of terms with her husband, Count Alexius Razumvosky. As the year wore on and Bestuzhev still held his own, Frederick grew anxious. He had already (15th April and 22nd May, 1744) signed conventions with France, Kaiser Charles VII,

---

[1] Frederick believed (or pretended to believe) and circulated the report that Tyrawley had placed 100,000 guineas at Bestuzhev's disposal for bribing purposes—a pure fiction.

and Hesse-Cassel, and was prepared to pounce at once upon the Queen of Hungary; but to embark on such an enterprise with Bestuzhev still paramount at St. Petersburg, was like leaving a strong hostile fortress in his rear.   As usual, when angry and disturbed, he becomes abusive.   The "extreme effrontery" of the Vice-Chancellor in steadily opposing his design to bring about an alliance between Russia, Prussia and Sweden, amazes him. [1]   He calls the growing influence of "ce méchant homme" "a mystery of iniquity," which he cannot fathom. [2]   At last he can wait no longer and seriously proposes to corrupt the man he cannot conquer.   On June 4th he wrote to Mardefelt: "Pressing circumstances and the prompt execution of my designs absolutely demand that you should change your tactics a little and employ all your *savoir-faire* to win over the Vice-Chancellor." [3]   Mardefelt is then authorised to spend as much as 150,000 crowns for that purpose, but to use every possible precaution lest Bestuzhev should reveal everything to the Empress, or take the money without changing his line of conduct.   "I must know the result before the end of the month," he adds, "so that I may see how I really stand with Russia. It is the last effort I mean to make, the *non plus ultra* of my endeavours."   Then, trusting to the skill of Mardefelt and the potent influence of the 150,000 crowns, at the end of August he openly threw off the mask, and invaded Bohemia at the head of 60,000 men, as "the protector of the Emperor of Germany and of German liberty." [4]   He

---

[1] Bestuzhev had dexterously thwarted this project by persuading the Empress to enter into an alliance with Sweden alone.   [2] *Pol. Corr.* Vol. III.

[3] *Ib.* Adding: "Pourvu que vous réussiez à ce que je n'ai rien à craindre de la Russie pendant cette année qui vient." *Pol. Corr.* Vol. III.

[4] In a letter to Elizabeth, however, he pretended that it was *her* cause alone he was fighting. "Ce que m'a le plus déterminé au part que je prends, est sans contredit pour venger Votre Majesté Impériale du peu de considération que la Reine de Hongrie fait de sa personne, de l'infâme conspiration du Marquis de Botta etc." Aug. 10th, 1744. *Pol. Corr.* III.

calculated, with his usual audacity, that this sudden irruption would overwhelm Maria Theresa before Russia had time to intervene.

Before quitting Berlin, however, an unwelcome piece of intelligence reached him, which, for the moment, filled him with consternation—this was no less an event than the expulsion from Russia of the French Ambassador, the Marquis de la Chetardie.

It was a capital blunder on the part of the French Government to send this already discredited diplomatist back to St. Petersburg at the most critical period of the War of the Austrian Succession, when the friendship of Russia was vital to the interests of France and her allies. Old Cardinal Fleury, who died at the beginning of 1743, would never have made such a mistake. La Chetardie was known to be personally odious to the Russian Ministers, and they regarded him with lively suspicion. To confide any political mission to such a discredited agent, therefore, was to condemn it to utter failure beforehand. Nor was La Chetardie's conduct, on his arrival, calculated to regain respect. On the Empress's birthday he appeared at Court with his right hand bandaged, and upon Elizabeth enquiring what had happened to him, he told an odd story of how he had been making experiments with gunpowder in a bottle, when the bottle accidentally exploded in his hand, and had injured it in such a manner that he was afraid he should lose the use of two of his fingers. The Empress, who had a strong sense of humour, thereupon observed with a smile, that she was very sorry, but that if a child had played with gunpowder as his Excellency had done he would certainly have deserved a whipping. The tale of the bottle was speedily the talk of the town, but one of those inquisitive persons who take such a lively and intelligent interest in their neighbours' affairs, speedily discovered that the Ambassador had really damaged his hand in a discreditable brawl with his colleague D'Allion, whose ears he had boxed and who had there and then retaliated by pinking the palm of his official chief with his rapier before the lacqueys of the Embassy could kick him downstairs. [1] After this La Chetardie naturally found himself more or less of a laughing-stock, and his mortification is mirrored in his despatches. He was well aware, indeed, that all letters were opened and examined at the Russian post-office before being forwarded to their destination, [2] but he took the precaution of effusively belauding the Empress in his ordinary despatches while expressing his real sentiments in private letters, which he wrote with his own hand in a new cipher which he regarded as absolutely undecipherable. [3] Unfortunately the Marquis fatally underrated the resources of his enemy the Vice-Chancellor. It happened that Bestuzhev had a secretary in his employment, Goldbach by name, who had a genius for finding the key to the most abstruse and complicated cipher-writing. To the ingenious Goldbach the unravelling of La Chetardie's hieroglyphics was the pastime of an afternoon, and Bestuzhev now had his enemy at his mercy. It was the practice of that astute Minister to lighten the labours of his Sovereign by systematically submitting to her a *précis* of all public documents, garnished with pungent marginal comments for her enlightenment and amusement; and he now furnished her with extracts from La Chetardie's correspondence with the usual elucidatory commentary. This time, however, Eliza-

---

[1] Wych to Carteret. 21st Dec. 1743 (*Record Office: Russia*).

[2] Bestuzhev introduced this system of espionage into Russia, borrowing the idea from Frederick the Great who was its original author. Frederick naturally protested loudly when his own invention was turned against himself.

[3] The fullest account of La Chetardie's expulsion is to be found in "*Dyelo o Markizye Shetardy i ob ego vuisuilkye iz Rossy.*" (Ark. Vor. Vol. I.) Compare *Solovev* and the *Despatches* of Wych (*Record Office: Russia.*)

beth was much more enlightened than amused. She could scarce believe her own eyes when she saw in black and white what the ever gallant and deferential Marquis said of her in private. She was "frivolous and dissipated," and not to be depended on; she abandoned herself to a "voluptuous lethargy;" the mere suggestion of business, however necessary, was sufficient to alarm her—and much more to the same effect. Furious at such treachery, the Empress dictated to Bestuzhev, on the spot, a memorandum addressed to La Chetardie, bitterly reproaching him for his want of honesty and courtesy, and commanding him to quit her capital within four-and-twenty hours. Armed with this document, General Ushakov, Prince Peter Golitsuin, Secretary Kurbatov and a captain and fifty men of the Semenovsky Guard proceeded, between 5 and 6 o'clock on the morning of June 17th, 1744, to the residence of the Ambassador, who was roused from his bed and compelled to appear before his visitors in his dressing-gown and listen while Kurbatov read the Empress's declaration and extracts from the Marquis's own deciphered correspondence. General Ushakov then bluntly told La Chetardie to select his suite without delay, as the soldiers in the hall were under strict orders to escort him to the frontier forthwith, and the sooner he was off, the better pleased her Imperial Majesty would be. The discomfited diplomatist had not a word to say; his voice trembled, his hands shook. Apprehensive lest still worse might befall him, he hastened to obey, and before evening he was gone. Six weeks later (July 26th) the Empress emphatically identified herself with the anti-French policy of her Minister by promoting him to the rank of Grand Chancellor of the Empire,[1] his friend and colleague,

---

[1] At the end of the year, moreover, she gave him land in Livonia, to the value of 100,000 rubles, and Ostermann's residence at St. Petersburg. (*Record Office: Russia*).

Michael Vorontsov, being at the same time appointed Vice-Chancellor.

Meanwhile the King of Prussia was carrying everything before him. Audaciously violating the territory of Saxony, in order to reach Bohemia by the shortest route, he captured Prague (16th Sept.) and speedily occupied the whole Kingdom, while General von der Marwitz invaded Moravia. In the extremity of her danger, Maria Theresa sent a special envoy, Count Rosenberg, to St. Petersburg, to express her horror at Botta's alleged misconduct, and, after appealing with dignity to the memory of the ancient friendship between the two Courts, she placed herself and her fortunes unreservedly in the hands of her Imperial sister. For two months Elizabeth hesitated while the Lestocq-Mardefelt-Zerbst clique did all in its power to prevent any assistance being sent to the distressed Queen of Hungary. But the Grand Chancellor was equally energetic on the other side, and he was far better informed than his opponents. The warning and pregnant despatches of his brother Michael, who had been sent from Berlin to Poland to counteract Prussian intrigues there, enabled him to exhibit "the philosopher of Sans Souci" to the Tsaritsa in his true colours, and he did not pick his words. "The King of Prussia," he said to the Empress, "has a restless, ambitious, agitating character, and is the chief cause of this unhappy German War. In violating the Treaty of Breslau, he solemnly broke his solemn word. It is absolutely necessary, your Majesty, for Russia to interfere. If my neighbour's house catches fire, I am bound for my own sake, even if he be my enemy, to help him put it out, and I am doubly bound to do so if my neighbour is also my friend." And then he revealed to her the treacherous behaviour of Frederick, how he had informed the Swedes that the Tsaritsa approved of his invasion of Bohemia; how he was stirring up Turkey against her in secret; how he impudently used the neutral Saxon territory as a stepping-stone to Bohemia, without asking the permission of the Elector; and how the Prussian Minister, Wallenrodt, had bribed and bullied the Polish deputies at Grodno, and had forcibly procured the dissolution of the diet there to prevent his anti-Russian intrigues from being discovered. Such an act of violence as the Grodno incident, argued Bestuzhev, was a blow at the supremacy which Russia had enjoyed in Poland ever since the days of Peter the Great, when Prussia was of no account in that kingdom. If, he continued, the King of Prussia were successful in the present war, Poland would be the next victim, and then Russia herself might suffer. Prussia was already far too powerful to be a safe neighbour. The balance of power in Europe must be restored instantly and at any cost. These considerations at last prevailed with the Empress, and she sacrificed her private resentment against Austria from patriotic motives. At the end of October, Rosenberg, who had undertaken that Maria Theresa should send a circular to the principal European Courts, expressing her regret at the intrigues imputed to Botta, at last received his long awaited audience, when Elizabeth assured him that henceforth she meant to consign the whole Botta affair to oblivion, and leave the peccant Marquis to the discretion of his own Sovereign. Simultaneously with this reconciliation, the tide of fortune began to turn strongly against the King of Prussia. The feeble strategy of Frederick's French allies enabled Austria to recall Prince Charles of Lorraine from the Rhine to Bohemia, where, obeying the prudent counsels of his chief of the staff, General Traun, he avoided general engagements by constantly taking up impregnable positions, and so skilfully harassed Frederick with his light troops, by intercepting his provisions and destroying his stores, that the exhausted Prussians, at the end of December, were obliged to hastily evacuate Bohemia and retire into Silesia, [1] followed by the triumphant Austrians. At the beginning of 1745 the prospects of Frederick were gloomier than they had ever been before. On January 8th a convention was concluded at Warsaw, between Austria, England, Holland and Saxony, to resist Prussian aggression. On the 20th suddenly expired the Franco-Prussian puppet, Kaiser Charles VII, whose name had hitherto served to cloak the nakedness of Frederick's pretensions. Almost simultaneously Russia bluntly refused him a succour of 6,000 men, which he had demanded in a letter written with his own hand to the Empress, conformably to his treaty with her. [2] He was still further alarmed by the persistent rumour of immense Russian armaments and the strenuous efforts of the Maritime Powers to induce the Tsaritsa to accede to the Treaty of Warsaw. In reality there was far less to be feared from this quarter than he imagined. Bestuzhev, indeed, was eager for war, but he knew that the finances were in disorder and the treasury empty, and he earnestly assured Lord Hyndford that he could not put even 30,000 men on a war footing for less than 1,250,000 Albert dollars per annum so long as the war lasted. His intervention project was duly submitted to the British Government, but was declared to be too onerous and exorbitant to be accepted in its entirety. [3] Finally, the knowledge that Austria was about to conclude a defensive alliance with Saxony, and that Saxony was arming rapidly, determined Frederick, alarmed for the safety of "my Silesia", as he called it, to make "the Saxons drink the cup of my wrath

---

[1] This retreat was accelerated by the point-blank refusal of Great Britain to lend any assistance to Frederick in a war which he himself had provoked.
[2] Tyrawley to Harrington, 22nd Jan. 1745. (*Record Office*, *Russia*.)
[3] Chesterfield to Hyndford. *Ib*.

to the very dregs." [1] To crush Saxony at once, was now, indeed, his best diplomatic move, for from Russia he had nothing more to hope. As a last pacific effort he had privately offered Bestuzhev, through Mardefelt, 100,000 crowns if he would acquiesce in Prussia's appropriating another slice of Silesia; but the Russian Chancellor had scornfully rejected the offer, and Mardefelt had become an object of suspicion ever since. Accordingly, at the end of May, Frederick openly declared war against Saxony.   Extreme was the agitation at the Russian Court when the news reached St. Petersburg. Elizabeth at once summoned a grand council of ministers and notables, and demanded their opinion on the situation individually. Vorontsov deprecated a military demonstration in favour of Saxony as likely to lead to a long war which the Empire had no means of supporting; Bestuzhev, on the other hand, strongly advised a vigorous intervention, and represented that now or never was the time to clip the wings of the artful and disquieting King of Prussia. In a subsequent private interview, he frankly warned his Sovereign that any further hesitation on the part of Russia, to take her proper place in Europe, might lead to the departure of all the foreign ministers from a Court where there was nothing for them to do. Elizabeth was silent and pensive for the rest of the day, and in the evening she summoned another extraordinary council for the following day, September 20th (at which Field Marshals Lacy and Dolgoruki were also to be present) to finally decide the question whether assistance should be given to Saxony or not. The council unanimously agreed that Saxony ought to be assisted. During the next fortnight, the Empress very carefully considered all the documents relating to the question, and then consulted a third council which

---

[1] Frederick to Mardefelt, May 6th, 1745. *Pol. Corr.* Vol. IV.

also unanimously advised intervention. Elizabeth thereupon signed a ukaz, commanding that the 60,000 men already stationed in Livonia and Esthonia should at once advance into Courland, so as to be nearer to the Prussian frontier and ready for every emergency; and ordered that a manifesto should be addressed to the King of Prussia, warning him that Russia considered herself bound to assist Saxony in case he invaded the territory of that Power. After signing these documents, Elizabeth, who had a humane horror of bloodshed, flung herself on her knees before an Ikon; called God to witness that she had acted conscientiously, and invoked the divine blessing on her arms. In a subsequent interview with the Grand Chancellor, however, she relieved her mind by reproaching him roundly with trusting too much to England, for, angry as she was with "the Shah Nadir of Berlin," as she now called Frederick II, she did not believe in the sincerity of the British Ministry. In this respect she showed that her judgment was clearer and sounder than that of her Minister. There can be little doubt, indeed, that at this time, the English Cabinet was simply playing with Russia. The safety of Hanover had already been secured by a secret compact with the King of Prussia, and, despite their sympathy with Maria Theresa in the abstract, the English Ministers now regarded the issue of the German War with comparative indifference, as quite a minor affair. This too was the real reason why Great Britain shrank from committing herself to a quadruple [1] alliance against Prussia, as proposed by Bestuzhev. Meanwhile Frederick, sure now of the neutrality of England, and shrewdly calculating on the tardiness of Russia's mobilization, had, despite the warnings and menaces of Elizabeth, already invaded Saxony, captured Gorlitz, and pushed on towards

---

[1] *I. e.* of Russia, England, Austria and Saxony.

Bautzen. The feeble Saxon army retired before him into Bohemia. Then Leipsic fell, and King Augustus, panic-stricken, fled from his capital, amidst the tears of the populace, and took refuge in Prague, followed by Michael Bestuzhev. The Prussians ravaged Saxony mercilessly, [1] Frederick declaring that if Saxony did not instantly come to terms, and renounce both the Austrian and the Russian alliance, he would not leave one stone upon another throughout the length and breadth of the Electorate. At the end of December, after the final crushing defeats of Hennersdorf and Kesselsdorf, both Austria and Saxony gave up the contest, and, on Christmas Day, 1745, peace was signed at Dresden, Maria Theresa [2] definitively ceding Silesia and Glatz to Frederick, and Augustus of Saxony paying him an indemnity of a million thalers. Thus, by his alert energy, the King of Prussia had, for the third time, baffled the designs of his enemies. But he was only just in time. Twelve days after the conclusion of the Peace of Dresden, and a week before the news thereof had reached St. Petersburg, a cabinet council, which lasted three days, was held at the Winter Palace, the Empress presiding. It was there and then unanimously resolved that Bestuzhev should inform Lord Hyndford that, if the Maritime Powers would advance Russia a subsidy of six millions, she would at once place 100,000 men in the field, and end the German War in a single campaign. As far as this, however, Great Britain was not prepared to go, so the King of Prussia remained unmolested.

---

[1] Michael Bestuzhev, an eye-witness of the campaign, reported to his Court that it would be 80 years before Saxony quite recovered from the effects of the Prussian devastations.

[2] On the other hand Frederick recognised Maria Theresa's consort as Kaiser, a great point with her. There had been some talk, earlier in the year, of the election of Augustus of Saxony, France in particular advocating the idea, but it fell thorough because Russia and Prussia were equally opposed to it.

Hampered as he was by the parsimony and backwardness of England, and the misgivings of his own Sovereign, Bestuzhev could not prevent the conclusion of a peace which he detested; yet there can be no doubt that the menacing attitude of the Russian Chancellor had profoundly impressed the King of Prussia, and induced him to moderate his demands in spite of his recent victories. And though foiled in his endeavours to assist the Queen of Hungary, Bestuzhev, before the end of the year, had at least succeeded in weakening the influence of Prussia at St. Petersburg. Before departing for Saxony, Frederick had committed the diplomatic blunder of requesting the mediation of Turkey and Russia at the same time, declaring with a sneer, at a public reception, that in his opinion the mediation of a Turk was every bit as good as the mediation of a Greek. The Sultan had thereupon addressed a letter to the Tsaritsa, piously expressing a desire to stay the effusion of so much Christian blood. Elizabeth was wounded in her tenderest point. That she, the devout mother of all the orthodox, should be placed in the same category with the descendant of the false Prophet, with Antichrist, revolted her, and her sentiments towards the King of Prussia were never the same again. [1] The expulsion of the Princess of Zerbst from Russia was also a very sensible blow to Frederick, and this, too, was the work of Bestuzhev. Madame Zerbst was, as the English Minister, Lord Hyndford, expressed it, "a lady not easily rebutted," but her zeal for the service of

---

[1] There had been some talk of an exchange of portraits between them, and Frederick had expressed his satisfaction at the opportunity which would be thus afforded him "à paître mes yeux dans les traits de la plus grande, la plus belle, et de la plus accomplie souveraine que l'Europe a vu naître," and to gaze constantly into "ses beaux yeux et dans cette physionomie remplie d'autant de charmes et de grâces que de majesté." *Pol. Corr.* IV. Elizabeth swallowed all this flummery without suspicion, till Bestuzhev gave her a glimpse at the *private* correspondence of the romantic Brandenburger.

the King of Prussia frequently outstripped her prudence, and more than once Elizabeth smartly snubbed her for interfering in political affairs. Nevertheless, presuming on her close relationship with the Grand Duchess, she persisted in her intrigues, and made herself so generally detested, that when, in September 1745, the watchful Chancellor intercepted a letter to her from her brother the Crown Prince of Sweden, condoling with her on her want of money, it was an easy matter for him to persuade the Empress that her august confidence and boundless liberality were both being abused by an ungrateful and extravagant woman, [1] and he boldly suggested that the Princess's private correspondence should now be overhauled. To this Elizabeth, after some hesitation, at last agreed, and the result was fresh discoveries of treachery, and a violent explosion of the imperial wrath, which made it impossible for Madame Zerbst to remain in Russia any longer. She departed loaded with loot of all sorts, [2] and the Empress gave her a parting gift of 50,000 rubles. At the final interview, the Princess threw herself at the Tsaritsa's feet, and begged pardon for any offence she might in ignorance have committed. "It is rather late in the day to think of that now," replied Elizabeth. "It would have been as well if you had always been as modest as you are at present." Thus Frederick lost his most trusted spy at the Russian Court.

Moreover, though the King of Prussia had succeeded in crippling Saxony, humbling Austria and retaining Silesia, his position throughout the year 1746 was highly precarious. His correspondence shows that he anticipated another war, this time with Russia, at any moment, and dreaded such a contingency exceedingly. All through the

---

1 "What does she do with all the money your Majesty gives her?" queries Bestuzhev in one of his suggestive marginal notes.

2 Amongst other things, two enormous boxes full of china.

year he was fluctuating between hope and fear. On April 21st he sent a courier to his Minister, Mardefelt, instructing him to offer the Russian Chancellor as much as 200,000 crowns to maintain peace. [1] Ten days later he considered it necessary to demand a categorical explanation as to the destination of the Russian troops reported to be moving on the frontier. On May 29th he strongly counselled his Minister to flatter and caress Bestuzhev to the top of his bent, in order to wheedle him out of his secret plans. On June 9th the new Prussian Ambassador, Finkenstein, is instructed to ask the Russian Chancellor, point-blank, what the Russian armaments mean. A week later he is grimly warned that his head will be in danger if he causes his master to take a single false step at a crisis when the very existence of the Prussian monarchy is at stake. [2] At last, finding it absolutely impossible to win Bestuzhev by the most dazzling bribes, and alarmed by the intelligence of a defensive alliance between Austria and Russia, 21 May/2 June, 1745, [3] Frederick resolved again to attempt to overthrow the Russian Chancellor. Nor did he despair of success even now, for Bestuzhev about this time was saddled with a fresh adversary who promised to be troublesome. This was none other than his former friend, the Vice-Chancellor Vorontsov,

---

[1] Letter to Mardefelt, 20th April, 1746. (*Pol. Corr.* Vol. VI.)

[2] Frederick to Finkenstein. (*Pol. Corr.* Vol. VI.)

[3] This treaty was brought about by the interception of a despatch from D'Argenson, the French Minister of Foreign Affairs, to Valory, the French Minister at Berlin, which the court of Vienna communicated to Bestuzhev. This letter disclosed that, as the King of Prussia found Russia to be the great obstacle to his designs, strong measures were necessary to keep her in check; every effort was to be made to egg on Turkey and Persia against her, and as a preliminary thereto, an alliance was to be contracted between Prussia and the Porte. On seeing this letter, Elizabeth at once agreed to a closer alliance with Austria. By this new treaty each of the contracting parties agreed to aid the other, within three months of being attacked, with 30,000 men, or with 60,000 in case Prussia was the aggressor. Frederick affected to see in this compact a plan for attacking him on the first opportunity.

who was formidable, not from any commanding qualities of his own, but because he had been a warm personal friend of Elizabeth from his youth up, and was married to her favourite cousin who had more influence with her than anyone else. In the earlier period of their intimacy, Vorontsov had posed as the protector of Bestuzhev, and shared and supported his political views; but when Bestuzhev was made Grand Chancellor and monopolized the conduct of affairs, Vorontsov was disgusted to find that he was little more than the humble satellite of this brilliant planet, and his pride revolted at the reflection. Accordingly he henceforth set himself industriously to oppose the plans of the Grand Chancellor—it was the only way he now had of asserting himself—and readily listened to the insinuations of D'Allion, Mardefelt, Lestocq and Bestuzhev's other enemies, who now regarded him as their last hope. In Frederick II's despatches, from 1745 onwards, Vorontsov is cryptically designated as "our important friend," while Lestocq is dubbed "our intrepid friend," and before either of them was well aware of it, they had both become Prussian spies [1] and hirelings. It was a slippery path to tread, beset with innumerable pitfalls, and Vorontsov, a timid, nervous, short-sighted man, was bound to stumble, and fall, sooner or later, especially with such an opponent as Bestuzhev lying in wait for him at every turn. His first indiscretion was to correspond with the already compromised Princess of Zerbst (now at Berlin) so indiscreetly that some of the letters fell into Bestuzhev's hands, who showed them to the Empress. Then the Vice-Chancellor and his wife, in a fit of pique, went abroad for the benefit of their health, for a few months, against the express wis hesof Elizabeth, who could

---

[1] There can be little doubt that Vorontsov communicated to Berlin the results of the secret negotiations going on between England and Russia during 1746 and 1747. (*Record Office: S. P. Russia.* 1746 and 1747.)

not bear to be parted from her cousin, even for a day. On their return, Vorontsov was received by the Tsaritsa with such marked coldness that it was evident to all the world that whatever influence he had ever had was well-nigh gone. The triumph of "Grand-Vizier Bestuzhev," as D'Allion called him, was now complete, and in the plenitude of his power he felt strong enough to disembarrass himself of another dangerous enemy, and, at the same time, deal the now desperate Prussian clique what was practically its *coup de grâce*. Taking advantage of Frederick II's gross discourtesy to the Russian Minister, Chernuishev, at Berlin, [1] Elizabeth formally demanded the recall of Mardefelt, from St. Petersburg, and the Prussian Court, after some demur, was obliged to comply with this request, on condition that Chernuishev [2] should also be recalled. On being informed by Bestuzhev that his passports were ready, Mardefelt could not restrain his anger. "I am well aware that your Excellency is the sole author of this dismissal," said he, "and I will neglect no opportunity of showing you my gratitude and rendering you a similar service on the very first opportunity." Mardefelt was superseded by Finkenstein, and Chernuishev by Kayserling, but neither Court gained by the change, for Kayserling was as determined an adversary of the Franco-Prussian system as even Chernuishev was, while Finkenstein was, from the Russian point of view, a past master in the art of intrigue.

The chronicle of the year would not be complete if I did not here allude to the death of the luckless ex-Regent, Anne Leopoldovna, in great misery and wretchedness. In 1744 Frederick II had advised Elizabeth to send Prince

---

[1] Frederick turned his back on Chernuishev before the whole Court, to mark his displeasure at the freedom with which that Minister had, three days before, discussed Prussia's anti-Austrian policy with Secretary Podewils.

[2] Chernuishev was transferred to London.

Anthony back to his friends in Germany, and transport the Princess and her children into a remote part of Russia so that nobody should know where they were. Then, he said, Europe would gradually forget them, and the Empress's throne would be secure. Frederick's "fatherly advice," as he called it, was followed, and the Brunswickers were first of all sent to the fortress of Schlusselburg. Four months later, however, they were transported to the remote Solovetsky Monastery near Archangel, travelling by night so that nobody should recognise them. The little ex-Tsar Ivan travelled under the name of Gregory, in a close carriage which he was not allowed to quit. The unhappy family set out for this dreary exile in great affliction. Anne Leopoldovna, who was near her confinement, was too weak, her husband too broken-hearted, to protest. On reaching the shores of the White Sea, the dangerous state of the ice made it impossible for them to cross over to the island on which the monastery was situated, so they had to be lodged in the Archbishop's house at Kholmagory, and it was finally decided that their stay at that rude little town, in the midst of a sub-arctic forest, should be permanent, as being less expensive than residence at the Monastery. There then they all lived together in a small, old-fashioned, wooden house, the father and the children (who were called Princes by courtesy even in this den) sleeping in the same room. Early in 1745 Anne gave birth to another son, who was christened Peter, and a year later to a third, named Alexius, expiring shortly afterwards. By the orders of the Empress, the body was conveyed to St. Petersburg, and buried with great pomp at the Aleksandrovsky Monastery, Elizabeth weeping bitterly on the occasion, and placing a wreath on the tomb.

In the course of 1747, Bestuzhev was able at last to put the finishing touch to the elaborate political system which for the last five years he had pursued with such

dogged tenacity, and in the face of such enormous difficulties, by concluding the long-coveted, but ever elusive
English alliance. Bestuzhev's predilection for England was,
in the eyes of France and Prussia, his greatest offence, and
the Ministers of those Powers at St. Petersburg, frequently
represented him to their courts as "the blind slave of Great
Britain." His own views on the subject are most clearly
exhibited, perhaps, in a memorandum which he laid before
the Empress in the course of 1745. [1] "The English alliance," he observes in this document, " is the oldest that
Russia has with any European Power, and is based (1) upon
the necessity for the mutual protection of both Powers
against any combination of Sweden, Denmark, Prussia,
Poland and France, as well as (2) upon their common welfare,
especially as regards commerce, the net result of which is
an annual balance of 500,000 rubles in favour of Russia.
Peter the Great knew well the value of the British Alliance,
and always did his best to preserve it by 'managing' Great
Britain as much as possible." The Empress was never so
enthusiastic an "Anglican" [2] as her Chancellor, and the
course of events more than justified her reserve; but after
her rupture with France and Prussia, she grew more reconciled to a *rapprochement* with the Maritime Powers, and
left Bestuzhev a free hand in the matter. But very soon
Bestuzhev was mortified to discover that the Maritime
Powers were by no means so eager to unite with Russia
as she with them. The English Ministers in particular,
were very content that Prussia should be held in check by
Russia's military demonstrations; but being strongly of opinion that more than enough money had already been paid
to secure Hanover, they were determined to get whatever
assistance Russia could give them in Germany at as cheap

[1] *Pis'ma Grafa A. P. Bestuzheva. (Ar. Vor. II.)*
D'Argenson called Bestuzhev by that name.

a rate as possible, and it must be admitted that not only
did they haggle like petty hucksters over the terms of the
various subsidy conventions made to retain in the service
of George II certain contingents of Russian troops, but they
treated Bestuzhev, their one friend in Russia, "the one man
who stood single in the gap against the Prussian interests," [1]
with a nonchalant ingratitude which would have thrown a less
devoted adherent into the arms of their enemies.   Bestuzhev
was by no means satisfied with the conditions upon which
the English Ministers proposed to accede to the defensive
alliance already concluded at St. Petersburg between Russia
and Austria, and he accused them of over-indulgence towards
the King of Prussia because they refused to subscribe the
secret article to that treaty which left the future disposition of
Silesia an open question, despite the treaty of Breslau. [2] But
the English Ministers stood firm.   "The King," wrote Chesterfield to Hyndford, "cannot guarantee to the Queen of
Hungary possessions which she herself has relinquished." [3]
The victories of Marshal Saxe in the Austrian Netherlands,
however, and the consequent danger of Holland, at last
drew Russia and Great Britain more closely together, and
the pressing question of the advance of a Russian auxiliary
corps to the Rhine engulfed all others.   On January 9th, 1747,
a conference took place at the Winter Palace, at which
Bestuzhev, Vorontsov, Field Marshal Lacy, and the War
Minister, Stephen Apraksin, were present, when Lacy proposed that 30,000 Russian troops, under the command of
Prince Ryepnin, should be placed at the disposal of the

---

[1] Tyrawley to Harrington, Feb. 12th, 1745. (*Record Office: S. P. Russia.*)—
E. g. they made the greatest favour of lending him £10,000 on the security
of his house, though they knew he had refused ten times that amount from
their enemies.

[2] England had already guaranteed to Frederick the full possession of Silesia
by the Hanover Convention.

[3] Chesterfield to Hyndford, 22nd May, 1747. (*Record Office: S. P. Russia.*)

Maritime Powers for two years, at a minimum cost of 150,000 ephim ducats per annum. [1] Two months passed in fruitless negotiations, till at last Bestuzhev, irritated beyond endurance by the delays of England and the attempt of the Court of St. James's to dock the amount of the stipulated subsidies, passionately exclaimed, in an interview with Lord Hyndford, that he saw he was about to become "the sacrifice of his good intentions towards an ungrateful Court," which hesitated at spending thousands in the common cause, when he, Bestuzhev, had saved the King and his allies millions. "France," he cried, "would gladly have given £200,000 per annum for the simple neutrality of the Empress." [2] After this, Hyndford advised compliance with the Russian demands, which were reasonable enough, and the negotiations proceeded more smoothly. Finally, in addition to holding a corps of observation, 30,000 strong, at the disposal of Great Britain on the Courland frontier, at a charge of £100,000 a year, the Empress consented to send another corps of 30,000 to the Rhine, on condition that £300,000 a year were paid for these troops by England and Holland, four months in advance, besides 150,000 ephim ducats for their maintenance during their passage through Europe. On Dec. 9th, 1747, the subsidiary treaty was signed at St. Petersburg, and on Jan. 28th, 1748, the day after the exchange of the ratifications, the Russian troops received orders to march. The event profoundly impressed the Courts of Europe. At London and Vienna there was great rejoicing. Maria Theresa, in the exuberance of her gratitude, wrote a warm letter to "her dearly beloved friend and sister," begging her to be one of the sponsors of her newly born son, the Archduke Peter Leopold Joseph, afterwards Joseph II, and Elizabeth complacently

[1] *Solovev:* Istoria Rossyi.
[2] Hyndford to Chesterfield, May 30th, 1747. (*Record Office: S. P. Russia.*)

accepted the flattering invitation. The King of Prussia, on the other hand, was much agitated by the mysterious Anglo-Russian negotiations of which he was kept duly informed by the treachery of Vorontsov and Lestocq, and nearly every despatch addressed by him to Finkenstein during 1747, speculates as to the destination of the Russian troops assembling on the frontier. His fear of "my great antagonist," as he now, without irony, calls Bestuzhev, is everywhere apparent, and he regretfully wishes that the enemies of the Chancellor were of a different kidney. When in the course of 1748, the Grand Chancellor suddenly becomes very polite to the Prussian Minister, Frederick at once suspects that "some fresh mystery of iniquity" is afoot. When Ryepnin's corps actually started, and Frederick discovered at last that its sole object was to impress France and make her more tractable, he was much relieved, but he secretly, though vainly, attempted to stir up the Poles against the unauthorized invaders of their territory. [1]

Meanwhile Prince Ryepnin, at the head of his 30,000 Russians, was slowly advancing through central Europe, so slowly indeed that both the Courts of Vienna and London were loud in their complaints to the Russian Ministers. But in truth the subsidiary corps had already accomplished all that had been required of it. The news of the approach of Ryepnin's army induced France, despite her brilliant triumphs, to accelerate the peace negotiations, and on 30th April, 1748, a preliminary convention was signed between the Court of Versailles and the Maritime Powers at Aix la Chapelle, which was confirmed by the formal treaty of Oct. 18th, to which Austria and her allies reluctantly [2] acceded. Thus, for the third time in fifteen years, the advance

---

[1] *Pol. Corr.* 1747 and 1748. Vol. V.

[2] Maria Theresa complained that England, by acting so hastily, had sacrificed her interests. England pleaded in excuse the tardiness of the Russians.

of a Russian contingent had checkmated the ambitious designs of France.

Never yet had Russia stood so high in the estimation of Europe as in the autumn of 1748, and she owed her commanding position entirely to the genius of the Grand Chancellor. By sheer tenacity of purpose, combined with the exercise of infinite tact, and in the face of apparently insurmountable obstacles, Bestuzhev had honourably extricated his country from the Swedish imbroglio; reconciled his imperial mistress with the Courts of Vienna and London, her natural allies; re-established friendly relations, on a firm basis, with both those Courts; freed Russia from the yoke of foreign influence; enabled her to assert herself effectually in Poland, Turkey and Sweden; compelled both Prussia and France to moderate their pretensions in the very hour of victory, and finally, and this perhaps was his greatest achievement, he had isolated the restless, perturbating King of Prussia, by environing him with hostile alliances. [1] Henceforth he was universally regarded as a statesman of the first rank, and rightly so, for it is not too much to say that during the interval between the death of Fleury and the ascendency of Kaunitz, Alexius Bestuzhev disputes with Frederick the Great the honour of being the greatest diplomatist in Europe.

And if abroad he was important, at home Bestuzhev was now well-nigh omnipotent. One by one, he had removed from his path all the obstacles to his progress, all the adversaries who had imperilled and embittered his triumphs. The last to go was Lestocq. The shameless venality, the unpatriotic intrigues of this dissolute adventurer had gradually opened the eyes of the indulgent Empress to his true character. Owing everything to Russia, he neverthe-

---

[1] Frederick's own confession in his despatch to Finkenstein, of Aug. 24th, 1748. (*Pol. Cor. Vol. V.*)

less had not scrupled to take money from her enemies.
Once or twice Elizabeth had remonstrated with her former
friend, but at last she withdrew her protection, and let
him rush upon his fate. One day the Grand Duchess
Catherine happened to meet Lestocq coming out of the
Empress's apartments. He appeared to be in great confusion and his face was very red. She would have accosted
him, for he was generally amusing, but he waved her off,
and, lowering his voice, said: "Don't come near me. I
am under suspicion and a person to be avoided." Think-
ing him merely a little drunker than usual, Catherine
turned away. This was on Friday, Nov. 23rd, 1748 ; two days
later Lestocq was arrested at his own house, and conveyed
to the fortress of St. Peter and St. Paul, under a military
guard. [1] He was accused of treasonable intrigues with the
Court of France and the King of Prussia, but would confess to nothing, although frequently and severely tortured.
When he found that he had nothing to hope from the
Empress, he inveighed bitterly against Bestuzhev, and, in
his desperation, attempted to starve himself, so that food
had to be forced upon him by artificial means. Finally
he was banished to Uglich. Frederick II was much disturbed by the removal of his chief spy and informer at
the Russian Court, especially as he had by this time
convinced himself that his second retainer, the timid and
ill-informed Vice-Chancellor, Vorontsov, was practically useless to him. [2] Moreover, it seemed at one time as if Vorontsov would share the fate of his friend Lestocq, for one
of the results of the latter's trial was to establish beyond

---

[1] See *Ob arest ye Lestoka.* (Ark. Vor. III); *Solovev ;* Catherine II: *Mémoires.*
Helbig's story (in *Russische Günstlinge*) of Lestocq sending the Tsaritsa a
ring and imploring her protection, is a fable.

[2] "Our important friend," he remarks with a sneer, " does not know what
"is going on at his own Court."

doubt the complicity of the Vice-Chancellor in the ex-surgeon's intrigues, and Bestuzhev, in the report of the affair which he submitted to the Empress, added a marginal note opposite to Vorontsov's name, to the effect that no man could serve two masters. Fortunately, Vorontsov possessed in his wife, the Empress's favourite cousin, an advocate to whom Elizabeth could refuse nothing, and now, as on so many other occasions, a few tears dropped *à propos* suspended his disgrace. But his influence was now completely destroyed, and though, at the Empress's express desire, he was allowed to countersign treaties and accept the gratuities usually given on much occasions, he was a mere puppet, the Grand Chancellor transacting all important business at his own private residence, without even consulting his colleague. Viewed politically, the fall of Lestocq signified the fixity of Russia's policy in the future, on the existing lines of the Anglo-Austrian alliance, and so the various foreign Courts regarded it.

CHAPTER VI.

THE COURT OF ELIZABETH.

1742—1749.

ELIZABETH's personality—Her amiability—Equity—Indolence—Extravagant splendour of her Court—Her favourites—Alexius Razumovsky—Cyril Razumovsky—Their amiable character—Anecdotes illustrating their generosity—Visit of the Empress to Kiev—General character of Elizabeth's Court—Entertainments—Opera Bouffés—The Court Theatre—The masquerades or metamorphoses—Elizabeth in male attire—Pilgrimages—Deterioration of morals—The rise of the Shuvalovs—Peter Shuvalov—His abilities and vices—Immense influence—Alexander Shuvalov—Ivan Shuvalov—He supersedes Razumovsky in the Empress's favour—Alarm of Bestuzhev—The Beketov incident.

AND now, during the lull in European politics, which makes the years 1748—1755, pregnant as they were in possibilities, perhaps the least eventful period of the Eighteenth Century, it becomes me to endeavour to draw a picture of the Court of Elizabeth Petrovna as it struck her contemporaries, and, as a Court is but the expression and the reflection of the Sovereign who is its soul and centre, we must first of all regard the Empress herself a little more narrowly. [1]

---

[1] The documents relating to this interesting subject are scant and scattered. The chief sources, apart from passing allusions in Solovev, Kostomarov and the despatches of the various Foreign Ministers, are as follows: (1) *Mémoires de Cath. II.* (2) *Pi'sma Grafa A. P. Bestuzheva* (Ark. Vor. 2); (3) *Instruktsy*

Elizabeth Petrovna, although no longer the ravishing, exquisite madcap, "always on the hop," whom grave diplomatists judicially pronounced to be the most exquisite creature in existence, [1] was still one of the most handsome, one of the most fascinating women in Europe. Lord Hyndford described her in her 38th year as "worthy of the admiration of all the world." [2] Catherine II tells us that at forty her somewhat puissant, but marvellously well-proportioned, figure appeared to admiration in male attire, while all the movements of the stately Tsaritsa were so graceful that one could gladly have gazed upon her for ever. Nothing else in the room seemed worth looking at when she was gone. Her once brilliant complexion, indeed, now needed the assistance of cosmetics; but her large blue eyes, "so like a merry bird's," were as brilliant as ever, while her luxuriant hair, of the richest auburn hue, was the crowning charm of a singularly majestic and imposing loveliness. But her salient, her most irresistible attraction was a natural kindliness expressing itself in a ready courtesy, an impulsive sympathy, which came straight from the heart. La Chetardie frequently alludes to her as debonaire, and that delightful word exactly describes her. She was gentle, affable, and familiar with all who approached her, yet always with a due regard to her dignity, and her playful gaiety was without the slightest tinge of malice. It was good to be with her, folks said. She seemed to radiate joyousness.

dlya lite naznashaemnikh sostoyat pri Velikoi Kniginye (Ark. Vor. 2); (4) *Notice sur ma Vie*, par le Comte A. R. Vorontsov. (Ark. Vor. 5); (5) *Ébauche du portrait de sa Majesté l'Imp. Elisabeth* (Ark. Vor. 22); (6) Vasilchikov: *Semeistvo Razumovskikh;* (7) Shcherbatov: *Povrezhdenie nravov v Rossy;* (8) Bantuish-Kemensky: *Biografy rosseskikh generalissumesov;* (9) Dashkova *Mémoires;* (10) Ruilyaev: *Staroe Zhit'e;* (11) Statesdamui ... Russkago Dvora v XVIII stolyetiya.

[1] For a description of Elizabeth at sixteen, see Bain: *Pupils of Peter the Great,* pp. 122—124.

[2] *Record Office: S. P. Russia.* Hyndford to Harrington. Nov. 30th, 1745.

Catherine II also possessed a charm of manner which was well-nigh irresistible, but with her benevolence was always more or less a matter of profound calculation. It was not so with Elizabeth. To make people happy was a necessity of her nature; she loved to see smiling faces around her, and considered that distress of every kind had an imperative claim upon her. Her horror of bloodshed made the very idea of war hateful to her, and she wept bitterly at the news of every victory won by her arms. She took care that her soldiers were so well-clad that casualties from stress of weather were almost unknown, and on receiving intelligence of the earthquake at Lisbon, she offered to rebuild part of the city at her own cost, though she had no diplomatic relations with Portugal. We have seen how at the beginning of her reign, she resolved to abolish capital punishment. The Ukaz to that effect was, by the advice of her Ministers, never promulgated, lest malefactors should multiply; but she took care to commute every capital sentence as it came before her. Again, when Peter Shuvalov submitted to her his codification of the Russian laws, which bristled with cruel and vexatious fiscal penalties, the Empress indignantly declared that it was "written not with ink, but with blood," and refused to sign it. One of her most engaging qualities was her fondness for young people, children especially, and all little folk were passionately devoted to her. She also very frequently gave children's parties, eighty to ninety little couples sitting down to supper with their governors and governesses at separate tables. The Princess Dashkova tells us that she took "the affectionate interest of a good godmother" in the private affairs of the youths and maidens of her Court, and, match-maker as she was, repeatedly helped struggling young lovers out of their pecuniary difficulties. On one occasion, the Princess, then a mere child, was so affected by the tone of maternal ten-

derness with which the Empress congratulated her on her
engagement, that she burst into tears, whereupon Elizabeth,
tapping her gently on the shoulder and at the same time
kissing her cheek, said with a smile: "Come, come, my
child! compose yourself, or all your friends will fancy I
have been scolding you." For, like most warm-hearted people,
the Tsaritsa had a naturally quick and impetuous temper,
and, when fairly roused, would scold and bully for an hour
at a time, without stopping to pick her words, till she grew
purple in the face. Yet when the paroxysm was over, she
was as radiant as ever; never bore the slightest resentment,
even under the most trying circumstances; and the words
"Vinovata, Matushka!" [1] uttered with becoming contrition,
always disarmed her. And if hasty and choleric, she was
also just, equitable, and a great peacemaker. It is one of
her chief glories that, so far as she was able, she put a
stop to that mischievous contention of rival ambitions at
Court, which had disgraced the reigns of Peter II, Anne
and Ivan VI, and enabled Foreign Powers to freely interfere
in the domestic affairs of Russia. Her Ministers had not
only to serve *her*, but to live in harmony with one another.
We have already seen how she protected the Bestuzhevs
against Lestocq and Trubetskoi, and how she would not
sacrifice Vorontsov to Bestuzhev; we shall see presently
how, for a long time, she held the balance equally between
the Chancellor's party and the Shuvalovs.

Nevertheless this bright picture has its darker side. One
of the chief faults imputed to the Empress Elizabeth is
her indolence. Lord Hyndford, on one occasion, complains of "this lady's mortal backwardness in all sorts of
business or anything that requires one moment's thought or
application," and although there is much of exaggeration,

---

[1] "Peccavi, dear mother!"

there is also something of truth, in this accusation. No doubt, as Solovev justly observes, her backwardness was not always due to indolence, but to a conscientious endeavour to consider doubtful questions from every possible point of view, and it is quite certain that, under the pressure of emergency, she took infinite pains to disentangle truth from falsehood, and would decide nothing till she had quite satisfied her own mind as to the subject in debate. It must also be remembered that, even judged by the low standard of her own age, [1] she was very ignorant, and therefore obliged to lean a good deal upon the opinions of others. But, after making every possible allowance, we cannot altogether acquit her of neglect of affairs. Frequently she left the most important documents unread and unsigned for months together, and Bestuzhev used bitterly to complain that she would not attend to business without a great deal of coaxing. There was the less excuse for her, moreover, because she had always plenty of time upon her hands. Literature naturally had no attraction for a Princess who regarded all reading (except the perusal of devotional books printed in very large type) as injurious to health. [2] And then she lived in such a haphazard way. She had no fixed times for lying down or getting up, and her meals were uncertain and irregular. A large portion of each day was spent in gossiping in her private apartments with her favourite women, Maura Egorovna Shuvalova, Anna Karlovna Vorontsova, Nastasia Mikhailovna Izmailovna, and a certain Elizabeth Ivanovna, a mysterious and not altogether reputable old lady whom the Tsaritsa frequently employed on dark and dubious errands, and whom the witty Stroganov

---

[1] She was never quite certain, for instance, whether Great Britain was an island or not, and her spelling was even worse than the spelling of Frederick the Great.

[2] She considered too much reading as the cause of her beloved sister Anne's death.

therefore dubbed "Le ministère des affaires étranges", in contradistinction to the Grand Chancellor, who was "Le ministère des affaires étrangères." Her devotions, however, for she rigorously observed the innumerable feast and fast days of the Orthodox Church,[1] occupied no small part of her leisure. In the summer she hawked and hunted, and, in winter, took horse exercise in the vast covered riding-school built in the reign of Anne for the favourite Biren. She was an excellent shot, a fearless and graceful rider, and could, in her best days, outwalk the strongest of her guardsmen. Nor was she altogether without æsthetic tastes, being passionately fond of music[2] and the drama, and taking a great interest in architecture. No other Russian Sovereign ever erected so many churches, and the celebrated Winter Palace, Rastrelli's masterpiece, was built under her supervision, though she did not live long enough to inhabit it.

But building was by no means her most costly pastime. For every hundred rubles she expended on the permanent embellishment of her capital, she wasted a thousand on the transitory pleasures of her Court. Lavish to the verge of extravagance, and loving pomp and show with all the ardour of a sensuous, semi-barbarous Oriental, it was the great delight of Elizabeth Petrovna to pose as the majestic central figure of brilliant assemblies and gorgeous pageants, and her court was indisputably the most splendid in Europe. Her cousin Anne, before her, had indeed astonished foreigners by the gorgeousness of her appointments,[3] but Anne's crude

---

[1] She was very severe upon any remissness on this score. Even the Grand Duchess Catherine did not escape. Once she arrived late at Mass, and after service the Empress sent for her and roundly rebuked her for giving to the embellishment of her person the time set apart for the service of God.

[2] In this respect she compares favourably with her successor Catherine II, to whom all music was only so much noise.

[3] For a full description of the Court of the Empress Anne, see Bain: "Pupils of Peter the Great," Chaps. IV and VIII.

and bizarre magnificence lacked the veneer of grace, elegance and refinement which characterized the court of Elizabeth. For, though in many respects a Russian gentlewoman of the old school, [1] and intensely patriotic, Elizabeth Petrovna was far more intelligent and receptive than Anne Ivanovna, and, especially where her pleasures were concerned, borrowed freely from the luxuries of Western civilization. Hence the accusation of reckless extravagance so often and so justly brought against her by Prince Shcherbatov and other *laudatores temporis acti*. Sir Cyril Wych, as early as 1742, when Elizabeth was still comparatively economical, described the Court of St. Petersburg as the most expensive in Europe, and protested that his allowance could not meet even current expenses. This extravagance manifested itself principally in the habiliments, equipages, retinue and banquets of the gentry and nobility, the Empress herself setting the example in this respect. She is said to have changed her clothes half-a-dozen times a day, and although she lost 4,000 dresses at the great Moscow conflagration of 1747, fifteen thousand more were found in her wardrobes after her death, most of which had only been worn once. And the Empress took care that her courtiers should live up to this high standard of display. At the wedding of the Grand Duke Peter, [2] all public officials were given a year's salary in advance that they might be able to make a brave show on the occasion, and a special ukaz laid down sumptuary regulations for the pageant. Every member of the first and second class in the table of grades was to have two heydukes and *not less than* eight lacqueys attached to each of his carriages, and as many more as he could afford. But the *jeunesse dorée* of Peterhof and

---

[1] *E. g.* she kept a jester, one Aksakov, for her private entertainment.
[2] The whole function followed closely the ceremony observed on the wedding of the Dauphin with the Infanta of Spain.

Tsarkoe Selo needed little prompting.   Their natural vanity
and luxuriousness met the Tsaritsa's wishes half way.   It
soon became the ambition of every young Russian noble
to outshine his neighbour, and at last even the most expensive
galloon was generally looked down upon as common and
vulgar.   Sergius Naruishkin, accounted the greatest dandy
of the age in Russia, won great favour by going to the
wedding of the Grand Duke, in a carriage [1] inlaid all over,
even to the wheels, with crystal mirrors, and wearing a caftan
ablaze with jewels, the back of which was made to imitate
a tree, the trunk being represented by a broad golden
band in the middle of his body, while the branches were
indicated by lines of silver running up the sleeves to the
wrists, and the roots by similar lines running down to the
knees of the breeches.   The immensely wealthy Ivan
Chernuishev, who had travelled widely and did more than
any other man to import foreign luxury into Russia, used
to order twelve suits at a time, and the very liveries of his
pages were of cloth of gold.   Yet even he could not compete
with Count Alexander Razumovsky and his brother Cyril.
The elder Razumovsky was the first to wear diamond
buttons, buckles and epaulets; while Count Cyril, on being
appointed Grand Hetman of the Cossacks, departed for
Glukhov, the seat of his Government, where he lived in
regal state, with an immense retinue which included a body-
guard, a *troupe* of actors, and half-a-dozen French cooks,
including the famous *chef*, Barridian, who received a salary
of 500 rubles (£125), and was considered even superior to
Duval, the *chef* of Frederick the Great.   On one occasion
Cyril bought up 100,000 bottles of wine, including 6,800
bottles of the best champagne, then a fashionable novelty,
which he freely distributed among his friends.   Far less

---

[1] It cost £7,000.

generous was Chancellor Bestuzhev, whose immense cellar was, after his death, given by Catherine II to Prince Orlov, who sold it for an incredible sum. Prince Shcherbatov instances it as a sign of the degeneracy of the times, that pine-apples and English horses were first introduced into Russia, at enormous expense, by Peter Shuvalov, who lived so recklessly that he left behind him a million rubles' worth of debts, although his standing income for years was 400,000 rubles (£100,000). [1] Peter Shuvalov was particularly proud of the magnificence of his dessert; his brother Alexander, on the other hand, boasted that he was the chief propagandist of champagne in Russia. Then there was Field Marshal Stephen Apraksin who had hundreds of suits of clothes, a jewelled snuff-box for every day in the year, and required more than five hundred horses to drag his private baggage when he took the field against the King of Prussia; [2] and Count Peter Borisovich Sheremetev, the richest man in the Empire, whose dresses were heavy with gold and silver, and who always went about surrounded by a whole army of domestics almost as brilliantly attired as himself. It is recorded of him that he kept such an ample table that once, when the Empress and her by no means tiny Court looked in upon him unawares, he was able to entertain them all sumptuously with what was actually provided for the use of his household on that particular day. The lesser nobles naturally imitated the magnates, and the result was a rapid declension from the simplicity of the old Russian mode of life, and a growing fondness for costly and unnecessary exotic luxuries which ministered to vanity and dissipation with often the most

---

[1] He made as much again by underhand means.

[2] He took to camp, in fact, all the luxuries of a great city. It was the same gentleman who refused a gold-hilted sword from George II because it was not bejewelled.

serious consequences. This was bad enough, but still worse remained behind, for the Court of Elizabeth was not only the most extravagant, it was also the most licentious in Europe, and for this also the Empress must be held primarily responsible.

I have already, [1] very briefly, alluded to the earlier escapades of Elizabeth, and, without attempting in any way to excuse the inexcusable, I will only add this much by way of partial palliation, that the Tsaritsa, at least during the first half of her reign, seems to have attempted the hopeless task of gratifying appetite without offending conscience, and to have tempered her licentiousness with a strong dose of asceticism. At least such seems to have been the case in the days of her semi-romantic attachment to Alexius Razumovsky, perhaps the least unworthy of all the palace favourites of history, whose singular career reads like a chapter from the Arabian Nights.

Alexius Grigorevich Razum, the second son of a simple Cossack shepherd dwelling in the remote Ukrainian village of Lemesh, was born on March 17th, 1709. [2] From an early age he tended his father's flocks, but his handsome face, amiable manners and sweet voice, attracted the attention of the village priest, who took a fancy to the lad and taught him reading, writing and singing. The *korchmar*, or little inn, kept by Razum's mother, stood near the church, on the post-road from Kozelets to Chernigov, and one day, at the beginning of January 1731, an imperial courier, Col. Vishnevsky, returning to Moscow from Hungary, whither he had been sent to purchase Tokay for the Empress Anne, stopped at and entered the little village church. Mass was proceeding, and primitive enough it was, yet the colonel was connoisseur enough to be struck by the beauti-

---

[1] Chap. IV.

[2] And consequently was only 10 months older than his Imperial Mistress.

ful voice of young Razum.   Such a jewel, he thought, was
meet for the delectation of a devout Empress, and he had
little difficulty in persuading the lad to accompany him to
the Capital, there to seek his fortune.   At St. Petersburg,
Alexius received proper training, and in a few years became one of the chief singers in the Court Chapel.   There
Elizabeth, then Tsarevna, first heard him, and was so
charmed that she had the youth presented to her.   His
beauty [1] impressed her even more than his voice had done,
and, at her request, the young chorister was transferred to
her little Court, where, for a time, he held the humble
position of *bandurist* or lute-player.   On the banishment
of Elizabeth's earlier paramour, Alexius Nikiforovich Shubin
to Kamschatka, Razumovsky, as he now began to be called,
stepped into the exile's shoes and became the Tsarevna's
chief *Kammerjunker.*   After her accession she rapidly promoted him.   He became, in quick succession, a lieutenant-
general, a Count and a Field Marshal.   The last dignity
he accepted very unwillingly, observing on that occasion:
"Your Majesty may create me a Field Marshal if you like,
but I defy you or anybody else to make a decent captain
of me."   And a still higher distinction awaited him.   The
event was kept a profound secret, and is necessarily very
obscure, but there are very strong grounds for believing
that the Empress was privately married to Razumovsky
at Perovoe in the autumn of 1742, at the instigation
of her confessor, Father Dubyansky, a worthy priest who
concealed very great talents beneath an extremely simple
exterior, and was, for a long time, the Empress's good angel.
There were no children of the marriage, though long after
the Empress's death, impostors came forward claiming to
be her descendants.   The mythical Tarakhanovs are an

---

[1] He is described at this time as a tall stately youth with a bronzed complexion, wonderful fiery black eyes, and finely arched black eyebrows.

invention of credulous gossip-mongers. Only one man guessed at both the influence and the ability of Dubyansky, and that was Chancellor Bestuzhev, who fraternized with him and Razumovsky from the first, and their secret but steady support, united to his own adroitness, enabled him for many years to hold his own against all adversaries. The kinsfolk of Razumovsky naturally benefited by his change of fortune. Even his old mother, Natalia, was invited to Court. There is a story that when the worthy old peasant woman, all rouged, powdered and bedizened, was being conducted through the Palace in order to be presented to the Empress, and caught sight of herself in a large mirror which she now saw for the first time, she imagined that her own gorgeous reflection was the advancing Tsaritsa, and plunged down on her knees before it as previously instructed. She soon had the sense to see that a Court was no place for her, and contentedly returned home to her little inn in the distant Ukraine, despite all the entreaties of her son, who insisted, however, upon keeping his younger brother Cyril, to whom he was as good as a father. Alexius himself, indeed, was now too old to learn much, though he took care to surround himself with those most likely to be serviceable to him and make up for his own deficiences—such men for instance as Vasily Evdoki-movich Adadurov, the author of the first Russian grammar, and ultimately Curator of the Moscow University, whom he made his secretary; Alexander Petrovich Sumarakov, the dramatist, and Ivan Perfilievich Elagin, one of the noblest and most cultivated Russians of his day. His brother Cyril hᵉ sent abroad for two years, and educated at his expense at Königsberg, Berlin and Paris. The young Cossack returned to Russia in 1745, an accomplished man of the world, and at once took a prominent position at Court, where his *bon ton* and amiable *savoir-faire* made him a prime favourite. Although he affected French elegance, and introduced many foreign modes and habits, he was always a Russian at heart, protected Russian authors, (notably Sumarakov) and officiated as the first President of the reorganized Academy of Sciences. Elizabeth loaded him with gifts, and made him marry her cousin Ekaterina Ivanovna Naruishkina (much against his will according to Catherine II). Subsequently he was made a Count and Grand Hetman of the Cossacks. He owed these distinctions not so much to his own merits, considerable as they were, as to the solicitation of his elder brother, whose influence was paramount during the first seven years of Elizabeth's reign. The Empress, during this period, adored her husband and was never happy without him. Whenever he had the gout (which was pretty frequently, for he was something of a *bon vivant*) all the court festivities were suspended, and the Empress nursed him in his apartments, which adjoined her own. His tastes and preferences were always consulted at feasts and banquets, and, for a time, the peculiar dishes of the Ukraine were all the vogue at Court. Moreover, he was the only person in Russia allowed to eat flesh on fast-days, the Empress obtaining for him, through Bestuzhev, from the Patriarch of Constantinople, a special dispensation which she would never have thought of asking for herself. Even the masterful Maura Egorovna Shuvalova, who was supposed to be able to turn the Empress to wrath or mercy as she listed, had to give way to him; while her husband, Peter Shuvalov, quietly submitted on one occasion to a whipping in public from the ex-Cossack-shepherd, when that gentleman happened to be more than usually tipsy. Like most Malo-Russians, indeed, Razumovsky was rather given to excess in liquor, but this, I may say, was his only serious fault, and his brother Cyril was free even from that. Both the Razumovskys

10

were naturally shrewd, honest, single-minded souls, and it says much for their innate integrity and stability, that all the splendours, all the vanities of the most riotous of Courts, were unable to spoil them. Magnanimous, unselfish and benevolent they remained to the end of their lives. "I know of no other persons," observed Catherine II authoritatively, [1] "who, amidst such boundless favour at Court, were so universally beloved as these two brothers. Riches and honours never turned their heads, and boundless luxury, with all its adjuncts, never spoiled their hearts. They remained cool-headed and sober-minded in the midst of a very whirlpool of intrigue and not very decent delights." Innumerable are the authentic stories of the generosity of these unique *parvenus* who benefited thousands and injured none, but I have only space for two, which, entertaining in themselves, present us likewise with little tableaux of the manners of the period.

The Grand Hetman, Count Cyril, kept open house for rich and poor alike, and a certain needy old soldier who had consumed all his substance in a fruitless lawsuit, took advantage of this hospitality, and dined at Razumovsky's table every day. Soon he grew very familiar with his host's mansion, and used to amuse himself after dinner by strolling leisurely and curiously through the splendid apartments. One day his peregrinations led the old fellow into an inner chamber, where he perceived Count Cyril playing at chess with another magnate. A chess-player himself, the old soldier remained watching the progress of the game in silence, till, perceiving that Razumovsky was on the point of making a false move, he could not restrain a loud expression of disapproval. The Hetman looked up astonished at this unexpected interruption. "Perhaps you will

---

[1] *Mémoires.*

show me my mistake then!" cried he. The humble guest did so in fear and trembling, and Razumovsky followed his advice and won the game. From that day forth the old man vanished, and though Razumovsky frequently enquired: "Where is my mentor?" and made frequent enquiries about him, he was for a long time nowhere to be found. Only after a long and diligent search was the old soldier at last discovered in a wretched tenement in the poorest part of the city, at the last extremity. The Hetman at once sent his own doctor to look after the poor old man, kept him supplied with plenty of nourishing food, and, when he was fairly on his legs again, placed his own purse at his disposal that he might prosecute his suit to a successful issue.

On another occasion when the Hetman was giving a grand banquet in honour of the Austrian envoy, Prince Esterhazy, the Ambassador produced a costly gold snuff-box which he had received from the Empress, and passed the curio round that the company might inspect it. Shortly afterwards Esterhazy, feeling the want of a pinch of snuff, put his hand in his pocket for his snuff-box, and it was gone. The company was very mixed, and the snuff-box was very valuable, so that the embarrassment of Razumovsky, who did not even know the names of half his guests, was extreme, especially when the agitated ambassador began to insinuate that his treasure had been stolen. Springing to his feet, the Grand Hetman at once turned out all his pockets, exclaiming at the same time in a loud voice: "Gentlemen! you see I set the example. I hope everyone here present will follow it, so that his Excellency may be fully satisfied that we have not got his snuff-box." Everyone instantly obeyed, with the exception of a shabby-looking old man at the extreme end of the table, who, in a tremulous voice, desired to speak a few words with his host in private.

They retired together accordingly, followed by the evil glances of the rest of the company. Once alone with the Grand Hetman, the old man timidly explained that for a long time past he had been in the habit, not only of feeding every day at Count Cyril's bountiful table, but of taking away with him each time some food for his destitute family, who had scarce enough to keep body and soul together, and with that he emptied his pockets of morsels of food of different sorts with which he had stuffed them. At that moment a heyduke knocked at the door, and told Razumovsky that the snuff-box had been found, the Ambassador having thrust it by mistake into his bosom instead of into his pocket. Thereupon Count Cyril, with a smile, helped the old man to refill his pockets, and thenceforth granted him a pension on which he and his family could live honourably.

The Razumovskys had the sense never to meddle with politics. The open-handed Count Cyril was content to play the grand seigneur magnificently at Court, while his elder brother Alexius, naturally pious and owing so much to the Church, was devoted to his spiritual mother, and the clergy always found in him a powerful and constant friend. Not only did he boldly plead their cause before the Empress,[1] but he gave immense sums for the building of new churches, and interested himself greatly in missionary[2] work. Three hundred and sixty thousand heathens are said to have been christianized by his efforts in the diocese of Novgorod alone. He also did much for his native province of Malo-Russia, and it was at his suggestion that the Empress undertook her longest expedition—the celebrated pilgrimage

---

[1] It was through his instrumentality that the vexatious anti-ecclesiastical legislation of the Empress Anne was very greatly mitigated.

[2] He was one of the first to send missionaries to the Caucasus and Kamschatka.

to Kiev—then at the very confines of her realm. It was on the 9th July, 1744, that Elizabeth set out for the ecclesiastical metropolis of her realm with a suite of 230 persons, including a couple of Archbishops, and the little Grand Duke and Duchess. The beginning of the journey was unfortunate. A conspiracy, whether real or imaginary it is difficult to decide, against the Empress's life, was discovered at Glukhov, which resulted in a part of the Imperial cortège having to change its route and proceed directly to Siberia, and, for the next few days, her Majesty was in a ferocious humour. But the clouds dispersed as she proceeded on her way, and the reception accorded her at Tolstodubovo, on the border of the Ukraine, was of the most imposing and enthusiastic description. Visiting all the innumerable monasteries and shrines on her way, the indefatigable Empress reached Kiev on Sept. 9th. The whole city turned out to meet her, and her solemn entry was a triumphal progress. At the gates, the students of the Theological Academy, the first in Russia, awaited her, attired as Greek gods, heroes and monsters, and from their midst there advanced to meet her an aged man with a long white flowing beard, dressed in royal robes, with a golden crown on his head and a golden sceptre in his hand. He represented the great Saint Vladimir, Grand Duke of Kiev, who greeted her Majesty as his orthodox successor, and surrendered to her the keys of the obedient city. She passed beneath the Golden Gates of Yaroslav in a carriage drawn by two winged Pegasuses and driven by Phaeton himself, amidst tumultuous acclamations. In later days she used to look back upon the two weeks of her visit to Kiev as the happiest episode of her life, and, on leaving the city, she raised her streaming eyes aloft and exclaimed: "Do but love me, oh my God! in Thy Heavenly Kingdom, as I love this gentle and guileless people!"

It will readily be imagined, from what has been said of the character and surroundings of the Tsaritsa, that the Court of Elizabeth must have been a delightful abode for anyone rich enough to cut a fine figure there. To the majority of the Russian nobility, still haunted by the dark memories of the Court of Anne, it must have appeared an earthly paradise. The oppressive atmosphere of suspicion and alarm which, under the saturnine Anne Ivanovna, had pervaded the highest circles, and made every Russian gentleman start apprehensively at his own shadow, was dissipated by the radiant joviality of a sovereign whose boundless good-nature banished everything melancholy or malign from her presence. Such barbarous pleasantries as the wedding in the Ice Palace, [1] would have been impossible under the humane Elizabeth. Nor was there any alien tyrant like the mercenary and vindictive German, Biren, to stand between Sovereign and subject. No Germans, no Frenchmen, but light-hearted Malo-Russians were now in vogue, and the Malo-Russians are to the Russians proper very much what Irishmen are to Englishmen, a lighter and brighter offshoot of the same national stock. There was, in point of fact, nobody now to domineer the Court or embitter its joys. The Grand Chancellor Bestuzhev, indeed, who would tolerate no interference in the department of foreign affairs, had persuaded the Empress to forbid all social intercourse between the Russian gentry and the foreign embassies at St. Petersburg, but otherwise he did not interfere with the pastimes of the Court. His Arguses [2] certainly kept him well informed of all that was going on; but nobody wanted to relieve the crabbed, peevish old statesman of the onerous burden that only his shoulders were strong

---

[1] See Bain: *Pupils of Peter the Great*, Chap. VIII.

[2] Lord Hyndford said that he had in his pay a whole army of spies at Court, from the highest lady-in-waiting to the meanest chambermaid.

enough to bear, and his elaborate system of espionage was, after all, purely precautionary. Indeed he injured nobody who did not first try to injure him, and occasionally he even did old acquaintances a good turn, as, for instance, when he pleaded with the Empress for his former patron Biren, and procured for him an increase of his pension. The Court, therefore, freely abandoned itself to its pleasures and frolicked gaily round the frolicsome Tsaritsa. Its chief diversions were banquets, at which Russian profuseness was now mated with French refinement, balls, masquerades, operas and plays both native and foreign. [1]

The Italian opera bouffé and ballet, introduced by Locatelli, seem to have been originally intended for the delectation of Alexius Razumovsky, who, like most of his race, was very sensible to the charm of music. No expense was spared on these entertainments, and the most famous singers and dancers were imported from Germany, France and Italy to take part in them. Locatelli's *premier*, the celebrated eunuch Manfredini, received an enormous salary, and his chief *danseuse*, Niodini, taught the ladies of the court to dance the menuet. Sometimes, however, the ballets were danced by the young cadets of the Infantry Corps of Nobles. Locatelli also gave public *réunions* at his house, at which tea, coffee and light refreshments were served, a new form of entertainment in those days, largely patronised by the court. There was, moreover, a *troupe* of Malo-Russian artists who sang the melancholy melodies of the Ukraine before the Empress.

The drama, both native and foreign, also received great encouragement. Russian plays of a sort had originally been got up by Count Boris Grigorevich Ysupov, Commander

---

[1] One mark of increasing refinement was the disappearance of the Court jester. Elizabeth had one buffoon, Arakshev, whom however, she kept exclusively for her private entertainment.

of the Corps of Noble Cadets, with the assistance of the
dramatist Sumarakov, in order to keep his young people
out of harm's way during the Empress's absence at Moscow.
On Elizabeth's return to St. Petersburg, one of these plays
was acted before her and so delighted her that she made
play-acting a regular amusement of the court, and transferred the stage to the inner apartments of the Palace.
She also provided the young actors with magnificent costumes and even lent them her own jewels occasionally.
Gradually the rough native products were superseded by
the masterpieces of the French stage, and at last the
"Comédie Française", as it began to be called, was played
regularly twice a week at court.   There can be no doubt
that these entertainments had a humane and enlightening
influence, and considerably widened the mental horizon of
the rising generation.   Count Alexius Vorontsov, a contemporary, assures us that it was by frequenting the Court
Theatre that he first acquired a taste for literature and art,
and that towards the end of Elizabeth's reign there were
very few Russian youths who were not thoroughly familiar
with the works of Racine, Boileau, Corneille, Molière and
Voltaire.

But the pastime the Tsaritsa loved best was the *bal-
masqué*, and this was but natural in one who was incom-
parably the most graceful dancer of her day.   At the
Russian Court the entertainments went by the name of
Metamorphoses, possibly because the women very frequently
masqueraded as men, and the men as women.   This
was a favourite whim of the Empress, whose own stately
and imposing figure was admirably set off by male attire,
which she affected on every possible occasion.   Lord Hyndford, who once had the honour of kissing her hand when
she was dressed in the uniform of her Life-Guards, was
much impressed by her appearance on that occasion.   "She

marched at the head of the company," he tells us, "into the great hall where the whole corps of brave fellows, consisting of upwards of four hundred, had the honour to sup with her."—"Your Lordship," he adds, "can hardly conceive how well the habit of an officer became the Empress, and I am persuaded that those who had not known her, would, by her air, have taken her for an officer but for her fine face."—Catherine II, also a connoisseur, is still more flattering: "A masculine habit suited the Empress marvellously well," she remarks. "She had the finest legs I have ever seen (far finer than any man's) and a foot of admirable symmetry. She danced to perfection, and was equally graceful whether dressed up as a man or a woman. One day, at one of the Court balls, I was watching her dance a menuet. She approached me when it was over, and I took the liberty to say to her that it was very fortunate for us poor women that she was not a man, as, dressed as she then was, even her portrait would be sufficient to turn all our heads.—She replied in the most gracious manner in the world, that if she were a man, it would be to me that she would give the palm.—I stooped to kiss her hand, by way of thanking her for this unwonted compliment, but she anticipated me by taking me in her arms and embracing me before the whole Court." [1]—Elizabeth's favourite costume was that of a Dutch sailor, and, in that character, she always insisted upon being addressed as Mikhailovna; [2] but she was quite as effective as a French Musqueteer or a Cossack Hetman, and danced equally well the stately menuet and the dashing Russian plyaska. She was also very fond of English country dances, and Chernuishev, who first introduced them, had no reason to regret

[1] *Mémoires.*
[2] In remembrance of her father who, while working as a shipwright in Holland, went by the name of Mikhailov.

it. These Metamorphoses were given at Court twice a week, as a rule, except of course on fast-days, and all costumes were allowed except those of pilgrims and harlequins, the Empress considering the former as profane and the latter as indecent. About four hundred couples was the average attendance, and the halls in which they danced were fragrant with blossoming orange trees, and cooled by illuminated fountains and cascades.

The Court, as a rule, migrated every three years to Moscow for twelve months, Elizabeth having a great fondness for the old capital and its beautiful environs. It was on these occasions, moreover, that she performed vows made during illnesses, which generally took the shape of pilgrimages to famous shrines. Her mode of procedure was as follows. Being of a very full habit, pedestrian exercise became irksome to her after middle age, and if, for instance, she had vowed to walk sixty miles, or a hundred miles to a monastery or church, she would set out from Moscow accompanied by her suite, and go on foot six miles, returning on horseback or in her carriage to the capital, and renewing her pilgrimage next day at the point she had reached the day before, until the whole distance was gradually traversed. It is therefore not surprising if these religious exercises sometimes occupied the whole summer, and proved very tiresome and expensive to her unfortunate retinue, which often included the foreign Ministers. Her favourite residence when she stayed at St. Petersburg was the country mansion of Gostilitsa, where she spent a great part of her time hunting, hawking and shooting, in male attire. She gave the place at last to her husband, who frequently entertained her there with great splendour, especially on her name day, March 17/28, which was generally observed as a sort of high festival at Court. Her favourite town residence at St. Petersburg was the

Anichkovsky Palace, which, in 1756, she also presented to Razumovsky.

Speaking generally, it may be said that, from 1742 to 1749, Elizabeth's Court was more Russian than French; but from 1749 to the end of her reign, it was certainly more French than Russian, although the Russian language was never relegated to a subordinate position as was the case during the reign of Catherine II. The growth of Gallic influence coincides with the rise of the Shuvalovs and the retirement of Alexius Razumovsky into the background. It also coincides with a very distinct deterioration of morals in the higher circles of the court, though, for the matter of that, her Imperial Majesty's own morality, despite her religious exercises, had never been uncompromisingly austere. There is no doubt, however, that in this respect she grew worse as she grew older.

In the spring of 1749, one of the imperial pages, Ivan Shuvalov, was suddenly promoted to the rank of Kammerherr. Rumour instantly whispered that, in all probability, the handsome and amiable youth had been fortunate enough to win the particular regard of the Empress, and any lingering doubt upon the subject was at once removed when, shortly afterwards, apartments were assigned to him at the Palace, close to those of the Empress. The elevation of the new favourite soon led to the advancement of his two uncles, Peter and Alexander Shuvalov, whose influence was henceforward to steadily increase, and towards the end of Elizabeth's reign become paramount.

The Shuvalovs were not of very ancient or illustrious lineage, and the nobles of old Boyar descent generally regarded them as mere upstarts. The first eminent member of the family was Major General Ivan Maksimovich, at one time Governor of Archangel, and the father of Peter and Alexander, to whom he gave an excellent education.

They were both attached to the Court of the Tsarevna Elizabeth by the Empress Anne, whose constant policy it was to surround her cousin with second-class people, but although poor and plebeian, both the Shuvalovs were men of superior abilities and insatiable ambition. Peter, in particular, was highly gifted, and had an extraordinarily keen eye to the main chance. He took the first step on the rung of Fortune's ladder when he married the Empress's prime favourite, Maura Egorovna, and very soon completely wormed his way into Elizabeth's confidence, at the same time taking infinite care not to offend anybody who could by any possibility do him the least injury. Partly by means of the most thorough-going obsequiousness (he is said to have cringed to the very serving women who rubbed the Empress's feet at night), partly by dint of remarkable industry and really superior ability, he gradually rose to the highest offices in the State, died a Count and a Senator, and ultimately exercised as absolute a control over domestic, as ever Bestuzhev exercised over foreign affairs. Morally he was altogether contemptible. His rapacity was insatiable, his hypocrisy unmitigated, [1] his duplicity unfathomable. He amassed millions at the expense of the treasury by vexatious commercial monopolies, which he was the first to introduce into Russia, and 15,000 poor people are said to have been scourged and sent to Siberia for resisting or evading his iniquitous imposts, notably the salt tax. His enmity was peculiarly dangerous because it was always veiled by the most insinuating *bonhomie*. He had a singularly mobile face which could reflect every imaginable mood at a moment's notice, and he would frequently assure his victims, with upturned eyes full of tears, that he took the liveliest interest in their wel-

---

[1] He used frequently to go about with a large prayer-book that the Empress might remark his devoutness.

fare and deeply sympathized with them in their misfortunes at the very moment when he was compassing their ruin. Yet even Peter Shuvalov was no mere lazy parasite, as Biren had been, and his services to his native land were considerable. If he enriched himself first of all, he showed others the way to get rich also. He taught the naturally improvident Russian peasant the value of economy by establishing savings-banks; reformed the coinage, which he placed on a sounder footing than it had ever been on before, and did very much to stimulate trade and commerce. Nor while cultivating the arts of peace did he neglect the science of war. He greatly improved the Russian artillery; invented a new species of howitzer which did terrible execution during the Seven Years' War; and out of his economies (or his exactions, as his enemies called them) he set on foot an army of 30,000 men for the Empress's service. The elder Shuvalov, Alexander Ivanovich, made by no means so much of a stir in the world as the alert and ingenious Peter, indeed the chief sphere of his operations was the much dreaded Secret Chancellery of which he became the terrible Chief Inquisitor. He was little more than the reflection of his younger brother, whose lead he dutifully followed in all things. Catherine II tells us that his revolting functions as Torturer-General had so affected his nerves that, under undue excitement, he could not control the muscles of the right side of his face, which twitched convulsively whenever he was very pleased or very angry. [1]

The best of the Shuvalov trio, after all, was the nephew who so complacently prostituted himself for the good of his uncles, indeed, if we could only forget that Ivan Shuvalov

---

[1] Catherine, however, hated the Shuvalovs far too much to do them justice. Count M. C. Vorontsov tells us that Alexander Shuvalov was a very honest fellow, but that he had: "Un œil à démi fermé et qui clignotait toujours."

filled the degrading and ridiculous office of minion to a woman old enough to be his mother, we might find much in his character to admire, and even to applaud. Even Catherine, the sworn enemy of his family, describes him as a studious youth of pleasing manners and a generous heart. A young man in his exceptional position might have done infinite mischief, but he seems to have been always modest, unassuming and disinterested. His services to literature were considerable, and he well deserves the title of the Russian Mæcenas which his grateful contemporaries bestowed upon him. He was a generous patron of all the struggling native writers of his day; unearthed and promoted eloquent young preachers; corresponded with Voltaire and freely distributed among his poorer fellow-students the principal literary novelties of the day, which he received regularly from Paris. [1] It was he, too, who gave the Empress the happy ideas of founding the University of Moscow, and the Academy of Arts at St. Petersburg,

The elevation of young Ivan Shuvalov at first seriously alarmed the ultra-sensitive Grand Chancellor, who regarded it as a blow aimed at his supporter Alexander Razumovsky, and consequently at himself likewise. He therefore instantly took measures to protect both his friend and himself against the insidious assault.

Among the cadets who acted before the Empress at the Court Theatre, was a very handsome youth of eighteen or nineteen, Nikita Afanasievich Beketov by name, who generally played the part of first lover at these entertainments. It at once occurred to Bestuzhev that such an Adonis was made for such a susceptible Cytherea as Elizabeth, and he took care that the youth should frequently come in the

---

[1] The Princess Dashkova tells us that he interested himself in everyone who loved learning. It was through him that the negotiations with Voltaire for writing a Life of Peter the Great were primarily conducted.

Empress's way. What the Chancellor had anticipated very soon came to pass. The Empress was very favourably impressed by young Beketov. Soon it was generally remarked that the youth was more handsomely dressed than his comrades, and his diamond rings and buckles, and superior laced cuffs and ruffles, began to excite their astonishment and envy. Presently Alexius Razumovsky made him his adjutant, and shortly afterwards he was promoted to the rank of Colonel, with apartments in the Palace—there could now be no reasonable doubt that he shared with Ivan Shuvalov the particular favour of her Imperial Majesty, apparently with the approval and consent of her husband! This infamous *ménage à quatre*, so to speak, lasted for about twelve months, and then it was suddenly exploded by the artful counter-mining of Peter Shuvalov. Approaching the too credulous Beketov, one day, this arch-intriguer said to him, with his usual unctuous suavity: "My dear young friend, I notice with regret that the late hours you are obliged to keep, have greatly impaired the freshness of your complexion. Now our gracious Sovereign does not like withered faces, take this ointment then from a well-wisher, and use it regularly for a few days, and you will soon see a difference." The simple youth gratefully accepted the insidious gift, but instead of restoring the bloom to his cheek, it very speedily covered his features with a foul eruption, to which the Countess Shuvalova, previously instructed by her husband, took care to direct the Empress's attention, at the same time insinuating that Beketov was a notoriously evil liver. [1] The horrified Tsaritsa fled at once to the rural seclusion of Tsarkoe Selo, and Nikita Afanasievich was forbidden the Court. He fell ill of grief and chagrin, but ultimately accepted the Governor-

[1] Catherine gives another and even fouler version of the cause of Beketov's disgrace.

ship of Astrachan, and disappeared from Court. So now
Ivan Shuvalov reigned without a rival, Bestuzhev making no
further attempt to oust him from the imperial favour. Indeed
the acute Chancellor soon perceived that his alarm had
been premature. Young Shuvalov was unambitious, and
of a gentle, pacific nature. He desired to live at peace
with everybody, and was almost as friendly with the
Razumovskys as with his own kinsfolk. He and Count
Cyril failed, indeed, to reconcile the Chancellor with Peter
Shuvalov, but they at least succeeded in mitigating the
hostility of the antagonistic Ministers and preventing any
open collision. This spirit of mutual forbearance and toleration
was, as already observed, peculiar to the Court of Elizabeth,
and by no means its least pleasing feature.

But it was not from within but from without, it was not
from domestic rivals but from foreign adversaries, that the
blow was to come, which ultimately hurled Bestuzhev from
power. At present, however, there was no sign of diminished
influence, no token of any impending danger. Abroad the
political horizon was absolutely clear; at home, since the
marriage of his worthless son with the youthful Countess
Razumovskaya (5 May, 1747), his influence with the Empress
seemed greater than ever, and he had free access to her
every hour of the day. For seven years longer the Grand
Chancellor was to repose triumphantly on his hard-won
laurels.

CHAPTER VII.

RUSSIA AND GREAT BRITAIN.

1749—1755.

THE European situation—Antagonism of Russia and Prussia—England opposes Russia's anti-Swedish plans—Rupture of diplomatic relations between Russia and Prussia—Poland—The Courland question—Saxony—Difficulties of the Grand Chancellor—Michael Bestuzhev and Madame von Haugwitz—Estrangement between the two Bestuzhevs—England's fear of Prussia—The Anglo-Russian negotiations—Bestuzhev's energetic efforts on behalf of England—The Conventions of 1755.

THE seven years of feverish repose which succeeded the War of the Austrian Succession, was nothing more than an armed truce between apprehensive and dissatisfied adversaries, nothing more than an indispensable breathing-space between a past contest, which everyone felt to have been inconclusive, and a future contest which everyone knew to be inevitable. Both the Peace of Aix and the Peace of Breslau had been forced from without upon active belligerents. In the first case the unexpected intervention of Russia had arrested the triumphal progress of the French armies, in the second the sudden desertion [1] of England had compelled defeated but still defiant Austria to surrender

---

[1] Desertion, that is to say, from the point of view of Austria.

her fairest province to the King of Prussia. The consequences of these prematurely suppressed hostilities were an
unnatural tension between the various European Powers,
an anomalous rupture of diplomatic relations in time of
peace,[1] a loosening of time-honoured alliances, and a cautious, shifty groping after newer and surer combinations.
The determining factor of this universal distrust was undoubtedly the King of Prussia. Perhaps no one man ever
did so much to demoralize diplomacy as this Proteus of
politics. His manifold and monstrous chicaneries and infi-
delities, his insatiable ambition, scandalized even that cynical age—at least until his critics had become his imitators
and his disciples, His capital offence, however, in the eyes
of his contemporaries, was, naturally, his success. He alone
had snatched a substantial prize out of the political hurly-
burly, he alone had profited by the struggle which had convulsed Europe. Frederick, too, was uneasy and apprehensive in the midst of his triumphs, and so far from diminish-
ing his armaments after the war was over, he prudently
increased them. He had nothing, indeed, to fear for the
present from exhausted Austria, but the attitude of Russia
continued as menacing as ever. Bestuzhev, in fact, did
not leave his redoubtable antagonist out of sight for an
instant, and for the next few years the diplomatic duel
between the Prussian King and the Russian Grand Chancellor
was carried on with ever increasing acerbity, principally in
Sweden, Poland and Turkey.

The Russian Ambassador at Stockholm, just then, was
the adroit and energetic Nikita Ivanovich Panin, who, under
Catherine II, was to occupy much the same commanding
position as Bestuzhev occupied under Elizabeth. He had

---

[1] First as between Russia and France, then as between Russia and Prussia,
England doing her utmost to prevent the renewal of any diplomatic relations
between these Powers.

been sent to Sweden to sustain the pro-Russian *Cap Party* against the Franco-Prussian *Hat Party*[1] which was in the ascendant and threatened to be dangerous. The adherents of Russia, however, were so few and incapable that Panin's mission was almost hopeless from the first. So vigilantly did the Hats watch all his movements, that it was only with the greatest difficulty, and after the most extraordinary precautions that he succeeded in smuggling the 5,000 rubles, sent to him for bribing purposes, into Stockholm by way of Copenhagen. The courier who brought the money had to feign illness at a small inn outside the capital, to escape detection, and Panin and his secretary both disguised, were obliged to visit him by stealth next day, and bring the money into Stockholm done up in small parcels beneath their mantles. What Russia feared most of all in Sweden was the re-establishment of a strong monarchy on the ruins of the corrupt and tumultuous parliamentary system which had already reduced the rival northern kingdom to the rank of a third-rate power, and rendered her harmless to her neighbours. Frederick II was suspected at St. Petersburg of favouring absolutism in Sweden, and as the death of the decrepit Swedish King, Frederick of Hesse, was daily expected, and the Crown Prince Adolphus Frederick was a mere tool in the hands of his brilliant and masterful consort, Louisa Ulrica of Prussia, the danger to Russian interests in Sweden was regarded as very serious at St. Petersburg. On Jan. 4, 1750, Panin went the length of addressing to the Swedish Senate a peremptory declaration, which the King of Prussia described as an ultimatum of six folios interlarded with coarse and odious expressions, in which the Russian Minister demanded guarantees that the actual form of govern-

[1] For an account of the rise and character of these two Factions see Nisbet Bain: *Gustavus III.* Vol I.

ment in Sweden should not be altered in a monarchial sense. Frederick thereupon, through the medium of his Minister Podewils, requested Gross, the Russian Ambassador at Berlin, to beg the Empress to cease all interference in Swedish affairs, as the King's obligations towards the Court of Stockholm, and his desire to preserve the peace of the North, would compel him to defend Sweden in case of attack. Now, as Panin had already secretly advised the despatch of an army-corps; as Bestuzhev was prepared to support Panin, and the Empress herself was much incensed by what she regarded as the ingratitude of the Crown Prince of Sweden who owed his position to her, another European war in the course of 1750 seemed highly probable. It was happily averted by the refusal of Great Britain to lend herself in this respect to the plans of her Russian ally. The treaty, or rather the treaties of alliance concluded between the two countries in 1747, were very far from preventing dissensions arising on various current questions, and it soon became evident that the interests of the Court of St. Petersburg and the interests of the Court of St. James's were by no means identical. Both Chernuishev, the Russian Minister at London, and his colleague, Panin, at Stockholm, were strongly of opinion that by the terms of the last treaty (27 Nov./9 Dec., 1747) England was bound to pay the Imperial Government a subsidy for the maintenance of Russian troops in Finland. The English Ministers, on the other hand, categorically refused to recognise the justice of this argument, and steadily declined not only to pay out any subsidies for such a purpose, but even to countenance the anti-Swedish policy of the Empress at all. "I am bound to tell you frankly," said Newcastle to Chernuishev, "that our Court, which has only just succeeded in freeing itself from one ruinous war, is not at all disposed to plunge into the hazards of a second one." [1] The English Ministers also considered the reply of the Swedish Government to the Russian ultimatum as reassuring and satisfactory, and the Austrian Government expressing the same opinion, Russia was obliged to withdraw her pretensions, especially after Lord Hyndford had delivered a similar message to Bestuzhev, and the French and English Ministers at Stockholm, for once acting in unison, had even succeeded in assuaging the martial zeal of the Swedish Senate. The only result of this contest was the absolute rupture of diplomatic relations between Russia and Prussia. Frederick II, already incensed beyond measure by an Imperial rescript issued by Bestuzhev, ordering all Russian subjects belonging to the Baltic Provinces, but actually in the Prussian service, to return to their homes, deliberately went out of his way to publicly slight Gross, [2] the Russian resident at Berlin. Thus that diplomatist was expressly forbidden to visit the new Palace of Sans Souci and was ostentatiously passed over when all the other foreign Ministers at Berlin were invited to a state banquet at Charlottenburg. Gross lost no time in informing Bestuzhev of these fresh instances of royal impertinence, and by the rescript of October 25, 1750, he was recalled from Berlin. Before the year was out Warendorff, the Prussian Chargé d'Affaires at St. Petersburg, also received his passports. Thus Russia was now isolated diplomatically from both Prussia and France.

In Sweden, England had considered it necessary to oppose the plans of Russia, but in Poland and at the Porte, both Powers acted together, and their ambassadors successfully resisted all the intrigues of France and Prussia. Purely oriental affairs, however, were of very minor importance

---

[1] Martens: *Recueil des Traités*, etc. Vol. IX.

[2] Frederick's aversion to Gross was notorious. His principal offence was that, acting under instruction, he had persuaded several Russian officers to quit the Prussian service.

throughout the reign of Elizabeth, and even in Poland the one constantly recurring question, the desirability of abolishing the fatal *liberum veto*, the chief cause of the chronic political anarchy of that unhappy country, excited no more than a languid interest.   There was, indeed, a patriot party in Poland itself, headed by the great Potocki family, which clearly perceived that Poland must perish unless this inveterate gangrene were boldly cut out of the body politic, and the Elector of Saxony, in his own interests as King of Poland, also desired the abatement of the nuisance. But he dared not move without the consent of Russia, and Russia, naturally enough, would consent to no reform of the Polish Constitution which might resuscitate her ancient but now moribund rival.   All she would do was to protect the Poles from despoilers whose claims were less valid than her own, and here again the King of Prussia was the rival most to be feared.   To watch and thwart his manœuvres on this debatable ground, was at present the chief mission of Elizabeth's ministers.   In the course of 1750 that erratic meteor, Maurice of Saxony, suddenly appeared at Dresden and Berlin, and at the latter place where he was received with the most flattering distinction, he revived his claims to the Duchy of Courland,[1] relying on the support of Prussia, Saxony, and of Poland herself who was the suzerain of Courland.   The prospect of a Marshal of France, and that too the victor of Fontenoy, occupying a princely throne on the very confines of Russia, caused a flutter at St. Petersburg, and Bestuzhev was so alarmed that he strongly advised Elizabeth to release and reinstate Biren as Duke.   To this proposal, however, though strongly supported by a large faction in Poland itself, the Empress would not listen.   In vain the

---

[1] He had been elected Duke some thirty years before, but the Russian troops and Menshikov had driven him out of the country.

Republic sent a special envoy, Gurowski, to plead for Biren, and offer Bestuzhev a bribe of 25,000 ducats; in vain Bestuzhev, afraid to approach the Tsaritsa again on the subject himself, employed his friend Razumovsky to insinuate it to her in private. Elizabeth remained firm, and Gurowski was dismissed after a stay of four months at the Russian Capital. In fine, the ducal throne of Courland remained vacant as the Empress would not release Biren, and the Poles refused to accept Maurice, although it was reported that he was to marry a sister of the King of Prussia and receive the active support of that potentate. The English Minister at Warsaw, Sir Hanbury Williams, was of great assistance to Russia in counteracting the Franco-Prussian intrigues, and he even carried the war into the enemy's country, by attempting to detach the Elector of Saxony from the French alliance. The Elector at first expressed his willingness to change sides if England would give him the same amount of subsidies as he received from France, and if Austria would guarantee him against all danger from the side of Prussia. This was in 1750. In 1753 the Russian Court went a step further, and endeavoured to induce Austria and Saxony actively to assist each other in case either were attacked by the King of Prussia. Austria was not unwilling to agree to this, but Saxony shrank back out of fear of Frederick and would only give such a guarantee if assured beforehand of the coöperation of Great Britain.

The King of Prussia was well aware of what he was wont to call the machinations of England against him, and he frequently alludes to her envoys in Russia and Poland in disparaging terms—an infallible sign of his uneasiness and alarm. Guy Dickens, the new English Minister at St. Petersburg, he calls "a vain, noisy, vehement and headstrong man, who has never acted in an easy or natural manner"; whilst Hanbury Williams is described as "an extremely dangerous man who is to be well looked after

in case he does mischief." [1]   It is upon the Russian Chancellor, however, that he pours out the vials of his fiercest
wrath.   "It would be a happy event in many respects,"
he wrote to Warendorff, his Chargé d'Affaires at St. Petersburg, shortly before the definitive rupture of diplomatic
relations with Russia, if it "would please Providence to
withdraw from this world him to whom you refer." [2]   But,
in point of fact, Bestuzhev had even more need of the
protection of Providence than his royal adversary.   He was
frequently heard to complain at this time that his enemies
were more numerous than the hairs of his head, and we
know from the despatches of Guy Dickens, [3] that, from 1753
onwards, "the rage of parties at the Russian Court was
never carried further" than it was at this period.   "All
kinds of intrigues and artifices," he writes, "are being
employed on each side to ruin, crush and destroy one
another."   Bestuzhev's own irritable temper, moreover, had
not improved of late.   The long possession of almost unlimited power had made him masterful and dictatorial; his
paroxysms of anger became more frequent and more violent
and, not content with snubbing his colleagues, he sometimes
even went the length of lecturing the foreign Ambassadors
instead of listening to them. His domestic life, moreover,
was very unhappy.   His son had proved a failure and a
scandal; his wife took the young scoundrel's part against
his own father, and presently his brother Michael was
superadded to the number of his enemies.   The cause of
the rupture between the two brothers is somewhat curious.
Ever since his departure from St. Petersburg, after the
Lopukhin tragedy, the elder Bestuzhev had resumed his

---

[1] *Pol. Corr.* Vols. VII—VIII.

[2] Oct. 20, 1750. Warendorff had dutifully reported that the Grand Chancellor was suffering from a severe attack of colic.

[3] *Record Office. S. P. Russia,* 1753—4.

ambassadorial peregrinations, and represented his country at the Courts of Berlin, Dresden and Vienna successively. At the Saxon Capital in 1747, this almost septuagenarian diplomatist conceived a romantic attachment[1] for the widow of the Royal Oberschenk, Madame von Haugwitz, and eagerly desired to marry her. As, however, his first wife, who, it will be recollected, had been sent to Siberia five years previously, minus her tongue, was still alive, and the Empress was known to have very strict views as to the indissolubility of marriage, Michael Bestuzhev was placed in a very awkward predicament. It is true that he had quite satisfied himself that his former marriage had been annulled *per se* by his wife's felony, and he consequently regarded her as dead to him; but whether her Imperial Majesty would take the same view was somewhat problematical. On the other hand, he seems to have persuaded himself that the notorious soft-heartedness of the Empress might induce her, for once, to condone a little irregularity of this sort, and accordingly he applied to his brother to plead his cause with her. But the Chancellor, well aware that on this point her Majesty would be inflexible, and fearing to compromise himself by any such advocacy, absolutely refused to interfere, and when his brother still persisted in besieging him with supplicating letters, he returned them unopened. Michael Bestuzhev, thereupon, turned to his brother's rival, Count Michael Vorontsov, who listened to him with deep sympathy, but was powerless to help him. The old diplomatist was in despair, and his later letters are not without a pathetic note. "For the sake of my health, my domestic comfort and the clearing of my conscience," we find him writing to Vorontsov at the end of 1747, "and in order that after my death I may appear before my Creator blame-

---

[1] The best authority for this curious case is: "*Pisma Grafa M. P. Bezt-uzheva k Grafu M. L. Vorontsovu.* (Ark. Vor. II.) Compare *Solovev.*

less, I implore her Majesty of her benevolence, to allow
me to marry again, and so end my life in this world decently
and orderly after thirty-seven years of public service, and
twenty-eight of diplomatic activity." He assures Vorontsov
that Madame von Haugwitz's conduct has always been most
exemplary, and that in birth and rank she is fully his
equal, so that the union would be in no way derogatory.
For two years the correspondence continued, and then, on
the eve of his departure to Vienna as ambassador, Bestuzhev,
receiving no reply to the numerous petitions sent by himself
and the lady to the Empress, felt obliged (30th March, 1749)
to go through the ceremony of marriage with Madame von
Haugwitz before the Greek priest at Leipsic, "after the due
performance throughout Holy Week of all proper and customary Christian devotions." He duly informed the Empress
of what he had done, and expressed the hope that, "as a
kind and humane "mother, she would look with a tender eye
upon his conduct "and approve of it." But although Vorontsov
and both the Razumovskys pleaded for him, Elizabeth would
not give her sanction to the union, and the unfortunate Ambassador was consequently exposed too much humiliation during
his residence at Vienna. Maria Theresa, indeed, gave Madame
von Haugwitz a private audience, at which she was treated
with much sympathy and all the distinction due to her rank;
but, with many strong expressions of regret, the Empress Queen
informed Michael Bestuzhev, through her Kammerherr, Baron
Kettler, that, so long as his irregular union was not formally
legalized by an Ukaz, the etiquette of the Court must prevent
her from receiving Madame von Haugwitz publicly. The
fond old man bitterly resented the slur thus cast upon his
wife whom he loved devotedly, and whose death seems to
have been hastened by grief and chagrin,[1] and assuming,

[1] She died of consumption on the 22 Aug. 1757, after living to see her
estates in Saxony ruined by the exactions of the Prussians, and pawning her

rightly or wrongly, that, but for his brother's neutrality, the difficulty might have been surmounted, he bore towards him ever afterwards an implacable hatred. Moreover, from and after 1753, Alexius Bestuzhev's other enemies began cautiously to raise their heads once more. Vorontsov, thanks to the secret influence of his own wife and the Countess Shuvalova, regained to some extent the Imperial favour, and he and his confederates attempted to persuade the Empress that the Grand Chancellor was actually in the pay of England, and received large bribes from that Power. Bestuzhev, however, whose hands and conscience were equally clean in this particular, succeeded in putting all his enemies to shame by a really brilliant stroke of sardonic humour. I have already alluded to the comparative poverty of the Grand Chancellor, and the difficulty he found in keeping up an establishment commensurate with his rank. His official salary was only about £ 3,000 a year, and his official residence was so small and inconvenient, that he complained to the Empress that it was impossible for him to entertain the foreign diplomatists decently. The Empress thereupon presented him with a magnificent house in the best part of the city, but informed him at the same time that he must furnish and embellish it at his own cost. Bestuzhev, thereupon obtained, but only after the greatest difficulty, a loan equivalent to 50,000 rubles from the English Government, on the mortgage of the new house, and as, according to the curious custom of the times, he was obliged to produce a written certificate of indebtedness for every thousand rubles borrowed by him, together with a guarantee of repayment by a third party, he called upon fifty of his *personal enemies* to furnish him with the guarantees required.

---

diamonds and plate to enable her husband to eke out his miserable salary. Bestuzhev was utterly broken by the event, and did not long survive her. His letters on the subject are most pathetic.

By this adroit expedient, he not only dissipated, once for all, the persistent rumour that he was the hireling of England, but convinced the Empress that he was really poor and deserving of her generosity.

Having thus cleared the ground, so to speak, Bestuzhev could now proceed energetically to promote his favourite project of a strong Anglo-Russian alliance, with the object of "still further clipping the wings of the King of Prussia". His efforts were materially assisted by the very evident desire of Great Britain to meet him half way. The fact is too often overlooked, that up to the very outbreak of the Seven Years' War Frederick the Great had no more thorough-going adversary then the very Power which subsequently supported him through his mortal struggle with combined Europe by supplying him with the sinews of war. In April 1750, Mr. Guy Dickens, the new British Ambassador at the court of St. Petersburg, delivered to the Russian Chancellor a note in which he represented an attack by Prussia upon Hanover as inevitable,[1] and demanded that in such a contingency the Russian troops now mobilized in Livonia should enter Prussian territory, when Great Britain would be ready to provide all the necessary subsidies, and even increase them if necessary. This demand at first was not very well received at Petersburg. It was not forgotten that only a few months previously, Great Britain had pleaded an empty treasury, and an addition of £ 30,000,000 to the national debt as an excuse for not subsidizing a Russian army in Finland, yet now she was ready to spend millions to protect herself against Prussia!

---

[1] Frederick II, who even after the rupture of diplomatic relations with Russia was kept well informed of what was going on at St. Petersburg by the Dutch Resident there, who communicated circuitously with him via the Hague, declares, in 1752, that England's apprehensions as to Hanover were absurd, and yet two years later, we find him sounding the French Court as to the advisability of invading Hanover. *Pol. Corr.* Vols. IX—XI.

Moreover, the Empress, who throughout these tedious and troublesome negotiations displayed a truer political instinct than her Chancellor, was indisposed to risk a rupture with the King of Prussia and his allies simply for the sake of Hanover. For three whole years, therefore, she returned no definite answer to these new Anglican demands. Then the British Government began to grow impatient. On July 26, 1753, the Duke of Newcastle asked the Russian Ambassador at London, Count Chernuishev, whether he had got any news from his Court yet, and, on receiving a negative reply, cried, with some irritation: "Why "always 'no! no!' and our Minister with you always "says the same thing?" He then insinuated that Chernuishev no longer possessed the confidence of his own Court, and dismissed him after an interview which had scarcely lasted two minutes.[1] The discontent of the Court of St. James's, however, was quickly dissipated when the Russian Chancellor once more came forward as the defender *à outrance* of the British Government. On May 7, 1753, Bestuzhev presented to the Empress a memorandum, in which he demonstrated, with his usual wealth of illustrative detail, that the English Alliance was still the most advantageous for Russia. "In my most feeble opinion," con- "cluded the Grand Chancellor, "the interests and glory of "your Majesty imperatively demand that prompt succour "should be sent to save and defend an ally so natural and "so useful as the King of England. Such assistance should "be rendered as speedily as possible, and it can be affirmed "without fear of contradiction that as soon as the neces- "sary conventions have been concluded, and ukazes have "been issued for the mobilization of troops on the Livonian "frontier, the King of Prussia will immediately abandon

[1] Martens: *Recueil des Traités, etc.* Solovev: *Istoria Rossy; Record Office, S. P. Russia,* 1753—4.

"his projects, and Hanover will remain in the most per-
"fect tranquillity. And how glorious for your Majesty to
"see the designs of the hostile Courts put to nought, and
"the interests of all your Majesty's allies maintained
"by a simple military demonstration!" Elizabeth, after
careful consideration, approved of all the points of her
Chancellor's memorandum, and commanded him to enter
into negotiations with the English Ministers for subsidizing
a second Russian army corps destined to make an irruption into Prussian territory. By the terms of this fresh
convention, Russia engaged to concentrate on the Livonian
frontier 55,000 men, instead of the 30,000 originally be-
spoken, in return for a subsidy from England of 3,000,000
Dutch florins. The English Government, however, protested its inability to pay as much as 3,000,000 Dutch
florins, and in March, 1754, a new project was submitted
to Mr. Dickens by Bestuzhev, whereby England was required to pay for the invading army of 55,000 men £500,000
a year, besides £200,000 more for the maintenance of
another army corps to be stationed on the frontier. But
"English avarice," as Bestuzhev bitterly complained, would
not accept even this. The utmost the Court of St. James's
would grant was £350,000 a year for the diversionary
corps against Prussia, and £50,000 for the maintenance of
the extra corps on the Livonian frontier. No wonder if
the Grand Chancellor at last began to lose patience. The
interviews between him and Mr. Dickens now became
remarkable for a display of heat on both sides, and while
Bestuzhev peevishly declared that "he wished the negotiations with England were broke off," [1] Dickens significantly

---

[1] *Record Office*, *S. P. Russia*, 1754—5. Dickens, with equal petulance,
describes Bestuzhev as the most ungrateful wretch ever known, although the
ingratitude was really all on the other side. If Russian statesmen ever want
a pretext for expressing distrust of England, they will find it ready to hand
in her treatment of Bestuzhev.

hinted that the obstinacy of Russia might induce the King of England to listen to the proposals of the King of Prussia, who, he said, was daily making advances to accommodate his differences with England. But Bestuzhev was too much enamoured of the English alliance to abandon it in a fit of pique, and in the course of the summer of 1754, he presented a fresh memorandum to the Empress, advocating more strongly than ever the conclusion of an alliance with Great Britain. No further progress was made, however, till Mr. Dickens was superseded, in June 1755, by Sir Hanbury Williams, who had secret instructions to conclude the new convention with Russia as speedily as possible. On July 6, 1755, he submitted to a conference of Russian Ministers the following ultimatum: (1) the convention to be concluded was to extend to all the allies of his Majesty; (2) the total amount of the subsidies, in case of a diversion against Prussia, was to be £500,000 per annum; (3) the cost of the maintenance of the extra corps on the frontier was to be £100,000 per annum. After a fortnight's deliberation, the Russian Ministers informed Williams that the Empress considered the terms offered altogether inadequate. Williams replied categorically that he could make no change in his ultimatum. After ten days' further consideration, the Empress finally decided to sign the convention, and signed it was on Sept. 19, 1755. By the terms of this convention, Russia engaged to furnish an auxiliary corps of 55,000 men for a diversion against Prussia in return for an annual subsidy from England of £500,000 per annum, besides £100,000 a year for the maintenance of an extra corps on the frontier. Russia also undertook to supply from forty to fifty galleys, and, on the first appeal for help from England, to march 30,000 men into Prussian territory. This convention was to be ratified two months after signature, but at the last moment Elizabeth could not make up her mind to do so. It must be admitted that her scruples were honourable and patriotic. She suspected, not without reason, that England required a large proportion of the Russian contingent to fight her battles on the Rhine and in the Low Countries, and although the Empress was perfectly willing to proceed to extremities against her near neighbour, the restless and disquieting King of Prussia, it revolted her to barter away the lives of her soldiers, and send them far from their native land to die like so many cattle in a quarrel with which Russia had no concern. Two months of suspense elapsed and still the convention remained unratified. At last in December, 1755, the Grand Chancellor sent for Williams, and put this question to him in the name of the Empress: "In "case the King of Prussia were to attack Russia, what "assistance would Great Britain be prepared to render her?" Williams replied to this question by asking another: "Is the convention ratified?" On Bestuzhev's replying that it was not, the English Minister, profoundly mortified, declared that he thought he had been summoned to this conference to settle quite a different matter; that it was now three weeks since he had notified the arrival of the ratification from London; and that although he was quite willing to await the Empress's leisure still longer, on receiving an assurance that such further delay would not imply the rejection of the whole convention, he could not answer the question now put to him before the ratifications of the original convention [1] had been exchanged. It now seemed as if the whole negotiation must fall through, but once again the Grand Chancellor came forward as the energetic defender of England. On January 19, 1756, he presented a very lengthy report to the Empress, in which he demon-

---

[1] Compare Martens' "*Recueil des traités* etc.", and Solovev's *Istorya Rossy.*

strated the dangerous consequences of a rupture of the negotiations. If the convention is declared of none effect, he argues, the English ratification will be sent back to London like a protested bill of exchange; the King and the British nation will naturally regard this as an affront, and a great coldness will ensue between the two Courts. The Empress yielded once more to the arguments of her Minister, and ordered the ratification of the convention to be proceeded with at once; but she was justly offended by the style and tone of Bestuzhev's last effusion. As a rule his *promemorias* were couched in the most humble and obsequious terms; but on the present occasion his ill-humour so far got the better of his judgment, that he imputed the delay in the negotiations entirely to the machinations of his enemies, and petulantly threatened to resign if her Majesty were absolutely determined to annul the convention. Now, as a matter of fact, both his enemies, as he called them, and the Empress herself were quite at one with him as to the necessity of a war with Prussia; but they were not disposed to deliver themselves, bound hand and foot, into the power of the King of England, and place their troops at the absolute disposal of the Court of St. James's. The Empress was seriously offended with her Chancellor for thus subordinating patriotism to expediency and casting suspicion on the purity of her own motives, and she lost no time in showing it. When the ratifications were finally exchanged on Feb. 1, 1756, the Chancellor by the express command of her Majesty, and in the presence of his rival the Vice-Chancellor Vorontsov (an additional humiliation) handed to the English Ambassador an explicit declaration containing certain reservations, and definitely excluding Hanover from the operation of the convention. Williams' enthusiasm at the ratification of the convention was instantly damped by the delivery of this declaration. At first he absolutely declined to send it to England on the ground that, up to a certain point, it invalidated the convention itself; but on the Imperial Government refusing to take back the declaration, he accepted it [1] rather than see the whole convention torn to pieces. Yet this very treaty, which it had taken nearly six years to negotiate, and which had only been carried through after an infinity of trouble and worry, had already become mere waste paper. A fortnight before the exchange of the ratifications, an event had occurred at the other end of Europe which shattered all the cunning combinations of the Russian Chancellor; completely changed the political complexion of the continent, and precipitated a general European war.—On January 16, 1756, an offensive and defensive alliance was concluded at Westminster, between Great Britain and the King of Prussia!

[1] Especially after Volkhov, the Secretary of the Russian Foreign Office, had made it quite clear to him that the Russian troops must be employed exclusively against the King of Prussia.

CHAPTER VIII.

THE LEAGUE AGAINST PRUSSIA.

1756.

THE new Prussian Monarchy a menace to Europe—Kaunitz's report to
Maria Theresa as to the necessity of a new political system—The
German Neutrality Convention between Prussia and Great Britain—
Indignation in France—The Treaty of Versailles between France
and Austria—Alarm of Great Britain—Cynical levity of her policy—
Pitiable situation of Bestuzhev—Character of the Grand Duke
Peter—And of the Grand Duchess Catherine—Birth of the Grand
Duke Paul—Beginning of friendly relations between Catherine and
Bestuzhev—Illness of the Empress—Bestuzhev becomes obstructive—
Establishment of the Conference of Ministers—The Five Points—
Renewal of diplomatic relations between France and Russia—The
Mission of Mackenzie Douglas—The Mission of T. D. Bekhtyeev—
Anxiety of Great Britain—The intrigues of Hanbury Williams—
Recovery of the Empress—Russia accedes to the Treaty of Versailles—
Frederick's apprehension—Beginning of the Seven Years' War.

THE year 1756 marks the beginning of a profound and
far-reaching diplomatic revolution, which completely reversed
the traditional political systems of Europe and the consequences of which were to be felt throughout the remainder
of the eighteenth century. Hitherto, broadly speaking, the
balance of power had hung upon the rivalry of the Houses
of Hapsburg and Bourbon, a rivalry centuries old, which
had been the determining cause of most of the wars which
had convulsed the continent since the days of Richelieu.

The object of France in the last of these wars, the War
of the Austrian Succession, had been to establish her
supremacy in Europe by partitioning defenceless Austria,
and splitting up Germany into a set of petty dependent
principalities. But just as after, and in consequence of,
the Great Northern War, [1] (also, by the way, a war of
partition, Sweden in that case being the victim) to the
astonishment of Europe a new Great Power had risen up
in the shape of Russia, so too the War of the Austrian
Succession had created another and still more unwelcome
Great Power in the shape of Prussia, the only State which
had profited, and profited considerably, by that political
cataclysm. France had been most cruelly deceived in her
calculations. She had sought to make a tool of the young
Prussian Monarchy, and the young Prussian Monarchy had
reversed their respective parts and made a tool of her
august and semi-contemptuous patron and ally. France
had emerged from the struggle with loss of power
if not of prestige, while Prussia had become, not merely
respectable, but formidable. Another result of the war was
the drawing together of Austria and France, both now
animated by a common fear and distrust of Prussia.
Austria, having suffered and learnt the most from Frederick
II, was naturally the most resentful and the most per-
spicacious of Prussia's foes. The Peace of Aix had scarcely
been signed when the Court of Vienna seriously began to
reconsider its whole political system. In the Spring of
1749, the Empress Queen instructed Wenzel Anton von
Kaunitz, her favourite and most promising counsellor, who
had already laid the foundations of his great reputation by
his brilliant diplomatic services at the Congress of Aix,
to report to her in writing his opinion on the situation and

[1] 1698—1720.

advise her what system, in view of the change of circumstances, it was now the best policy of Austria to pursue. The document which Kaunitz thereupon laid before his Sovereign, was a masterpiece of political foresight and diplomatic astuteness, for, in point of fact, he boldly advised her to break once for all with an obsolete past and make fresh opportunities out of her present necessities. He pointed out, among other things, that although England was the chief of Austria's allies, she could not be counted upon in the case of another war with Prussia, a prophecy to be singularly verified by the event. Russia, he admitted, was Austria's natural ally, but as her system mainly depended upon the caprices of various individuals, neither was she to be regarded as a perfectly stable political factor. Saxony was even less reliable than Russia, for with all the will, she had not the power to help Austria. The chief enemies of Austria, he proceeded to observe, were Turkey, France and Prussia. Turkey's system, from the very nature of her Government, was quite incalculable; she must simply be well watched, and given as little cause of offence as possible. The King of Prussia, on the other hand, must always be regarded as foremost among the essential adversaries of Austria and as her most dangerous neighbour. Possessed of Silesia, he could at any moment, at the head of his formidable army, penetrate into the heart of the hereditary domains of the House of Austria and deal the monarchy a deadly blow, and it was highly probable that he *would* do so on the first opportunity, well persuaded, as he must needs be, that Austria would never forgive him for despoiling her of her fairest province, or neglect any opportunity of recovering it. The old system of alliances, therefore, having been proved to be obsolete, a new system was necessary. Every effort of Austria must now be directed to defending herself against the King of Prussia, and recovering her lost territory. But as it was impossible to attack Prussia without allies, and no active assistance was to expected from the Maritime Powers, it must be made worth the while of France to assist Austria against Prussia, especially as the active co-operation of Russia could always be relied upon.

But it proved a very difficult thing to overcome the prejudices of ages. In the autumn of 1750, Kaunitz was sent as Ambassador to Paris, and in May 1751, he reported that he saw very little hope of making a breach between the French and Prussian Courts. In the Spring of 1753, Kaunitz was recalled to Vienna to occupy the post of Chancellor, and Count Stahremberg succeeded him at Paris. On Aug. 21, 1755, alarmed at the rumours of a *rapprochement* between England and Prussia, Stahremberg sounded the Abbé Bernis, then the French Minister of Foreign Affairs, as to the advisabillty of a defensive alliance between the Courts of Versailles and Vienna; but the French Government still held back, pleading its previous engagements with Prussia, engagements which it could not break except in the case of extreme necessity. No such honourable scruples disturbed the conscience of the King of Prussia. As early as August, 1755, he had been approached by the British Government with the offer of an alliance whereby he was to engage not to disturb the peace of Germany, and formally undertake not to enterprise anything against Hanover at the instigation of France. [1] Frederick had been seriously alarmed by the subsidy treaty between Great Britain and Russia. He was also afraid that if he renewed his treaty with France (it had now only a few more months to run) he would be obliged, as a *sine qua non*, to attack Hanover, or, in other words, draw down upon himself the combined forces of England, Holland and Russia, whereas the friendship of England seemed to him to offer a sufficient

---

[1] Compare Martens: *Recueil des traités, etc.;* Frederick II. *Pol. Corr.* Vol. XII; Solovev: *Istoria Rossy;* Vondel: *Louis XV et Elisabeth.*

guarantee for the neutrality of Austria. Calculating, therefore, that the chances were, on the whole, in favour of the
superior usefulness of the English alliance, he signed
(16 Jan. 1756) the Treaty of Westminster with Great
Britain, commonly known as the German Neutrality Convention, whereby the two contracting Powers agreed to
unite their forces to oppose the entry into, or the passage
through, Germany of the troops of any other foreign Power,
under any pretext whatsoever. A secret article expressly
excluded the Austrian Netherlands and their dependencies,
as being extra-Germanic, from the operation of this Convention. [1]

It was most natural that Frederick should seek at once
the best possible protection against the storm which he
foresaw was about to descend upon him; but it was equally
natural that the French Government should regard his
sudden *volteface* as an act of diplomatic treason. The
Treaty of Westminster was signed, but not yet ratified,
when the Duc de Nivernois set out from Paris for Berlin,
officially charged to negotiate the renewal of the Franco-
Prussian Treaty of Alliance which would expire in July 1757.
Frederick frankly confessed his infidelity to his oldest and
most faithful ally, alleging, as an excuse, his fear of the
Russian Empress, and protesting at the same time that
his intentions were absolutely pacific. The news caused
equal amazement and indignation at Versailles, and the
French Government hastened to make reprisals. Louis XV
instructed his Ambassador at Vienna to inform the Austrian
Government that he would no longer refuse to negotiate
on the basis of the proposals rejected in 1755, and on
May 2, 1756, a defensive alliance was signed at Versailles
between the French and Austrian Governments. On the

[1] Compare Martens: *Recueil des traités, etc.;* Frederick II, *Pol. Corr.* Vol.
XII; Solovev: *Istoria Rossy;* Vondel: *Louis XV et Elisabeth.*

same day a secret treaty for the ultimate partition of Prussia was signed between the same two Powers, to which Russia, Sweden and Saxony were to be invited to accede.

If France had been alarmed by the Treaty of Westminster, still more alarmed was Great Britain by the Treaty of Versailles.   Yet had it not been completely blinded by a too exclusive self-interest, the English Government might well have reflected that other Powers also had their proper interests to look after, and that Silesia was at least as dear to Austria as Hanover could be to England.   Indeed it must be confessed that the cynical levity of England's foreign policy at this period reflected little honour upon her statesmen or her diplomatists.   Keith, the British Minister at Vienna, even had the assurance to remark to Maria Theresa that the Treaty of Versailles was a breach of the treaties already existing between Austria and Great Britain. To this the Empress-Queen replied, with her usual spirit, that it was not she, but Great Britain, who first had abandoned the old system by signing the Treaty of Westminster. "The King of Prussia and myself," she continued, "cannot go together.   I can have no part in any alliance into which he has entered.   I fear but two foes, the Turks and the Prussians; but the good understanding which now exists between *the two Empresses* guarantees me against the attacks of my most powerful enemies." [1]

This reference to her sister Empress was significant.   It clearly indicated what nobody had hitherto suspected, viz., that Austrian influence was stronger than British influence at St. Petersburg.   In this respect even the astute and well-informed King of Prussia had been deceived, as he was very soon to discover.   It was towards the Russian capital that every eye was now directed, and for the next seven

[1] Solovev: *Istoria Rossy.*

years St. Petersburg was to be the centre of the political activity of Europe.

It may be imagined with what feelings the intelligence of the Treaty of Westminster was received at the Russian Court. It was on 4/15 February, 1756, that Sir Hanbury Williams informed Bestuzhev of the conclusion of the Anglo-Prussian Convention. The British Minister was more than usually fertile in sophisms. He assured Bestuzhev that the new alliance aimed only at preventing a combined attack of France and Prussia upon Germany, and would not interfere in any way with the previous Anglo-Russian Convention. Bestuzhev was thunderstruck. He instantly perceived that his whole policy, the patient policy of a laborious lifetime, was collapsing. With difficulty he kept his countenance, and drily observed: "This new alliance will not, I fancy, be very agreeable tidings for the Empress."—"I hope," said Williams, "that your Excellency will put it to her Majesty in the proper point of view."—"But what does the Court of Vienna say?" insisted Bestuzhev.—"Oh," rejoined Williams flippantly, "if Austria seriously desires the prolongation of peace, she will say nothing." [1]

Williams's whole conduct is a fair sample of the frivolity with which Great Britain treated her allies at this period. As Solovev rightly observes, it would have been so easy for the English Ministers to have ascertained beforehand the true sentiments of the Courts of Vienna and St. Petersburg with regard to the King of Prussia. Instead of even trying to do so, they simply played for their own hands without the slightest regard for existing alliances, treated everyone who would not go all lengths with them as an ingrate or a traitor, and unscrupulously sacrificed their friends of to-day to oblige their enemies of yesterday. Williams, in par-

[1] Solovev: *Istoria Rossy.*

ticular, exhibited an arrogance and a rashness which rather befitted a headstrong dictator than a responsible diplomatist. He supplied his Government with utterly false views of the situation in order to justify his over-hasty predictions; he represented all the Russian statesmen as venal; he absolutely shut his eyes to the fact, obvious to everyone else, that the Anglo-Prussian had nullified the Anglo-Russian Convention, and he was even ready to sacrifice Bestuzhev, the only friend Great Britain still possessed at the Russian Court, to the vengeance of his enemies. The position of the Russian Chancellor, indeed, was now truly pitiable. He had expended all his energy in carrying through the alliance with England against the warnings of his colleagues and the wishes of his Sovereign —and now that alliance was proved to be utterly valueless to Russia. He had repeatedly and most confidently predicted that Prussia could never unite with Great Britain, or Austria with France, yet now both these alleged impossibilities were accomplished facts! Blunders such as these might perhaps have been pardonable in a rising young politician, whose very mistakes may often be a part of his political education, but in an ageing statesman with a diplomatic career of thirty years behind him they argued a serious decline of ability and inevitably suggested the expediency of his speedy retirement from affairs. The most bitter blow of all must have been the consciousness that he had forfeited the high esteem in which the Empress had hitherto held him. Even while she had trusted him, she had never liked him; but now how could she even trust a minister who had advised her wrongly, and to whom she had listened nevertheless, against her own better judgment? In an agony of impotent jealousy, the falling Chancellor perceived his ancient rival Michael Vorontsov, a man intellectually far his inferior, but strong in the friendship of Elizabeth and the support of the Shuvalovs, superseding him in the direction of affairs day by day and hour by hour. Yet, with a tenacity of purpose not without its pathos, the discomfited statesman still clung desperately to the power that was slowly slipping from his grasp. Nay, more, even now he did not quite abandon the hope of recovering his old ascendency. He was much too experienced a political gamester not to have a trump card in reserve. Two years previously, when the uncertainty of his position had first begun to dawn upon him, he had attempted to make sure of the future, while still enjoying the present, by secretly making pacific overtures to the Grand Duchess Catherine, whose superlative merits he had at last learned to recognise.

Up to 1753 the relations between the Chancellor and the little Grand Duchess had been anything but amicable. Catherine had grown to regard the saturnine old statesman as a sort of malignant ogre who dogged her every step with his Arguses and took a delight in tormenting her, while Bestuzhev looked upon Catherine as a precociously pert school-girl who required to be taught to keep her proper place. It was his hand that drew up the " Instructions " regulating the deportment and the discipline of the young spouses immediately after their marriage, for the guidance of the Choglokovs, whom, with the consent of the Empress, he had placed over the young Court, with strict directions to report regularly to himself as to the conduct of the Grand Duke and Grand Duchess. These patriarchal " Instructions "[1] give us a curious and interesting picture of what was expected of an orthodox Grand Duke and Grand Duchess in those days, as well as glimpses of the characters of the spouses for whom it was speci-

---

[1] Their full title is " *Instruktsy dlya lits naznachaemuikh sostoyat pri Velikoi Kniginye . . . i pri Velikom Knyazye.*" (Instructions for the persons attached to the service of the Grand Duke and the Grand Duchess.) *Arkh. Vor.* Vol. 2.

ally intended.   Maria Semenovna Choglokova, who was
appointed the Mistress of Catherine's household, was selected
for that responsible post because "she loved her husband and
had had many children by him." It was hoped and believed
that the little Grand-Duchess would be duly impressed by
this shining example of the domestic virtues. [1] Gospodina
Choglokova was to see to it that the Grand Duchess dili-
gently said her prayers in private as well as in public, and
was to give her good advice in case she neglected any of
her devotions.   She was to use her utmost endeavours to
make the Grand Duchess love, honour and respect her husband, and never on any occasion permit her to offend him,
or treat him with coldness.   She was also to do her best
to make the spouses live together "in the sweetest and
happiest manner, to the end that they may consummate the
heart-felt wishes of ourselves and our faithful subjects." [2]
The slightest appearance of ill-temper or coldness was to
be checked by reasonable counsel.   It was to be impressed
upon the little lady that the Grand Duke was not only her
lord, but would one day be her Sovereign likewise, and it
was therefore her plain duty to submit to his will.   Madame
Choglokova was further admonished to accompany the
Grand Duchess everywhere she went, and see that her intercourse with her gentlemen-in-waiting was never unduly
familiar or unbefitting her rank.   For example, none of
her gentlemen was ever to be permitted to whisper to her
or convey books or letters to her surreptitiously.   Still less
was the Grand Duchess to be permitted "any familiarity
or sportiveness with any page or groom of the bedchamber,
or coffee-server, or table-layer, or lacquey, to the disparage-

---

[1] As a matter of fact, the little rebel regarded Madame Choglokova as a
domestic dragon of the worst kind, and is malignantly delighted when the
poor lady's virtuous husband plays her false at last.

[2] The "Instructions" were of course drawn up in the Empress's name.

ment of her dignity." On the other hand, she was always
to receive courteously the physicians sent from time to time
to enquire after her health, and reply seriously to all their
interrogations. The Grand Duke was submitted to a similar
regimen. He was always to listen willingly and attentively
to the Clergy, and especially to his Confessor, when they
spoke to him concerning spiritual things. In view of his
tender constitution, "so liable to indisposition and so slow
to recover therefrom," [1] great care was to be taken as to
what he ate and drank and put on, and he was always to
answer the doctors clearly and circumstantially concerning
the state of his health. Every means was to be employed
to promote love and harmony between the spouses, and
great care was to be taken to prevent them from saying
rude, hasty and unbecoming words to each other in the
presence of their domestics. The reading of romances and
games with soldiers were to be strictly forbidden, in order
that the Grand Duke might the better employ his time in
a manner worthy of his high vocation. Above all things,
joking and jesting with menials was to be avoided. His
Highness, moreover, was to be carefully instructed in current history and politics, geography, the life of Peter the
Great, and to read regularly and carefully Russian books,
laws, codes and ukazes. He was also to give audiences
twice a week, on all which solemn occasions he was to
strive to be serious, pleasant, courteous, and constantly
good-humoured, avoiding anything like vulgarity or affectation in public. He was to listen rather than speak, ask
questions rather than volunteer opinions, so as to profit by
the science and experience of other people, constantly
bearing in mind that "reticence is the most necessary

---

[1] Peter was as feeble in body as in mind. His health was constantly in
danger and perhaps there was never a single day in his life on which he
could be said to be quite well.

quality in a great ruler." All familiarities with servants were to be prevented, "and no drums, tents, weapons or uniforms were to be introduced into, or used in, the private apartments of the Grand Duke " [1] by any of his domestics, under pain of dismissal.

The best available teachers were placed around the Grand Duke, under the superintendence of the Academician Stehlin, an able and conscientious governor. But they could do little or nothing for a pupil who was quite incapable of grasping abstract ideas, or giving his attention to anything requiring reflection or steady application. There can indeed be no doubt that Peter's case was one of arrested mental development. Without being actually imbecile, he was childish to an almost incredible degree, delighting only in toys and trifles and with little or no sense of his immense responsibilities. He was not naturally vicious [2] or bad hearted, as has sometimes been supposed ; his memory was extraordinary, and he was even capable of real enthusiasm and of a sincere though exaggerated hero-worship ; [3] but the utter frivolity and futility of his nature was becoming more and more apparent every day. The most disquieting feature of his character, however, from a political point of view, was his now notorious detestation of the country of his adoption. With an imprudence bordering upon idiocy, he lost no opportunity of publicly

[1] An allusion to Peter's childish fondness for games at soldiers.

[2] It is too often forgotten that all the bad accounts we have of this poor prince have all been catherinized so to speak, that is to say told us by the woman who suffered most from him and ultimately rid herself of him. Even that strong partisan of Catherine, the Princess Dashkova, admits that the Grand Duke was not naturally vicious. His drunkenness, a reproach so often brought against him, was due rather to a weak head than to habitual excess. If what his wife tells us of his physical condition be true, his so-called amours must have been purely platonic.

[3] *E.g.*, his enthusiasm for Frederick II, and his appreciation of the Abbé Bernis.

disparaging Russia and the Russians, and exalting Russia's enemies and rivals, notably Frederick the Great, whom he usually alluded to as "the King my Master." [1]   And this reckless Russophobe was one day to wear the imperial Crown! To thoughtful and patriotic Muscovites, such an outlook was scarcely reassuring.

And as if still further to complicate an already difficult situation, this poor *crétin* was the nominal consort of the most intelligent and the most audacious of European Princesses! The early married life of the Grand Duchess Catherine must have been miserable in the extreme. This essentially robust and expansive young woman, bubbling over with the desire of life and proudly conscious of almost unlimited capabilities, was bound by an iniquitous marriage to a sort of living corpse, to a creature scarce able to hold up his head, and as little able to discharge the duties of a husband as the functions of a Prince. Can we wonder if she plunged riotously into the dissipations of a licentious Court, and sought in the embraces of half-a-dozen successive lovers those joys which her ardent physical nature demanded, and which were altogether denied her in wedlock? Yet in this many-sided, richly endowed nature the cravings of the intellect were at least as imperious as the cravings of appetite.   From her childhood upwards, Catherine had had a veritable passion for literature, and, after her arrival in Russia, a large portion of her ample leisure was devoted to study and self-improvement. Before she was twenty, there were very few notable books in the domains of history and philosophy with which she was unacquainted, and

---

[1] On learning of the death of old King Frederick of Sweden, he exclaimed: "They dragged me into this accursed Russia where I must consider myself a monarch under arrest, whereas if I had been left free, I should now be sitting on the throne of a civilized nation." He meant Sweden. As the great-nephew of Charles XII and the great-grandson of Charles XI he had an indisputable right to the Swedish crown.

at thirty her knowledge of the masterpieces of France and Germany was intimate and profound.[1] She spoke French and German with equal ease, and at a later day she was to enrich the literature of both languages. Russian she had studied assiduously from the first, with the secret but unconquerable determination of one day ruling the country of her adoption, for she was quite resolved to die rather than occupy any other than the very highest place. Deep down within her heart, more intense, more absorbing even, than her love of pleasure or her love of learning, was her ruling passion— the lust of power. To gratify her ambition, she had already begun to practise, with all the art of a born comedian, those ineffably winning ways which fascinated everyone, male or female, high or low, whom she thought it worth her while to win; and to gratify that ambition she was prepared to venture everything, and lightly, almost gaily, commit or connive at crimes which the passionate but essentially benevolent Elizabeth would have shrunk from with horror. Up to 1755, the relations between the two Princesses had been more than cordial. Elizabeth, as I have already mentioned, loved young people, especially when they were merry, pretty and vivacious, and Catherine was liberally endowed with all these endearing qualities. Moreover, the aunt and niece possessed many tastes in common. Both

---

[1] The Swedish Minister, Count Gyllenborg, was the first to encourage her literary studies. It was he who advised the little philosopher of fifteen to read only the best books, *e.g.*, "Plutarch's Lives," "The Life of Cicero," "The Fall of the Roman Republic," by Montesquieu. Subsequently she fell in with the "Letters of Madame de Sévigné," which, she says, enthralled her. After "devouring" them, she procured and read the works of Voltaire. Montesquieu's "Spirit of the Laws" she also read with avidity, while the "Annals" of Tacitus produced a perfect revolution in her mind and first taught her to look at the dark side of things. Her German reading was equally extensive, and she perused every line of Russian she could lay her hands upon, notably two huge tomes of a Russian translation of the Ecclesiastical History of Baronius.

delighted in boisterous pastimes and athletic exercises. Both had a natural liking for the romantic and the adventurous. Both were daring horsewomen, accomplished dancers, amusing talkers. Both of them loved to go masquerading about in masculine attire with an escort of obsequious admirers. The bond of intimacy between them seemed to be still further established by the birth, after nine years of sterility, of Catherine's first child, [1] the Grand Duke Paul of tragic memory (Oct. 1, 1754), an event which secured the continuance of the dynasty, and was celebrated by a month of festivities of unexampled magnificence. [2]

I have already said that the relations between Catherine and Bestuzhev had hitherto been anything but amicable; but, towards the end of 1753, circumstances at length drew the ambitious Grand Duchess and the wily Grand Chanchellor together. Already Bestuzhev's position, though still paramount, was growing insecure, and he looked feverishly about him for additional support, against the hostile coalition of Vorontsov and the Shuvalovs. Nor, to do him justice, was his anxiety altogether personal. Like all patriotic and far-seeing Russians, the prospect of the succession to the throne of the irresponsible and capricious Grand Duke Peter, filled him with consternation. So long as Elizabeth lived, no danger to the State was to be apprehended; but, of late, the Empress had been ailing, and if she were to die suddenly, who was there to take her place? Bestuzhev

---

[1] It was the general opinion at Court that the father of the child was Sergius Saltuikov. The Empress had taken infinite pains to induce and even compel Peter and Catherine to consummate their marriage, but her good intentions in this respect had utterly failed. Then, according to Catherine, whose veracity, however, is very questionable, Elizabeth connived at a liaison which should secure the continuance of the dynasty, giving Catherine the choice between two of her most notorious lovers. I myself think the child was legitimate because Catherine always hated it.

[2] Peter Shuvalov, on this occasion, gave a *bal-masqué* which lasted forty-eight hours.

had already arrived at the conclusion that the only possible candidate was the little Grand Duchess. Of late he had been secretly but closely observing her, and the astute old statesman had at last persuaded himself that here he had to deal with no ordinary woman. Once convinced of this, his whole line of conduct changed. From being her jailer he suddenly became her friend. [1] His first advances to her were made through her lover, Sergius Saltuikov. Catherine readily met Bestuzhev's advances half way, and a secret alliance for mutual support was ultimately formed between them, the Grand Duke's chief adviser in the affairs of his Holstein Duchy, serving as their intermediary. [2] For the present, however, this tacit bond of union remained inoperative. The burning question of the day, which obscured all others, was the proposed substitution of a French for an English alliance.

Elizabeth Petrovna and the majority of her counsellors rightly regarded the Treaty of Westminster between Great Britain and Prussia as utterly subversive of the previous conventions between Great Britain and Russia, [3] and the intelligence thereof, duly reported by Bestuzhev, was received at Court with the utmost indignation. Bestuzhev alone still affected to regard friendship with England as compatible with active hostility against Prussia. He was well aware, indeed, that if Great Britain could no longer be counted upon for help against Prussia, the assistance of France would be indispensable, yet with his inveterate and inextinguishable hatred of France, he could not reconcile himself to the idea of an alliance with that Power under any circumstances,

---

[1] He even condescended to be the secret medium of her correspondence with two of her lovers.

[2] Vasilchikov: *Semeistvo Razumovskikh.*

[3] See the Imperial Rescript to Prince Golitsuin at London in: "*Iz bumag Elizavetinskoi Konferentsy.*" *Arkh. Vor.* Vol. III.

even when the needs of his country imperatively required
it. One of the masters of modern statescraft has laid down
the following axioms which no diplomatist worthy of the
name can venture to ignore: "No great Power can place
itself exclusively at the service of another. It will always
have to keep in view not only existing, but future relations
to the others, and must, as far as possible, avoid lasting
fundamental hostility with any of them." [1] And again:
"The clause *rebus sic stantibus* is tacitly understood in all
treaties involving performance." [2] Bestuzhev had hitherto
adopted similar political maxims; but there had always
been too much of the purely personal element in his diplomacy, and pique and passion now blinded both his patriotism
and his natural sagacity. Clinging frantically to a past
condition of things, and refusing to bow to the inexorable
logic of accomplished facts, his whole policy now became
purely obstructive and therefore purely mischievous. His
first act, on recovering from the shock of the Treaty of
Westminster, was to propose to the Empress the establishment of a Conference of Ministers, under her presidency,
to advise her on all important matters relating to foreign
affairs. [3] The Empress approved of the proposal, and, for the
remainder of the reign, the Conference, as it was briefly called,
became a permanent and paramount Department of State,
its first session taking place on Feb. 8, 1756. On February
22, after carefully considering a report of the College of
Foreign Affairs on the political situation, the Conference,
despite the counter-arguments of the Chancellor, decided

---

[1] Bismarck Autobiography, Ed. Butler II. 234.

[2] Ib. II. 30.

[3] This he did to compel his opponents to show their hands openly and also
to prevent secret intrigues against himself. The original members of this "Conference" were the Chancellor himself, the Vice-Chancellor Michael Vorontsov,
Peter and Alexander Shuvalov, Prince Nikita Trubetskoi, Count Buturlin.
Admiral Golitsuin and Stephen Apraksin.

that England's treaty with Prussia had practically nullified the Anglo-Russian Conventions of 1755, and that it was against the dignity of the Empress to continue to receive subsidies from Great Britain. At the Session of March 14, the Conference proposed, in order to "reduce the King of Prussia within proper limits, and, in a word, to make him no longer a danger to the Empire," [1] that the following five points should be adopted: (1) Russia should proceed to curtail the power of the King of Prussia, but should not act single-handed; (2) the Court of Vienna should be engaged by every possible means to act in concert with Russia; (3) France should be invited to assist in the curtailment of the King of Prussia; (4) permission should be obtained from Poland for the passage of Russian troops through her territories for the purpose of attacking the King of Prussia, and (5) the acquiescence of Sweden and Turkey in the operations against Prussia should be secured. These five points were to be the unalterable rule and basis of all future measures.   Poland, as a reward for her compliance with the demands of Russia, was to receive Royal Prussia [2] when conquered from Frederick II, and in exchange therefor was to cede Courland to Russia, besides agreeing to a rectification of boundaries, which should place the commerce of the Black Sea as well as of the Baltic in the hands of Russia.   Moreover, that no time might be lost, it was ordered that the army should be mobilized and increased, so that Austria also might be spurred on to more rapid action and the King of Prussia attacked in the Spring, and the Austrian Ambassador was summoned to the Conference and informed of these military operations, at which he expressed great satisfaction.   He was also instructed to inform his Court without delay, that her Imperial

---

[1] "*Iz bumag Elizavetinskoi Konferentsy.*" *Arkh. Vor.* Vol. III.
[2] East Prussia.

Majesty was ready to accede to a definite treaty with France, whenever invited to do so.

The desire of re-opening diplomatic relations with France was the most significant sign of the times, and pointed indubitably to the abasement of Bestuzhev. But, in point of fact, a French Agent was actually on the spot. This was Mackenzie Douglas, a Jacobite refugee in the French service, who, the year before, had been sent to Russia by the Prince of Conti to sound the dispositions of the Russian Ministers, and find out the lie of the land. His mission was fenced about with mystery. His instructions, written in microscopic characters, were hidden in the false bottom of his tortoise-shell snuff-box, and he was to pass as a dealer in furs, [1] and use the jargon of the trade in his correspondence with the French Government. Thus the English Minister, Williams, figures in the despatches as " black fox;" Bestuzhev is "lynx;" "the little grey skins" meant the Russian troops in the pay of England, and the phrase "sable skins are falling in value," was to signify that the influence of the Chancellor was declining. Douglas arrived at St. Petersburg in 1755, and at once requested Williams, as a fellow-countryman, to present him at Court. But Williams, regarding a Scotchman who was at the same time a Catholic as doubly suspicious, warned Bestuzhev against him, and the Russian Chancellor took his measures so promptly that Douglas had to fly, though not before he had succeeded in secretly communicating with Vorontsov. The result of his first mission was nevertheless considered so satisfactory, that he was sent to Russia a second time, [2] in the Spring of 1756. His instructions were to proceed with the utmost caution, and to trust nobody but Vorontsov,

---

[1] Vondel: *Louis XV et Elisabeth*, etc.

[2] On this second occasion, Douglas brought with him as his secretary, an effeminate-looking young man, the Chevalier D'Eon de Beaumont, like him-

and accordingly he waited upon the Vice-Chancellor at
9 o'clock on an April evening, and presented him with a
letter from the French Minister, Rouillé, thanking Vorontsov
for offering to find him a librarian, and send him samples
of Burgundy. [1]—"What librarian? what Burgundy?" exclaimed the mystified Vice-Chancellor.—"I am the librarian,"
replied Douglas, "and the samples of wine are the persons
who should be sent on both sides to renew our relations."—
Vorontsov, not unnaturally, begged his enigmatical visitor to
be a little more explicit, whereupon Douglas handed the Vice-
Chancellor a letter to the effect that the King his Master [2]
desired a resumption of those amicable relations between
France and Russia, which should never have been interrupted. After much hesitation and many misgivings, Vorontsov at last took it upon himself to introduce Douglas to
the Tsaritsa when he presented his credentials, was very
favourably received, and, at his suggestion, a secret Russian
Agent, Theodor Dmitrievich Bekhtyeev, a dependant of
Vorontsov's and a man of considerable tact and astuteness,
was, in the beginning of May, sent to Paris, *via* the Hague,
incognito, to feel the pulse of the French Government.
Bekhtyeev arrived in Paris in July, and was received with
the utmost distinction, not only by the French Government,
but also by the then all-powerful Austrian Ambassador, [3] Count
Stahremberg. He was unfavourably impressed by the lack
of ability and enterprise in the rulers of France. He describes the Marshals and Ministers as "all either very old

---

self in the service of the Prince of Conti. This was D'Eon's *first* appearance in Russia. His mysterious and romantic previous mission, of which
so much has been made, has now been proved to be purely apocryphal. Yet
romances of that sort die hard, and even now the mythical first mission of this
insinuating adventurer disguised as a maid-of-honour, is accepted by credulous lovers of the marvellous.

[1] Solovev: *Istoria Rossy.* Compare *Iz bumag, etc.*

[2] Vondel: *Louis XV et Elisabeth, etc.*

[3] *Pisma Th. D. Bekhtyeeva k Grafu M. L. Vorontsovu. Arkh. Vor.* Vol. III.

or very ignorant." The Comptroller-General, Séchelles, who had done so much for the navy, the War Minister, D'Argenson, and, especially, the ageing but still brilliant Marshal de Bellisle, alone impressed him favourably. He also reported that the prospect of a war with Prussia, in addition to the ruinously expensive maritime war already proceeding, was very unpopular, as although the revenue of France was now much larger than formerly, her expenses nevertheless were also disproportionately great. On the whole, however, his report was considered satisfactory, and the Russian Government proceeded to urge upon the Austrian Government the necessity for prompt and vigorous concerted action against the King of Prussia, before he had had time to concentrate his forces. But now the Court of St. Petersburg encountered unexpected and irritating difficulties. At this crisis the Court of Vienna exhibited a caution not far removed from timidity. This was due partly to the refusal of France to assist Maria Theresa in an *offensive war* against Prussia, and partly to a fear lest, by overhastiness, Austria might have to contend, for a time, single-handed against the whole might of the much dreaded Prussian King. Moreover, Esterhazy, the Austrian Minister at St. Petersburg, painted the condition of the 10,000 Russian troops already mobilized on the frontier in the darkest colours, and reported that the Tsaritsa had not a single competent general. Austria therefore preferred to await an attack which would constitute a *casus foederis* binding upon both France and Russia, besides making her position more correct diplomatically.

Meanwhile Great Britain was using all her influence to prevent or counteract a Franco-Russian alliance. The news of the treaty between France and Austria had naturally caused great excitement in London, an excitement intensified still further when the new Russian Ambassador, Prince

Alexius Mikhailovich Golitsuin, presented to the English Ministers the imperial declaration to the effect that, in the opinion of the Russian Ministers, the Treaty of Westminster had nullified the Anglo-Russian Conventions of 1755. The Duke of Newcastle expressed the hope that the Empress would not abandon her old ally. Golitsuin replied, very justly, that the Franco-Austrian Alliance was the inevitable consequence of the Anglo-Prussian agreement. Secretary Holdernesse went so far as to say to Golitsuin that if the Empress now left England in the lurch, it would be her ruin. "England," said he, "cannot possibly resist a combination of France, Russia and Austria, and must henceforth remain a purely American Power, without any influence on the Continent." [1] But Great Britain's principal hope, at this crisis, was in the energetic and unscrupulous Williams, her Ambassador at St. Petersburg. Williams was determined, at all hazards, to prevent the re-establishment of friendly relations between Russia and France, and in his zeal for "the good cause" was quite prepared to pose as a second La Chetardie, a king-maker in fact, and accomplish his purpose by a dynastic revolution in Russia itself. The failing health of the Empress in the beginning of the Summer of 1756, suggested to him and his friend Bestuzhev an audacious conspiracy. Williams gave Elizabeth but six months more to live at most, and, on her decease, he proposed to give the Grand Duchess a share in the Government, as being the only person, in his opinion, capable of ruling Russia. [2] Peter III was not to be actually superseded, but Catherine was to be proclaimed Empress Consort, and Bestuzhev, as Colonel of the four regiments of the Guards, and with the absolute control of the Admiralty and the

---

[1] *Despatches of Golitsuin,* cited by Solovev.

[2] Bestuzhev, on the other hand, preferred the absolute exclusion of Peter, and the proclamation of Paul, with his mother, Catherine, as Regent.

Departments of War and Foreign Affairs, was to stand by her side as Chief Councillor. The intermediary between Williams and Catherine was Stanislaus Poniatowski, a handsome young Polish nobleman, already one of the most brilliant and fascinating personages of his day, who united the quintessence of Western Culture with all the romantic *abandon* of a true Sarmatian. Poniatowski originally came to Russia as the Secretary of Williams, who treated him like a son; but subsequently, through the influence of Bestuzhev and Williams, he was accredited to the Russian Court as the Ambassador of Saxony. The impressionable Grand Duchess was irresistibly attracted by this dazzling Phoenix, and abandoned all her other lovers in his favour. Williams had a preternaturally keen nose for scenting out secret French agents, whom he repeatedly hunted down, [1] and so sure was he of the success of his scheme, that he did not hesitate to lend Catherine £10,000 the moment she asked for it. He also tried to frighten her by insinuating that any French Minister who might reach the Russian Court, would be certain to join with her enemies, the Shuvalovs, to exclude her from the succession. The Grand Duke also fell under the influence of Williams. During the illness of the Empress he had been invited to participate in the Conference of Ministers, and it is said that when Alexander Shuvalov handed him the protocol of the session at which it had been decided to renew diplomatic relations with France, Peter refused to sign it till the War Minister, Stephen Apraksin, with great difficulty, persuaded him to do so. Williams was furious when he heard of this act of weakness, as he regarded it. He maintained that if the Grand Duke had persisted in his refusal, the whole affair must have fallen through. As for Catherine, she was

---

[1] We have seen how he thwarted Douglas's first mission. A previous agent, Valcroisant by name, was also detected and exposed by him.

quite prepared to act at the decisive moment. She fancied she could depend upon the Guards, and had resolved to arrest the Shuvalovs upon the slightest provocation. Nevertheless, despite Williams, Bestuzhev and Catherine, the negotiations with France steadily progressed, and with such secrecy were they conducted, that it is extremely doubtful whether the intriguing trio knew anything either of the mission of Douglas or the mission of Bekhtyeev. [1] Rumours of these negotiations seem, however, to have reached Williams at last, and, becoming suspicious, he was inclined, with his usual impetuosity, to discard Bestuzhev as a traitor, and treat direct with the Shuvalovs. Catherine also privately gave the Shuvalovs to understand that if they would only do something for her now, she would do everything for them in the future. But it was not to be. Contrary to everyone's expectation, a change for the better took place in the Empress's condition at the end of October, and all Williams' schemes to prevent the Franco-Russian alliance instantly collapsed. It is true that Elizabeth was now little more than a wreck of her former self, and still so feeble that she could not go from one room of the palace to another without extreme fatigue; but she still preserved all her old spirit, and her mental powers were as vigorous as they had ever been. On being told by Vorontsov that Frederick II had threatened her with a manifesto in favour of the ex-Tsar Ivan, in case she attacked him, she exclaimed: "In that case I will order Ivan's head to be cut off," nay, she declared she was prepared, if necessary, to lead her army in person. In August the British Government, as a last pacific expedient, had begged the Russian Government to mediate between Austria and Prussia; but the Conference of Russian Ministers had informed Williams, in

[1] Apparently Frederick II was also ignorant of both these missions.

reply, that her Imperial Majesty, being also aggrieved by
the King of Prussia, could not take upon herself the office
of mediator. The invasion of Saxony by the King of Prussia,
shortly to be alluded to, accelerated the accession of Russia to
the Franco-Austrian Alliance, and rendered all pacific overtures impossible. At the Conference of September 2nd, after
first consulting the sick Empress, it was resolved unanimously
to attack the King of Prussia as speedily and as vigorously as
possible, and to see that the Elector of Saxony received
every satisfaction for this shameless attack " on his domains,
the measure of compensation to be estimated, not by the
amount of damage done, but by the enormity of the breach
of faith." A circular was also addressed by the Russian
Government to all the Courts of Europe, expatiating, in no
measured terms, on the unheard of treachery of the King
of Prussia in ravaging a friendly State with whom he had
no cause of quarrel and at a time of profound peace, and,
in a despatch to Golitsuin, the Russian Minister at London,
Williams was accused of " lending himself to the low and
shabby intrigues of the King of Prussia." And yet, after
all this, Williams in an interview with Vorontsov on Nov. 1,
actually insisted upon a joint mediation of Elizabeth [1] and
George II as the only remaining means of preventing a
bloody war, otherwise, he added, the King of Prussia would
be obliged, in sheer despair, to attack Russia. Vorontsov
haughtily replied that Russia feared nothing, and he then
requested to see the written authorization of the King of Prussia
for such proposed mediation, which Williams was unable to
produce. He had the effrontery, however, to tell Vorontsov
that he had actually despatched a courier to the camp of
the Prussian King, informing him of the departure of the
Russian Commander-in-Chief, Stephen Apraksin, for the

---

[1] Elizabeth subsequently refused her mediation as being incompatible with
her " dignity as a Sovereign, and the justice of the case."

front. Such a piece of impudence could not be overlooked. In reply to Williams, Elizabeth expressed her astonishment that the Ambassador should be so wanting in self-respect as not only to urge upon her once more to do what she had already categorically refused to do, but also to couple his demand with the threat that otherwise the King of Prussia would attack her. [1] Her resolution, she declared, was unalterable. After this Williams saw nothing for it but to quit Russia as speedily as possible.

On December 31st, the Russian Empress formally acceded to the Treaty of Versailles, whereby she joined the Franco-Austrian league against Prussia, Russia at the same time binding herself, by a *secret* article, to assist France if attacked by England in Europe, France at the same time contracting a corresponding secret obligation to give Russia pecuniary assistance in the event of her being attacked by Turkey. [2] It is, however, a significant fact that the secret articles of the partition Treaty of Versailles, as between France and Austria, were *not* communicated to the Court of St. Petersburg. [3]

It is not to be supposed that the ever alert King of Prussia was altogether ignorant of the intentions of his enemies; but, nevertheless, it is certain that at this, the crisis of his life, he was by no means so well-informed as usual. Either some of his ubiquitous and well-paid spies played him false, or, which is far more probable, his adversaries, taught by experience, were more circumspect; but the fact remains that, during the first six months of 1756, he acted upon incorrect, or, at least, incomplete, information, and was for a long time in the dark as to the true nature and magnitude of the danger he knew to be impending. He

---

[1] Solovev: *Istoria Rossy*, and *Iz bumag Elizavetinskoi Konferentzy.*

[2] Yet in the actual treaty itself Elizabeth expressly released France from the obligation of assisting her against Turkey or Persia, and Russia was not to be called upon to assist France against England in Europe.

[3] Martens: *Recueil des traités, etc.*

was well aware all along, that Austria was determined to attack him at the first opportunity, and that Saxony would go with her; but not till towards the end of June did he suspect the existence of the Franco-Austrian league, and, till the end of August, he flattered himself that British influence would prove stronger than Austrian influence at St. Petersburg, and thus keep the dreaded Moscovite in check. It is remarkable, too, that for a long time he refused to believe in the very possibility of such a reversal of historical precedent as the Franco-Austrian Alliance. Thus, on Feb. 21, he wrote to Klinggraeffen, his Ambassador at Vienna: "I cannot believe that Austria and France will form a league, their interests are too opposite, and France would never so far neglect her true interests as to aggrandize anew the House of Austria." [1]   Even as late as the middle of June he had still only surmises to go upon; but, on the 22nd of the same month, he wrote to Knyphausen, his Minister at Paris: "I begin to believe that mutual sacrifices have been stipulated, the Court of Vienna consenting to abandon the English to France, and France in the same way abandoning Prussia to Austria," and again, on the 29th, to the same diplomatist: "I am inclined to presume that there are secret articles in the treaty between France and Austria, which mean no good to me."   At the end of July, all doubts as to the attitude of France were removed by the declaration of Valory, the French Minister at Berlin, to the effect that if Prussia attacked the Queen of Hungary, "the King of France, her ally, would feel bound to succour her."   On the 31 July, Frederick wrote to his sister, Queen Ulrica of Sweden: "My situation is very critical, and I shall be forced to anticipate my enemies, in order to escape becoming their victim." [2]

[1] *Pol. Corr.* Vol. XII.
[2] *Pol. Corr.* Vol. XIII.

Frederick was also mistaken, or misinformed, as to the relative attitudes of Russia and Austria. He was, for instance, under the false impression that Austria was urging on Russia against him, but that the latter Power was not prepared and would postpone an invasion till the following Spring, whereas, as we have seen, the real state of the case was diametrically opposite to his supposition, and it was Russia who was urging on dilatory and timorous Austria. [1] In the beginning of June, Frederick learnt from the Hague that Russia had definitely renounced her obligations with England. In the beginning of July he told Mitchell, the British Minister at Berlin, that he was convinced at last that Russia was lost to them, and that the only way was to attack his foes before they had time to attack him. He had in fact resolved to begin what Bismarck has called "a preventive war," [2] and this was certainly his best policy. He took the first step in the middle of July by commanding Klinggraeffen, his Ambassador at Vienna, to demand an audience of Maria Theresa, and ask her, point-blank, whether she meant to attack him that year or not. In reply to Klinggraeffen's question, the Empress-Queen read him an answer from a little piece of paper, which she held in her hand, to the effect that, affairs in general having reached a crisis, she had judged it expedient to take measures for her own safety and the safety of her allies, which did not tend to anyone's prejudice. [3] Not content with what he rightly designated "an oracular ambiguity," Frederick (Aug. 12) instructed Klinggraeffen to instantly solicit another audience of the Empress, and demand a formal and categorical declaration that she had no intention of attacking him either that year or the next. Maria Theresa's

---

[1] Solovev: *Istoria Rossy.*

[2] *I.e.,* an aggressive war made to anticipate an attack under possible circumstances.   [3] *Pol. Corr.* Vol. XIII.

answer to this second demand also proving evasive, Kling-graeffen was directed to "return to the charge a third time," and again insist on a categorical reply, which also proving unsatisfactory, he was formally recalled from Vienna, and the diplomatic rupture between Austria and Prussia was an accomplished fact. In the course of September, Valory, the French Minister at Berlin, was recalled to Paris with almost indecent haste, and Rouillé, the French Minister of Foreign Affairs, told Knyphausen, the Prussian Minister at the French Court, in almost as many words, that his presence there in his official capacity was superfluous. Frederick, however, had already taken the decisive step. On August 26 he commanded Maltzahn, his Minister at Dresden, to wait upon the King of Poland and inform his Majesty that the King of Prussia, to his great regret, found himself under the painful necessity of entering Saxony with his army, in order to reach Bohemia by the shortest route. What followed is a matter of history. On Aug. 31st Frederick invaded Saxony with 60,000 men; seized Dresden; drove back into Bohemia (Battle of Lowositz, Oct. 1st) the Austrian army under Browne which had hastened to the assistance of the Saxons; captured the whole of the feeble Saxon army of 18,000 in its intrenched camp at Pirna, forcibly incorporating the rank and file with his own host; and in a few weeks had occupied the whole Electorate which he treated as a conquered province, and ravaged and blackmailed unmercifully, attempting to justify his conduct in the eyes of Europe by publishing and circulating a sufficient number of the diplomatic documents in the Archives of Dresden, to prove conclusively that Saxony had all along been in the league against him.—The Seven Years' War had begun.

CHAPTER IX.

THE CAMPAIGN OF GROSSJÄGERSDORF.

1757.

STEPHEN APRAKSIN appointed the Russian Commander-in-Chief—His character—Dilatory tactics of Apraksin—Advance of the Russian Army—
Memel and Tilsit taken—Strategy of Apraksin—Battle of Grossjägersdorf—Description of an eye-witness—Retreat of Apraksin after
the victory—Demoralization of the Russian Army—The Austrian
victories—Embarrassment of Frederick—Rossbach and Leuthen—
Fresh Convention between Russia and Austria—Russia left out of
the Franco-Austrian partition treaty—The Embassy of the Marquis
de l'Hôpital to St. Petersburg—His character—The Embassy of
Michael Bestuzhev to Paris—Russia's relations with England—Sudden
and dangerous illness of Elizabeth.

THROUGHOUT the winter of 1756—7, the Russian forces
were slowly massing on the north-western frontier. The
Commander-in-Chief, Apraksin, had been appointed in September 1756, and arrived at Riga with his staff to superintend
the mobilization of the army on November 21. It is a striking
proof of the dearth in Russia of military talent at the outbreak of the Seven Years' War, that such a man as Apraksin
should have been pitted against the foremost captain of the
age. This lack of good generals was mainly due to the
neglect, under the reign of the Empress Anne, of Peter
the Great's golden rule to form a school of native generals,
by carefully training promising young officers, under the
eye of intelligent and experienced foreigners. For this

neglect, Münnich, the military celebrity of Anne's reign, was largely responsible. A foreigner himself, he was chary of promoting natives who might supersede him. Of the other two capable captains who had contributed, in the earlier part of the century, to the martial glories of Russia, Lacy had died in 1751, and Keith, offended by the refusal of the Russian Government to give an asylum to his brother the ex-Jacobite, and piqued, besides, at not receiving the command of the auxiliary corps of 30,000 men sent to the Rhine in 1747, which was given instead to his junior, Prince Ryepnin, had, the same year, quitted the Russian for the Prussian service. Apraksin owed his appointment partly to seniority, partly to the friendship of the Empress, and partly to the fact that he had no enemy at Court. His friendship with the Grand Chancellor was intimate and of long standing, yet the Shuvalovs also regarded him favourably,[1] and he was on the best of terms with the Grand Duke and the Grand Duchess. He seems to have been an indolent, luxurious, good-natured, easy-going *bon viveur*, a slave to the grosser appetites, passionately addicted to the pleasures of the table, nervously apprehensive of offending anybody who could by any possibility retaliate, and, most damning of vices in a soldier, was strongly suspected of cowardice.[2] His previous career had been absolutely without distinction. The nephew of Fedor Apraksin, Peter the Great's Grand Admiral, he was born on July 30, 1702, entered the Regiment of the Preobrazhensky Guards while still a youth,[3] and had his first taste of campaigning under Münnich. He

[1] At Court the friendship of the Shuvalovs for Apraksin was attributed to the intimate liaison existing between his married daughter, the Princess Helena Kurakina and Peter Shuvalov. Vasilchikov: *Semeistvo Razumovskikh.*
[2] *E.g.*, he took a public whipping from Alexius Razumovsky without a word of protest.
[3] Bantuish Kamensky: *Biografy rosseskikh generalissumesov.*

was present at the siege of Ochakov, was sent home to lay the keys of Khotin at the feet of the Empress Anne, and emerged from the war with the rank of a Major-General. Subsequently he occupied the post of Ambassador in Persia. Elizabeth elevated him to the Vice Presidency of the War Department, and, on September 5, 1756, just before his departure for the front, made him a Field Marshal, an honour conferred at the same time on the ex-shepherd-boy, Razumovsky. Apraksin lingered for some weeks at St. Petersburg after his appointment to the supreme command. He was loth to leave the Capital during the illness of the Empress in view of resulting contingencies, for he was well aware that the Grand Duke Peter, the heir to the throne, detested the war with Prussia. He therefore invented all manner of excuses when urged to go, and complained again and again to the sick Empress of the bad condition of the army. [1] On one of these occasions Elizabeth was so excited by the jeremiads of her Commander-in-Chief, that, turning towards Peter Shuvalov, who had all along declared everything to be in perfect order, she passionately exclaimed: " You it was who magnified my forces before we declared war. Do you not fear God that you so deceive me? " The Empress's recovery, however, compelled Apraksin to go in his own despite. On October 28, he had a private audience of Elizabeth, at which he received his final instructions. On Nov. 10, 1756, he set out with his staff, and on Nov. 21, as already mentioned, he arrived at head-quarters at Riga. [2] The Government itself seems to have had little confidence in the capacity of its general, for it deprived him of all

---

[1] It is quite clear from Masslowski *(Der siebenjährige Krieg)* that the Army was indeed in a very unsatisfactory state, but that in itself was a most cogent reason for the Commander-in-Chief to be with his men, instead of hanging about the Court.

[2] The Empress sent after him a costly fine mantle, and a silver service weighing 18 puds. A pud = 40 lb.

initiative by subordinating him entirely to the directions of
the Conference of Ministers at St. Petersburg, even in the
most minute particulars. It was really foreign Diplomacy
and not the Russian Commander-in-Chief, that was to direct
the operations of the army. To do Apraksin justice he had
the moral courage to resent this preposterous interference
with his liberty of action, and to protest against the ignorant
commands of this far-distant and therefore ill-informed junto
of civilians. He refused categorically to undertake a winter
campaign with an army still in process of formation, and
unprovided with the most absolute necessaries, [1] and the
Conference at last reluctantly allowed his troops to go into
winter quarters along the Dnieper and in the province of
Pskov, where they remained till the beginning of February,
1757. Then the Conference again grew restive. The Grand
Chancellor in particular was much disquieted by the con-
tinuous inaction of his friend. His own position had by
this time become so critical, that his political existence
depended on a prompt and complete victory of Apraksin
over the Prussians. He was also apprehensive lest the dilatoriness of the Commander-in-Chief might be attributed to his own
secret machinations. He therefore earnestly urged Apraksin
to make a move and *do something*. But "the pacific Field
Marshal," as the wits of St. Petersburg already dubbed him,
hated being hurried. Moreover, he was aware that the Grand
Duke and the Grand Duchess disliked the war; he was very
anxious to do nothing against the wishes of the heir to
the throne and he seems to have persuaded himself that
the whole campaign was only meant to be a military
demonstration. He was furious therefore at the Chancellor's
importunity, and even sent one of his adjutants to town
to find out what it all meant. Only with the utmost diffi-

[1] Masslowski I. 128.

culty did Bestuzhev succeed in calming him, and, which was more to the point, sent him a note from the Grand Duchess herself, also urging him to be more expeditious. At a later day, as we shall see, Catherine had good reason to repent parting with this missive. So, at length, Apraksin did move, but it was not till May 17th that the main army, some 85,500 strong, [1] crossed the Lithuanian border. Apraksin's objective was Königsberg, the Capital of East Prussia, and all his operations were to be directed to the capture of that important place, which would make the whole of East Prussia easily tenable by the Russians. Königsberg once captured, circumstances were to guide him as to his subsequent movements against Brandenburg or the Kingdom of Prussia generally. Simultaneously with the advance of the main army, a strong siege-corps under General Fermor, was to operate against Memel from Libau, so as to divide, if possible, the forces of the enemy. This subsidiary force was to unite with the main army after the capture of Memel (and of Tilsit also, if possible), cross the Niemen, and proceed by the best practicable route towards Königsberg. On June 4, the main army reached Kovno, which Apraksin intended to make his chief *dépôt*, and there he remained till the 16th. The heat was intense, the roads were villainous, and the food supplied to the soldiers proved inadequate and inferior, no fewer than 11,000 were found to be on the sick-list before the campaign had well begun. On the 19th the army reached the Niemen, and on the 20th the Marshal crossed that river. Meanwhile Fermor had entered Prussian territory near Libau and captured Memel (June 24th), the Prussian general, Lehwaldt, retiring before him to Wehlau. So far the strategy of the Russians, if not brilliant, seems at least to have been correct. Apraksin

---

[1] Masslowski I. 151.

had been urged by the last rescript of the Conference, above all things not to let Lehwaldt escape and unite with the King of Prussia, [1] but this he found it impossible to attempt to do till he should have been rejoined by Fermor, who, in the meantime (Aug. 1) had captured Tilsit, and also crossed the Niemen. On the 24th and again on the 29th July, Bestuzhev thought it necessary to address urgent remonstrances to Apraksin, informing him that the Empress was seriously displeased at his long delay in Poland, and that the wags of the Capital were joking freely at his expense, and offering rewards to whomsoever should discover the whereabouts of the missing Russian Army. [2] Apraksin in reply attributed the slowness of his advance to the extreme heat and the difficulty of finding forage; but at last, Aug. 1st, the whole of the main army crossed the Prussian border at Stallupönen, and immediately began skirmishing with the enemy in a number of indecisive engagements, the Prussian light horse, however, steadily retreating before the Cossacks who did excellent service. On August 18th, Fermor, after a difficult march from Tilsit, rejoined the main army, and on August 23rd, it was resolved, at a Council of War, to cross the Pregel and march upon Königsberg via Allenburg. This route was three miles longer than the orginally intended route via Wehlau; but, on the other hand, the region on the other side of the Pregel was more richly provided with forage—an important consideration in those days. [3] The advance of the Russian army from Saalau, via Allenburg, comes within the category of difficult and dangerous manœuvres, for it practically amounted to an attempt to turn the enemy's army. Apraksin had, first of all, to fall

---

[1] Masslowski I. 179—80.
[2] Solovev: *Istoria Rossy*, 1757.
[3] Masslowski I. 201.

back on the Pregel, cross that river at Simohnen, and then, by means of a flank march, get to Allenburg, with the enemy in touch the whole time. [1] In executing this movement, he was obliged, for a time, to abandon his communications with Kovno, his principal *dépôt*, and, in case of disaster, he would have been limited to a single line of retreat *via* Grodno.   On Aug. 27, the Russian army successfully crossed the river, and only on the following day does the Prussian General, Lehwaldt, seem to have become aware of the fact that he had been outflanked.   Fully recognising the gravity of the situation, he resolved to quit, at once, his entrenched position on the right bank of the Pregel, and attack the Russians on the left bank. On the evening of August 28th the Prussian army, after crossing the Pregel, encamped on both sides of the village of Puschdorf, behind the forest of Norkitten, Lehwaldt having successfully masked his real movements by a sham attack upon Saalau.   Lehwaldt's position was now only seven or eight versts distant from Apraksin's, and he occupied all the exits from the forest leading into the plain of Grossjägersdorf. His offensive tactics took the Russians completely by surprise.   All Apraksin's efforts had been directed to drawing Lehwaldt out of his entrenched position on the right bank of the Pregel, nobody had anticipated for a moment that the Prussians would abandon their strongly entrenched camp of their own accord.   Moreover, the thick, almost impenetrable forest between Puschdorf and Norkitten, all the exits from which were occupied by the Prussian pickets, made it impossible for the Russians on the left bank of the Pregel to estimate the real strength of the enemy.   From the 28th to the 29th Angust, the Russian army was encamped in the neighbourhood of Grossjägersdorf, on a

[1] Ib. I. 205.

high level plain, [1] not far from the banks of the Pregel,
here a broad river flowing though a deep gully. This
plain was bounded on two sides by a large dense forest,
a verst or more in width, and traversed on the third
side by a very long and very deep ravine, with a small
stream flowing through it and falling into the Pregel. Consequently this plateau was girt about by almost impenetrable obstacles, with only two exits, one through a clearing
in the forest, and the other through an open space, about
half a verst wide, between the forest and the above-named
ravine. All the circumstances combined to make the position the strongest imaginable in case of an attack, provided
the Russian Generals were skilful enough to make the most
of these natural advantages. On the morning of August
28th everything was quiet in camp and there was no sign
of the enemy; at 4 o'clock the same afternoon, a false
alarm was given and a large part of the army was led
out from behind the forest into the plain of Grossjägersdorf.
There, however, nothing was to be seen of the enemy, and,
after burning a village and waiting under arms for three
hours, the troops returned to their original positions.
Everything was then quiet till 12 o'clock on the following
day (29th Aug.) when three signal guns were fired, and
again the army was marshalled in battle array. But still
the enemy did not show himself, so, after waiting under
arms till the day was beginning to decline, the soldiers
retired once more to their tents. The hostile armies were
so near that during the night the Russians could hear the
drums beating the tattoo in the hostile camp beyond the
forest of Norkitten, behind which the enemy was encamped.
Late the same evening the whole army was ordered to
move forward in the direction of the enemy, with provisions

---

[1] Bolotov: *Zapiski*, Vol. I; Masslowski I. 212—259.—Bolotov, be it remembered, was an eye-witness of the battle.

for three days, and to remain under arms all night, and at break of day (Aug. 30) the advance-guard and the second division, with the baggage in the rear, began to march alongside a crescent-shaped wood, behind which the bulk of the army was still massed, in order to turn the enemy's position. Before, however, all the proper dispositions could be taken, the Prussians anticipated an attack by themselves attacking, "hoping to throttle us like a hen in her nest," to use Bolotov's homely simile. In the very midst of the confusion of starting off, the cry was heard: "The enemy is upon us!" About eight o'clock in the morning, the cavalry of the Prince of Holstein drove in the reconnoitring Cossacks and Hussar detachments, and attacked the 2nd Moscow Regiment, which gallantly repelled the assailants. The suddenness of the attack produced the utmost confusion and dismay in the Russian camp. The air was full of clamour and tumult. The Generals could not believe that the enemy was already upon them. "Our commanders," says Bolotov, "ran about wildly, forgetting everything and not knowing what to do." The greater part of the Russian regiments was behind either the forest or its own baggage, and could not, for the time, reach the field of battle. Fortunately, the rapidly forming regiments accidently hit upon the safest and most advantageous positions, eminences commanding the whole field. The regiments of the Lopukhin division, without awaiting orders from head-quarters, forced their way at last through the baggage, and took up a position left and right of the 2nd Moscow Regiment, but as the Division of Fermor did not move simultaneously, this hasty and hazardous deployment created a gap between the regiments of the 2nd Division and the regiments of Fermor, which did not escape the attention of Lehwaldt, who at once hurled twelve of his battalions, under Dohna, into the gap, with the intention of breaking through the Russian centre. Favoured by a depression of the ground, Dohna's battalions advanced unseen, and attacked the Russians so suddenly that anything like a regular formation on their part was impossible. " What dispositions we took, and what directions we followed," remarks Bolotov, "came from God alone."—Moreover, the Russian regiments were inadequately supported by the artillery, and the ammunition for the newly invented Shuvalov howitzers, on which they chiefly relied, was behind the forest, and therefore unprocurable. Yet despite there disadvantages, and the absence of reserves (the bulk of the army still standing idle behind the forest), the hitherto untried Russian regiments, for two whole hours, resisted the onset like a stone wall till their powder quite gave out, and they were compelled to fall back upon the forest, with the loss of half their officers, including General Zuibin, General Vasily Abramovich Lopukhin, (who, mortally wounded, fell into the enemy's hands, and was torn, still breathing, from his captors by a spirited rush of his devoted grenadiers) and fifty per cent of the rank and file. The fate of the Russian army now hung upon a hair. The Prussians had already penetrated to the baggage, and the cry of " Fly! fly!" was becoming general, when defeat was suddenly converted into victory by four regiments of the reserves, hitherto standing behind the forest, who, enraged at doing nothing while their comrades were being massacred, and, apparently, without waiting for orders, [1] " forced their way somehow through the forest, to the relief of their co-religionists." [2] The forest was so dense that an individual could scarce have forced his way through it at all, but, directed by the

---

[1] "They resolved to go or *possibly* were sent," observes Bolotov. Even Masslowski, Apraksin's apologist, is forced to admit that they "gingen man weiss nicht auf wessen Veranlassung."

[2] Bolotov: *Zapiski.*

groans of their suffering and dying comrades, and throwing away their muskets and cartridge boxes, in order to get along better, the reserve regiments fortunately emerged at the very place where they were most wanted, and fell upon the flanks of the Prussian grenadiers who, after a quarter of an hour's hard fighting, were, in their turn, forced back. While this was proceeding in the centre, Fortune was also favouring the Russians on the right wing where the 1st Russian Grenadier Regiment, effectually supported by the Shuvalov howitzers, repulsed the attacks of the Prussian Dragoons. Meanwhile on the left wing, the Cossacks, skilfully led by Serebryakov, had enticed the Cavalry of the Prince of Holstein into the jaws of fifteen of the best Russian battalions well provided with artillery. The Prussian squadrons, eagerly pursuing the light Cossack horsemen, "flowed onwards like a rapid stream, and dashed full upon our front," close upon the heels of the flying Cossacks, the Russian infantry opening their ranks to enable their own cavalry to pass through to the rear and rally. Those of the Prussians who succeeded in breaking through the Russian front began massacring everybody in their way till the batteries in reserve were brought to bear upon their cramped squadrons, when, caught like mice in a trap, they were mown down to the last man. This characteristic engagement on the left wing, was the final act of the Battle of Grossjägersdorf The Prussians had been repulsed on all points, and retreated behind the protecting forest from which they had first debouched. Their total loss is estimated by Masslowski at 4,163,[1] the same authority puts down the Russian loss at 5,989.

---

[1] They also lost 29 guns, eleven of which were of heavy calibre. The effective strength of the Russian army before the battle was 55,000, of the Prussians 24,000. Eleven of the thirty-one Russian Generals present were placed *hors de combat*.

Grossjägersdorf is one of the most casual victories on record. It was won by the sheer courage of raw troops suddenly attacked by an enemy they were marching to outflank. The inexperienced divisional-commanders, suddenly confronted by a critical emergency, instantly rose to the occasion, and did their duty like men, but of anything like orders or directions from head-quarters there is no trace. It was a headless host which beat back the veteran legions of the King of Prussia. Lehwaldt, according to Solòvev, attributed his defeat to a sudden flank attack in overwhelming force by Rumyantsev. According to Bolotov, the Prussian commanders subsequently represented the Russian position as impregnably entrenched and bristling with artillery, whereas he emphatically affirms that not a spadeful of earth was ever thrown up by the Russians. He may not have been a military expert, but he was on the spot and used his eyes. The whereabouts of the Commander-in-Chief during the struggle still remains an insoluble enigma. [1] He was not, apparently, skulking behind the baggage, as his enemies presumed and proclaimed; but it is pretty plain from his confused and confusing bulletin describing the battle, that he must have contemplated the engagement from some securely remote standpoint among the reserves. He had certainly less to do with the victory than the simplest Cossack. "The battle was won," remarks Bolotov, "not by the skill of our general, but by the valour of our soldiers and the grace of God." Still, however won, a victory it was, and a victory which relieved the Russian Government of a heavy anxiety. It was at 7 o'clock on the morning of September 8th that the inhabitants of St. Petersburg were aroused from their slumbers by one hundred and one salvos

---

[1] Even Masslowski observes: "Es ist sogar schwer zu bestimmen wo er (the Commander-in-Chief) sich während der Schlacht eigentlich befand."

from the guns of the citadel, announcing the triumph of the Russian arms. At eight o'clock the evening before, a special courier, Major General P. Panin, escorted by trumpeters, had brought the news of the victory to the Empress at Tsarkoe Selo. But the joy of the Court was so quickly changed to indignation, when a fortnight elapsed and there was still no news of the prosecution of hostile operations. At last came the mortifying intelligence that, in consequence of want of forage and the rapid progress of the enemy, Apraksin had found it necessary to fall back upon Tilsit, to provide his troops with food and forage. What had actually taken place was this. For two days after the battle, the army remained at Grossjägersdorf to bake bread, celebrate the victory, and obtain intelligence of the whereabouts of the enemy. Lehwaldt had at first fallen back on Wilkindorf, leaving the road to Königsberg completely open, [1] but, instead of taking advantage of the opportunity thus offered to him, Apraksin, after engaging in a series of complicated and inconclusive manœuvres, held, September 7, a Council of War, at which it was decided to retire upon Tilsit, in order, as "the pacific Field Marshal" informed the Empress, "not to expose to disaster troops already exhausted by severe marches in a hungry [2] land." On September 8 began this demoralizing retreat of a victorious army pursued rather than followed by an enemy of only half its numerical strength. The wretched roads, the drenching rain, the lack of proper food for the men and of forage for the horses – all these things seriously diminished the mobility, and gradually

---

[1] A day later he rectified his mistake by occupying a position behind the Alle at Wehlaw.

[2] *I.e.*, wasted ... Apraksin's despatches, by the way, are full of timid counsels and whining excuses. His main object seems to have been to preserve the army "intact," as if an army were meant for show and not for fighting.

ruined the fighting capacity of the host.   The contempt of
the soldiers for a commander who lay for the greater part
of the day in his sumptuous waggon bedstead, listening to
the gossip of his doctor and a couple of old Grenadiers,
was unbounded, and expressed itself in the most scathing
terms.   "Shame and anger was on every face, and curses
upon our commanders came from every mouth," says Bolotov.   By the time the army had reached Tilsit, more than
a seventh part of the rank and file (8,996) was on the
sick-list, and the remainder so demoralized that another
Council of War (24 Sept.) decided unanimously that Tilsit
was untenable, and that the only way to save the *débris*
of the host from utter destruction was to avoid a combat,
and fall back still further upon Memel.   While still on the
march to the latter place, with his temporary head-quarters
at Lapienen, Apraksin received a Ukaz commanding him
at once to retrace his steps, and resume the offensive.   A
Council of War held on October 9, replied, unanimously
and categorically, that "it was of no use trying to make
possible the impossible," the Commander-in-Chief adding
that it was useless to attempt to fight against nature, and
that to order the army to winter in those regions was
tantamount to devoting it to destruction. [1]   Yet even these
arguments did not seem convincing to the Conference of
Ministers, and immediately after the reception of the decision of the Council of War at Lapienen, another Ukaz, signed
by Elizabeth herself, and commanding Apraksin to occupy
East Prussia and again attack Lehwaldt, reached him (16 Oct.)
just as he was approaching Memel.   It is plain that under
the difficult circumstances, and with a thoroughly exhausted
and demoralized army, it had by this time become a physical impossibility to execute such exorbitant demands, and

---

[1] Masslowski I. 264; Solovev: *Istoria Rossy.*

such, in substance, was the tenour of the declaration which another Council of War instantly sent back to St. Petersburg. All the signatories of this declaration solemnly assured the Empress that they had convinced themselves by actual experience of the impossibility of resuming hostilities, and would joyfully answer for their opinions with their heads. Twelve days later another Ukaz was issued, removing Apraksin from the command of the army, and submitting his conduct of the campaign to the judgment of a Court Martial.

Absurdly peremptory as were the commands of the Conference of Ministers to the equally unfortunate and incapable Apraksin, they are very excusable and intelligible when we reflect that another Russian victory following hard upon the victory of Grossjägersdorf, would, in all probability, have brought the King of Prussia to his knees, and terminated the war in a single campaign. A month after the battle Frederick himself wrote to his sister, the Margravine of Bayreuth: "If this lasts through the winter, I am lost," and much about the same time the Russian Vice-Chancellor wrote to Bekhtyeev at Paris that, if Russia continued successful, he hoped to see peace in the course of the winter. In point of fact the position of the King of Prussia in the autumn of 1757 already seemed desperate, and this, too, in spite of his brilliant successes in the early spring. It had been Frederick's intention to invade Bohemia, in the hope of overthrowing Austria so quickly, and so completely, that her confederates would be deterred from taking up her quarrel, and the beginning of the campaign appeared to justify his anticipations. After a murderous conflict, he succeeded in defeating the Austrians under Prince Charles of Lorraine before Prague (May 6) and shutting up the vanquished army in the city; but there his triumph ended, for Marshal Daun, advancing with a fresh army, relieved Prague and drove back the Duke of Bayern, who had been sent against him. Frederick thereupon hastened to the scene himself, and attacked Daun at Kolin (June 18), but was routed with the loss of 14,000 men and 43 guns. The consequences of this overthrow were disastrous indeed to the King of Prussia. Not only was he now forced to evacuate Bohemia forthwith, but he had, at the same time, to make head against all his other enemies. who, encouraged by the success of the Austrians, now fell upon him simultaneously. A French army, under D'Estrées, occupied all the Prussian territory westward of the Weser; defeated the Duke of Cumberland at Hastenbeck (26 July); conquered Hanover and Hesse; and compelled the whole Anglo-Hanoverian army to capitulate at Kloster-Zeven. The Austrians, meanwhile, had pressed forward into Upper Silesia and Lusatia, and their most brilliant cavalry-officer, Francis Nadasdy, at the head of his Magyars and Croats, had defeated the Prussian General, Winterfeld, at Moys (7 Sept.), a victory which left both Breslau and Berlin exposed. The Prussian armies were decimated, exhausted and discouraged; the Generals had lost all hope of fresh successes, and even Frederick's own relations already gave up his cause for lost. And now, at the most critical moment, when only one more vigorous blow seemed wanted to bring the common enemy down, "the pacific Field Marshal" had suddenly abandoned all his conquests, and retired precipitately before an enemy whom he had badly beaten! The immediate result of this retreat was to release the army of Lehwaldt, and enable Frederick to clear Pomerania of the invading Swedes. [1] Then, relieved for the moment from the pressure of the Muscovite Colossus on the East, he turned swiftly to the West

---

[1] Sweden had joined the anti-Prussian league in Sept. 1757.

against the French, who, in the meantime had advanced as far as Weissenfels, and, as all the world knows, well-nigh annihilated them at Rossbach (5 Nov.), immediately afterwards marching southwards towards Silesia, almost the whole of which had been occupied by the Austrians, whose threefold larger army he pounced upon at Leuthen (5 Dec.), utterly .defeating it, and regaining possession of the whole province, except the fortress of Schweidnitz. Nevertheless, the net result of these astonishing victories was to leave the belligerents pretty much as they had been at the beginning of the year and cement still more closely the heterogeneous coalition against the common foe, who had so very nearly succumbed at the very outset of the struggle. It seemed impossible that this royal stag could, in the long run, escape destruction at the hands of the encircling band of Kings and Princes who were bent on hunting him down.

For meanwhile the march of political events had been more rapid and more effectual than the marching and counter-marching of Marshal Apraksin. At the very beginning of the year (22 Jan.) a fresh convention had been concluded at St. Petersburg between Russia and Austria, confirmatory of the old alliance of 1746. This new convention was a direct consequence of the sudden invasion of Saxony by the King of Prussia, and contained an additional obligation binding the high contracting parties not to lay down their arms till Silesia and the county of Glatz had been recovered from the King of Prussia. Each of the contracting parties agreed to employ at least 80,000 men against Frederick. Assuming that the repose of Europe could not be solidly established, so long as the King of Prussia possessed the means of troubling it, their Imperial Majesties engaged to direct all their efforts "to render this

service to humanity"[1] by acting in concert with any other
Powers they might consider to be in the same dispositions
as themselves.   Sweden also was to be invited to join the
league, and was to be promised advantages proportionate
to the part she might take in the abasement of the King
of Prussia.   Saxony was to receive an adequate indemnification for the wrongs she had suffered from the same potentate
—of course at his expense.   Finally, Austria undertook to
pay 1,000,000 rubles a year, in subsidies, to Russia so long
as the war lasted.

Apparently, however, the Court of Vienna considered
that the alliance with France was more precious and profitable than the alliance with Russia, inasmuch as it took
particular care *not* to inform the Court of St. Petersburg, as
already mentioned, of the secret negotiations simultaneously
proceeding with the Court of Versailles.   The famous
Treaty of Versailles, between France and Austria, providing
for the partition of the dominions of the King of Prussia,
and concluded the same day as the definite treaty of alliance between these two Powers (to which latter treaty, it
will be remembered, Russia acceded on the 31st Dec. 1756)
was not officially communicated to Russia at all.   As to
any indemnity for Russia's assistance (and her assistance,
be it remembered, was of capital importance), nothing definite had yet been settled.   In this respect, indeed, all
that Russia had to go upon was the personal assurance of
Maria Theresa that she was ready to take all necessary
measures to satisfy the just claims of Russia, and indemnify
her for all the sacrifices she had made, or might make, in
the common cause.[2]   Such an assurance was ambiguous
at best, but it seems to have been insincere as well as
ambiguous, for it is certain that both France and Austria

---

[1] Article 6, in Martens' *Recueil des Traités*.
[2] Martens' *Recueil des Traités etc.;* Solovev: *Istoria Rossy.*

strongly objected to any territorial aggrandizement of Russia. By the Treaty of May 1, 1757, between these two Powers, the claims of all the other partners in the anti-Prussian confederacy to territory to be wrested from Frederick II were admitted and settled beforehand, but Russia, the chief factor of the whole combination, was left entirely in the cold, Russia, the French Ministers sophistically argued, was merely an auxiliary Power, and therefore had no right to conquests.[1] Bekhtyeev, the Russian Minister at Paris, was quite aware of this unsatisfactory state of things, and he advised his Government to make a formal convention beforehand with France, Austria and Sweden, for securing possession of Courland in exchange for East Prussia. Vorontsov, however, prudently advised the Empress to wait till the Prussian Duchy was actually in her hands, and there, for the present, the matter was allowed to rest.

But the great diplomatic event of the year was the ostentatious resumption of the long interrupted friendly relations between Russia and France. Appointed to the post of French Plenipotentiary at the Russian Court, in September,[2] 1756, it was not till June 1757 that the Marquis de l'Hôpital, at the head of a magnificent suite, finally reached St. Petersburg. Paul Gallucio de l'Hôpital, Marquis de Châteauneuf, was a nobleman of commanding presence and courtly manners, who had served his king with honour, if not distinction, both in the Cabinet and in the field. But, though but fifty years of age, he was already a confirmed invalid, racked with gout and rheumatism, and therefore, one might fancy, more enamoured of repose than of promotion. Yet he himself is said to have eagerly offered[3] to quit his comfortable sinecure as French

[1] Bekhtyeev: *Pisma.*   [2] Not June, as Vondel represents.

[3] Bekhtyeev: *Pisma.*—The shrewd Bekhtyeev describes him as wealthy and affable, but not very knowing.

Minister at Naples in order to represent his country at what was essentially a fighting post at a strange and distant Court full of political pitfalls. Nor did he possess the ability requisite to cope with the difficulties of a situation which would have tried to the uttermost the capacity of a Stainville or a Vergennes. He was indeed alert and adroit and possessed all the courage of an old soldier and all the grace of a finished courtier; but his judgment was defective, his appreciation of men and things was too prompt to be profound, and, with the best will in the world, he misled his Court repeatedly by representing facts not as they actually were, but as he thought they ought to be. [1] Nevertheless, his charming manners, his ready wit, and his truly patrician liberality made this *"fort galant homme"* a *persona gratissima* at the Russian Court, the moment he appeared. L'Hôpital was lodged in the beautiful and spacious mansion but recently vacated by the rival diplomat, Sir Hanbury Williams. It stood by the side of a little canal, which, from the moment when L'Hôpital took possession of the house, was yclept by the wags of St. Petersburg, "Le Pas de Calais." Elizabeth, in particular, was enchanted by the magnificence and the *éclat* of the new embassade, which was very numerous and splendid, and included in its ranks half-a-dozen young men of the first nobility. The Empress and the Ambassador met for the first time at a Court ball given shortly after his arrival, and each of them was very favourably impressed by the

---

[1] Speaking from a pretty large experience, I can safely say that I know of few despatches so inaccurate as those of the Marquis de l'Hôpital. Very often he does not seem to have even used his eyes. Thus *e.g.*, he represents the Grand Duchess as at the head of a formidable faction at Court, actively opposing the wishes of the Empress, whereas, as a matter of fact, throughout the reign of Elizabeth, Catherine occupied an altogether subaltern position, and never possessed the slightest political influence. Again he represents Elizabeth as "swearing a mortal hatred" against Catherine, a pure fiction, "yet unable to resist her usurpations etc., etc. "

other. "Her Majesty," writes L'Hôpital, "wore a costume at once costly and imposing. Her powder, her large hoop-petticoats, her diadem of precious stones, and the splendour of her dress, enhanced the nobility of her carriage and the natural charm of her features. With a smile on her lips, she goes from group to group, addressing herself to the women especially, with that air of affable benevolence which is the very basis of her character." When L'Hôpital advanced towards her to kiss her hand, she conversed familiarly with him in French; expressed her satisfaction at seeing at her Court an Ambassador of the Most Christian King, and, with great sympathy, desired to know all the details of the recent attempt on the life of Louis XV, by the fanatic Damiens. L'Hôpital had been particularly charged to insinuate himself into the good graces of the Vice-Chancellor, and this he effectually succeeded in doing. In the name of his Monarch, he presented Vorontsov, who was somewhat of an antiquarian, with a beautiful and costly set of gold medals, illustrating all the chief events of the history of France, specially chosen from among the royal collections, and proposed that young Vorontsov should be sent to Versailles, to complete his education at "*l'École des Chevaux Légers*," the seminary of the noble families of France. "The King my master," said he, "told Cardinal Bernis what pleasure it would give him to see the nephew of your Excellency educated there." Altogether the Marquis de L'Hôpital was a success at St. Petersburg, and his frequent and splendid entertainments (for he kept open table nearly every day) added greatly to the pleasures of the Russian Court. [1]

[1] Besides his openly accredited Ambassador at St. Petersburg, Louis XV employed the Chevalier D'Eon as a sort of private agent, through whom he intended to communicate directly with the Empress, Vorontsov acting as the intermediary between them. That D'Eon was directly instructed by Louis XV

The Ambassador whom Russia sent to Versailles, at the same time that the Marquis de L'Hôpital was sent to St. Petersburg, was a diplomatist of equal distinction and still greater decrepitude. It was the Grand Chancellor's brother, [1] Michael Bestuzhev, who was selected to occupy this all important post. In the middle of June, 1757, this rolling-stone of diplomacy (for the last thirty years he had been revolving from Court to Court) arrived at Paris with his wife. Both of them were in a miserable state of health. "The wife of Bestuzhev," wrote Bekhtyeev to Vorontsov, [2] "is a piteous sight to see. She is a living skeleton, scarce able to breathe, and speaking only in a whisper. Her Saxon estates have been so ravaged by the Prussians that they do not bring her in enough to eat. It is a marvel to me how she got here alive." According to the same authority, her husband was very little better. He was suffering so severely from eczema, that he could not bear even a dressing-gown on him, and gout so crippled his hands that he could not put pen to paper. For the first three weeks after his arrival, he was confined to his bed, and fit for nothing. Even when sufficiently recovered to go to

there can be no doubt. Bekhtyeev's *Pisma* are decisive on that point. His mission was kept so secret, that neither L'Hôpital at St. Petersburg nor the French Cabinet were aware of its existence, and Vorontsov was expressly cautioned by Louis XV not to let L'Hôpital—his own Ambassador at St. Petersburg—know anything about it! D'Eon too, though no coward, affected to be afraid of L'Hôpital. As, however, this very mysterious mission appears (so far as it aimed at anything definitive at all, for, it seems to me, to have been mainly due to Louis XV's inveterate love of intrigue and mystification) to have been directed to the attainment of quite secondary objects, *e.g.*, the election of the Prince of Conti to the Ducal throne of Courland. I need say little more in these pages of the ambiguous chevalier who has already obtained far more attention than he really deserves.

[1] How pleasant this must have been to the Chancellor, may readily be imagined. Yet the two brothers still kept up a semblance of amity, and even dined together, "but," says Williams, "their faces were enough to turn the milk upon the table sour."

[2] Bekhtyeev. *Pisma;* M. P. Bestuzhev: *Pisma.*

Versailles, the poor old man complains pathetically of all the stairs he has to climb, and all the corridors he has to traverse, in order to pay his respects to the innumerable members of the royal family. "Running up staircase after staircase is no doubt excellent practice for young legs," he wrote to his friend, Vorontsov, "but it is a little too much for me at my age." He also complains that Paris is twice as dear as Vienna, and that his allowance is altogether inadequate to meet his expenses. Nevertheless, despite his bodily infirmities, Michael Bestuzhev was certainly the best representative whom Russia could, at this crisis, have despatched to France. Perhaps no other contemporary diplomatist had such a grasp of the political situation, or understood the *minutiæ* and the intricacies of continental diplomacy so intimately as he, and his dignified bearing and resolute manner soon won for him a respect and a confidence denied to all the other Ambassadors at Paris. [1] Very shortly after his arrival, he succeeded in amicably adjusting the serious differences which had arisen in Poland between the Russian and French Ministers, by convincing Cardinal Bernis that the French representatives at Warsaw were exceeding their instructions, and acting injuriously to the common cause. At his public audiences, moreover, he spoke more authoritatively than any of his diplomatic colleagues, "and with such assurance," adds Bekhtyeev, "that it is impossible not to rejoice at the good impression produced thereby upon the French Ministers."

The preference of Russia for France was, naturally enough, regarded by the English Government as an act of the blackest perfidy; indeed the relations between Russia and Great Britain, during the year 1757, were strained almost to breaking-point. In May, Prince Golitsuin wrote

[1] Bekhtyeev: *Pisma.*

from London that the victories of the King of Prussia had made the English people prouder than ever, and glad that they had exchanged their old ally for their new. He himself was instructed to complain to the British Cabinet of the conduct of Williams at St. Petersburg, and demand his withdrawal, which Lord Holdernesse assured him should take place at once. In June, Golitsuin was informed by Holdernesse that George II was deeply offended at the threats against the King of Prussia contained in the Russian Empress's recent Manifesto to the Powers, and he himself threatened that England and Prussia would unite to prevent the passage of any foreign regiments through Germany, [1] whereby the Russian troops were plainly meant; but Golitsuin, at the same time, reassured his Government by informing them that such a combination was impossible inasmuch as Great Britain had no army and would think twice before sending a fleet to the Baltic. The Russian Foreign Office, however, (11 July) in a rescript in reply to the English declaration, expressed its surprise and displeasure at such a strange mingling of angry threats and pacific assurances. The present policy of the English Government, it continued, was directly contrary to its previous compact with Russia. England had done nothing to stop the King of Prussia, who had been the first to begin hostilities, and it was inconceivable why Great Britain should now try to prevent the other Powers from coming to the assistance of weak and oppressed Saxony. "If," concluded the Empress, "England attempts in any way soever to take measures against our army or our fleet, we shall regard such an attempt as a rupture of all existing treaties between us, and shall adopt such other measures as may correspond with our honour and dignity."

---

[1] Despatches of Golitsuin, cited by Solovev.

But now, at the very moment of its triumphant conclusion, a sinister event suddenly threatened the Franco-Russian understanding with destruction. On the Feast of the Nativity of the Blessed Virgin (Sept. 19) the Empress went on foot from the Château of Tsarkoe Selo to the Parish Church, which was only a few yards distant, to hear mass. The service had scarce begun, when, feeling indisposed and not wishing to disturb the congregation, Elizabeth quietly left the Church, and was descending the small slope, which is the nearest way to the Château, when she was seized with a fit, and fell down unconscious on the grass, in the midst of a small crowd which had been curiously watching her movements. None of her Majesty's suite had accompanied her from the Château to the Church, but they had followed her immediately afterwards, and were shocked to find her lying senseless on the ground in the midst of a crowd, sympathetic indeed, but too frightened to render assistance. They at once covered her face with a white handkerchief and sent for doctors and a litter, for Elizabeth was a very big heavy woman, and had hurt herself in falling. She was conveyed back to the Château as soon as possible, and remedies were applied, which, after an anxious suspense of nearly two hours, succeeded in reviving her. But she recognized nobody, and her speech was almost unintelligible. There was great consternation at Court, and the publicity of the affair made it doubly embarrassing, as the catastrophe could not be officially contradicted. For some days the Empress lay in a state of lethargy, without regaining the free use of her tongue, and although the natural vigour of her constitution ultimately asserted itself, and she partially recovered, the shock [1] had an important influence

[1] Count A. R. Vorontsov, a contemporary, attributes in his "*Notice sur ma Vie*," the seizure to "maux hystériques occasionnés par sa trop de sensi-

upon the rest of her life.   Her health was never the same afterwards; for fear of similar accidents occurring to her in public, she appeared less seldom at Court than heretofore; aged considerably, and began, for the first time in her life, to be apprehensive of purely imaginary dangers.   From this time, too, must be dated that fear of death which constantly haunted her during the last few years of her reign.

And the illness of the Empress, quite apart from the other political changes presently to be mentioned, of which it was the immediate cause, expedited, if it did not actually occasion, a domestic event of the first importance—the fall of the Grand Chancellor.

bilité."   It is true that the loss of life at the Battle of Grossjägersdorf had deeply affected her, but imprudent diet, against the advice of her doctors, was also a predisposing cause.

CHAPTER X.

THE FALL OF BESTUZHEV, AND THE CAMPAIGN OF ZORNDORF.

1758.

INSECURITY of Bestuzhev—Examination of Apraksin—Arrest of Bestuzhev—
Anxiety of Catherine—The trial of Bestuzhev—Catherine's pathetic
letter to the Empress—Her midnight interview with Elizabeth—The
Empress finally mollified—The new Commander-in-Chief, General
Fermor—The winter campaign of 1757-8—Disorganization of the
Russian army—"Letter from a traveller from Riga"—Campaign of
1758—Advance of Fermor into Prussian territory—Bombardment of
Cüstrin—Battle of Zorndorf—Subsequent operations—Elizabeth's dis-
satisfaction with Fermor—Differences with the Court of Vienna—
Firmness of Elizabeth—Opinion in France—And in England.

DURING the last two years, the political *existence* of Alexius
Bestuzhev may be said to have hung upon a hair, which
not one of his innumerable enemies had the courage to
sever; his political *influence* had long since departed. The
negotiations with France had been carried on behind his
back, and without his knowledge, and finally he had been
obliged, as Chancellor, to subscribe the definite treaty
between his own Court and the Court of Versailles, and
thus set his seal to an alliance which he had always vehemently opposed and still detested. Further than this humiliation could scarcely go, and we may well wonder why this
haughty and masterful old statesman did not resign his office
rather than give his official sanction to what he regarded
as an abomination. But by this time the inordinate love

THE GRAND DUCHESS CATHERINE.

of power, the pleasurable sensation of being the first subject in the land, had deadened within him all the finer
feelings of self-respect, and he clung desperately to the
shadow of authority long after its substance had departed.
That he, the notorious and inveterate enemy of France,
should still remain, even nominally, the highest official in
the realm, was of course not only a crying anomaly, but
might even become, in view of possible contingencies, a
positive peril to the Franco-Austro-Russian Alliance, so
that we cannot be much surprised if L'Hôpital and Esterhazy,
the Ambassadors of France and Austria at the Court of
St. Petersburg, used their utmost efforts to remove from
their path this diplomatic obstruction. Moreover, the Austrian
Chancellor, Count Kaunitz, already a power in Europe,
who looked for incalculable benefits from the new triple
alliance, which was his own political masterpiece, vowed
he would never forgive the Russian Chancellor for opposing
the combination, and henceforward that bitter hater threw
the whole of his immense influence into the scales against
his already tottering Russian colleague. And now we come
to one of the most obscure and enigmatical episodes in
Russian history. The retreat of Apraksin, which, naturally,
infuriated the French and Russian Courts, and the almost
simultaneous illness of the Tsaritsa, plunge us incontinently
into a dark, trackless labyrinth of intrigue, in which we
have little more than bare conjecture to guide us. Bestuzhev's enemies at once connected these two events, and
argued that the Chancellor had secretly instructed his friend,
"the pacific Field Marshal," to hold his army in readiness
to support a projected *coup d'état* in case of the Empress's
death. There is not one grain of truth in this accusation,
which, nevertheless, has been accepted as an absolute fact
by many modern continental historians, almost without
question. The retreat of the army was ordered, not by

Apraksin personally, but by a unanimous council of war held a *full fortnight* previous to the Tsaritsa's sudden seizure and three weeks before the intelligence of that event could by any possibility have reached the ears of the General Staff. I believe, indeed, that the dilatoriness of Apraksin's earlier operations were not *entirely* due to want of provender and stores, and that he meant, as far as he dared, to respect the wishes of the prussophil Grand Duke Peter by not pressing the enemy too hard; but there is no proof of any deliberate plot to employ the army for anything but purely military purposes. Esterhazy and L'Hôpital thought otherwise, however, and it was owing, mainly, to their energetic representations that Apraksin was suspended from his command and summoned to St. Petersburg. On reaching Narva, he was detained in custody, and, while receiving an assurance of the imperial clemency, was commanded to deliver up all his papers, as it was strongly suspected by the Shuvalovs that among them would be found some letters from Bestuzhev and the Grand Duchess. For six weeks Apraksin's correspondence was minutely examined, but even the ingenuity of malignant hatred could find nothing in them to compromise either the writer or those to whom he had written. Still the foreign Ministers were not satisfied. "Why," they seem to have argued, "should there have been any correspondence at all between these persons?" Meanwhile the wretched Apraksin lay in a fever of agony and terror at Narva, sick both in mind and body, and with no one to attend to his wants but his devoted wife, Agripina Leontievna, who never quitted him for an instant. He vehemently protested his innocence throughout and addressed, from time to time, the most abject appeals to the Empress, [1] imploring her to have mercy

---

[1] Compare: *Iz bumag J. J. Shuvalova. Sb. of Imp. Russ. Hist. Soc.* Vol. IX; Solovev: *Istoria Rossy.*

on "the lowest of her slaves," and protesting that if he had
done amiss, it was from sheer ignorance and stupidity. On
January 29th, 1758, Alexander Shuvalov, the director of
the Secret Chancellery, was sent down to Narva to examine
the prisoner, but Apraksin solemnly swore that he gave no
promise whatever to the Grand Duke or Duchess, and
"received no inspirations whatever in favour of the King of
Prussia." He also declared, again and again, that he had done
nothing throughout the campaign without first consulting a
Council of War, and General Fermor, who had succeeded
him in the command of the army, fully bore out the words
of his former chief. Thus, for the sake of consistency,
Fermor ought also to have been suspended and arrested.
But this was a case in which consistency (and justice too,
for the matter of that) was quite out of the question, for
it had been resolved beforehand to make a scapegoat of
Apraksin, in order to get at Bestuzhev and so appease the
anger of Russia's allies by a double sacrifice. Well aware
of this, Bestuzhev defended himself with characteristic skill
and unscrupulousness. For fear of consequences to himself,
he was the first to turn round upon his old friend Apraksin
on hearing of his arrest, and attacked him fiercely in the
Council-Chamber where Peter Shuvalov as hotly defended
the fallen Field Marshal. Not content with this, Bestuzhev,
to further justify his conduct in the eyes of Russia's allies,
as well as to prove that "the young Court" [1] was as anxious
as anybody to promote the good cause, showed to Herr
von Prassé, an *attaché* of the Saxon Embassy, and to an
Austrian *attaché*, General Bakkow, three letters from Catherine
to Apraksin, urging him to hasten on his operations. Bakkow
duly informed Esterhazy of these letters, and Esterhazy,
more than ever anxious to ruin both Bestuzhev and Apraksin,

---

[1] The Grand Duke and Grand Duchess.

represented to the Empress, who was now recovering from her seizure, that both the Grand Duchess and the Grand Chancellor had been in secret communication with Apraksin during the past campaign, and that the whole affair looked very suspicious for them both. From October, 1757, to February, 1758, every effort was made by the foreign camarilla at the Russian Court to oust Bestuzhev, who doggedly defended himself, though now only too well aware that the Empress herself regarded him with positive dislike. She had other causes of displeasure against him besides the matter of the Catherine-Apraksin correspondence. He had protected and defended the intriguing Stanislaus Poniatowski, despite the Imperial displeasure thereat, in order to oblige the Grand Duchess whose lover that handsome reprobate had now become; he had procured the Polish Order of the White Eagle from the King of Poland for his confidant and *protégé*, Privy Councillor Stamke, also contrary to the Empress's wishes; he had absented himself from Court functions, of late, without sufficient reason. But all these things, though they created bitterness and hostility, could never, in themselves, have brought the Grand Chancellor down. By a curious irony of fate, it was reserved for England, involuntarily, indeed, but none the less effectually, to complete the ruin of her chief, or, rather, her only, well-wisher in Russia,

On the departure of Hanbury Williams from St. Petersburg, Robert Keith, the British Minister at Vienna, was nominated to St. Petersburg. L'Hôpital and Esterhazy at once took the alarm. If Bestuzhev could still contrive to defend himself single-handed against all their intrigues, what might he not do if he had such a powerful and energetic friend as Keith at hand to help him? It was impossible, it is true, to prevent the arrival of Keith at St. Petersburg; in fact he was on his way and had actually reached Warsaw; but Keith could only be dangerous so long as Bestuzhev re-

mained the chief diplomatic personage at the Russian Capital;
it was indispensable, therefore, to overthrow Bestuzhev before the arrival of Keith. L'Hôpital, therefore, acting under
direct orders from his Court, approached Vorontsov confi-
dentially, and represented to him emphatically, what an
anomalous and indecent state of things it was, that a person
who had justly forfeited the confidence of her Majesty and her
Allies, should still possess the control of the foreign affairs of
the Empire. The timid and conscientious Vice-Chancellor
hesitated at first to proceed to extremities against his rival;
but, upon L'Hôpital threatening to reveal everything to Bestuzhev, if he, Vorontsov, did not instantly move in the matter,
the Vice-Chancellor took counsel of Peter Shuvalov, and the
pair of them thereupon represented to Elizabeth that the
credit of Russia was suffering from the pernicious influence
of Bestuzhev abroad, which they represented as very much
greater than it actually was. The Grand Duke also was induced
to complain to his Aunt of Bestuzhev's conduct, and especially of his political intrigues with the Grand Duchess. The
Empress long hesitated to proceed against the Chancellor
on mere suspicion, however strong, till at last she was persuaded that the only way of getting at the truth of the
conspiracy alleged against Bestuzhev, Apraksin and the
Grand Duchess, was to thoroughly examine the Grand Chancellor's papers, and this could not be done till he had been
formally arrested. So, finally, the Empress, still infirm and
full of nervous fears sedulously encouraged by Peter Shuvalov, gave way and signed the order for Bestuzhev's arrest.
On the evening of February 21, 1758, the Empress summoned the Conference of Ministers, and the Chancellor was
ordered to attend it. He sent word back that he was
indisposed, but his plea of illness was treated as an act of
disobedience, and he was peremptorily commanded to come
without further delay. On passing through the antechamber

he must have recognised at once what he had to expect, for it was filled by a detachment of the Guards fully armed. Bestuzhev had scarcely entered the Council-Chamber, when his arch-enemy, Prince Nikita Trubetskoi, arose and roughly informed him of his disgrace, at the same time carrying his brutality so far as to tear from the aged statesman's breast, the broad blue ribbon of the Order of St. Andrew.[1] The other members of the Council had the decency, however, to loudly protest against this gratuitous act of violence. The Captain of the Guards was then called in and to him Bestuzhev surrendered his sword, and, getting into his carriage, was escorted back to his own house, where he was told to consider himself under arrest, a strong cordon of troops being placed around the premises to prevent his escape.

Early next morning, Catherine was privately informed by Poniatowski that the Chancellor, the Court jeweller Bernardi, who used to run various little errands for her, Adjutant Elagin, an intermediary between herself and Poniatowski, and Adadurov, her former Russian tutor, had all been arrested. Although somewhat reassured by a verbal message from Bestuzhev, sent through an old fiddler, bidding her not to lose heart as he had already burnt all his papers, the arrest of so many of her intimate friends, pointed only too clearly to an attempt to implicate her in the alleged conspiracy. "It was with a poignard in my heart, so to speak," she tells us, "that I dressed myself and went to mass that morning."[2] The same day there was a grand wedding, followed by a ball at Court, at which Catherine, concealing her growing alarm behind a mask of careless gaiety, took care to be present. Perceiving Prince Trubetskoi among the guests, she approached him, and enquired saucily: "Well, your Excellency, have you discovered more crimes

---

[1] Corresponding in dignity to our Order of the Garter.   [2] *Mémoires*.

than criminals, or more criminal than crimes?"—"Madame,"
replied Trubetskoi stiffly, "we have only obeyed our
instructions. The enquiry is proceeding, and"—he significantly added—"we hope to be more successful presently."—
Field Marshal Buturlin, another member of the Conference,
whom she next approached, was still more cynical: "Yes,"
said he, "Bestuzhev is arrested, and now we are trying to
find some reasons for justifying the arrest."

Trubetskoi, Buturlin and Alexander Shuvalov, all three
the Chancellor's personal enemies, had already been
appointed to try him, but, so far, their enquiry had been
anything but successful. It was indeed almost too much
to expect that a cunning old fox like Bestuzhev could
ever be taken by surprise, and he had had ample time
for getting rid of all compromising documents. It is
more than probable that he had intended, in case of
Elizabeth's death, to set aside the Grand Duke in
favour of little Paul, with Catherine as Regent, and no
patriotic Russian would now think of blaming him for such
an intention. His enemies also were convinced in their own
minds that such had been his design, but search as they
might[1] they could not discover a jot of incriminating evidence. His cross-examination also elicited nothing, and his
replies were considered so unsatisfactory by the Empress,
that he was threatened with the question extraordinary if
he was not more communicative. He stoutly denied that
he had hidden away any secret correspondence with the
Grand Duchess or Apraksin, or that there was any such

---

[1] I am very strongly inclined to think that Catherine did meddle in the
matter, for both she and Bestuzhev seem to have thought that the Empress's
days were numbered, and they were bound to look after themselves, but
there is no evidence against her. Her own asseverations of innocence go
for nothing. She was notoriously untruthful, and besides, in her terrible
situation, a casuist would perhaps say that falsehood was only a means of
self-preservation and therefore justifiable.

correspondence to hide. He denied that he had had any secret
conferences with Poniatowski, or that he had harboured
any design, present or future, for altering the succession.
Exasperated at the barrenness of the enquiry, his three
judges at last (March 15) exhorted him to make a clean
breast of everything, or to the torture-chamber he should
go. The Empress was particularly embittered against him
for protecting Poniatowski, and for his dealings with the
Saxon Court generally; but he explained, plausibly enough,
that, knowing of the hostile designs of l'Hôpital and Esterhazy, he had simply tried, in self-defence, to induce the
Court of Dresden to impress the Courts of Vienna and
Paris with a better opinion of himself. Finally, when the
Commission, at its wits' end for evidence, accused him to the
Empress of obstinate reticence and duplicity, and the old
statesman had every reason to fear that the knout, the last
resort of Russian criminal procedure, would be applied to
him, he solemnly swore before his judges, that he had
spoken the whole truth, and confirmed his oath by taking
the Sacrament upon it in their presence. After this the
devout Empress expressed herself satisfied of his veracity.

All this time the Grand Duchess remained in a horrible
state of suspense and anxiety. Thanks to the precautions
of Bestuzhev, and her own prudence, she flattered herself
that she had nothing to fear, for all proofs of her supposed
complicity in the Apraksin affair had been destroyed;[1] but
she knew she had seriously offended the Empress by
dabbling in politics at all; she knew that the dominant
Shuvalovs hated her, and would stick at nothing to
compass her ruin, and she had not a friend at court who
could assist her. Esterhazy, to whom she appealed for
advice, counselled her to ask her husband to plead for her

---

[1] See note on page 241.

with his Aunt, but at this her pride revolted for she knew
that the Grand Duke was delighted at her discomfiture.
The future now began to look dark indeed, and at last,
after much anxious thought, Catherine resolved to turn to
the Empress direct. This was certainly her wisest course.
She knew that the tender-hearted Elizabeth could not
endure the sight of tears, and that no humble suppliant
had ever yet appealed to her in vain. Accordingly on May 29,
1758, Catherine addressed a pathetic epistle to the
Empress,[1] in Russian, imploring the favour of an audience,
and concluding with these words: "When I think of your
"Majesty's kindness to me, my eyes gush out with water.
"The whole remainder of my life will be full of obedience,
"love and sincerity, if, only for a brief space, I may be deemed
"worthy to look upon your Majesty's face." This letter,
her fellow-student, young Ivan Shuvalov, who, all along,
had taken no part in the intrigues of his uncles, undertook
to deliver privately,[2] and, on parting with the Grand
Duchess, he gave her a good piece of advice : "At the
first interview," said he, "be sure to be very meek, and
all will go well with you." The letter was duly delivered,
but several days passed, and still Catherine received no
reply. She was much distressed, and one of her maids,
Catherine Cheregorodskaya, perceiving her in tears, persuaded her mistress to allow her to tell her uncle, who happened to be one of the Empress's confessors, the whole
story. By the advice of this good priest, Catherine
pretended to be seriously ill, and sent for him to hear her
confession, as she "feared her soul was in danger." He
came and sat on the edge of the bed, while she confided
everything to him, and told him how anxiously she

---

[1] *Sb. of Imp. Russ. Soc.* Vol. III.
[2] According to Catherine's own *Mémoires,* written, however, twenty years
after the event, she gave the letter to *Alexander* Shuvalov to deliver.

awaited a response from the Empress. He promised
to do what he could for her, and advised her to remain in
bed till she heard from him again. The worthy man was
as good as his word, and, the next day, he informed
her, through his niece, that the Empress had promised to
see her the same evening. All that night she was up and
dressed. At one o'clock, Alexander Shuvalov knocked at
her door and informed her that the Empress was awaiting
her. She arose and followed him, through the dimly lit
corridors of the Palace, to Elizabeth's bedchamber.[1] It was
a large long room with three windows in it, and between
the windows nearest to the door by which Catherine had
entered, was a toilet-table with a golden toilet-set upon it.
In one of the basins of this toilet-set were three folded
letters, the letters which Catherine had written to Apraksin.
In the background of the room stood the Grand Duke,
uneasily shifting from one leg to the other, and Alexander
Shuvalov, the left side of his face convulsed with that spas-
modic grin which always betokened extraordinary excitement. The form of another man was dimly outlined behind
a curtain—this was Ivan Shuvalov, Catherine's friend and
Elizabeth's favourite. Up and down the vast chamber the
massive figure of the Empress, in a gorgeous dressing-gown,
was pacing slowly to and fro. All these circumstances the
quick-eyed, keen-witted Grand Duchess took in at a glance,
and she instantly conceived her plan of action. In an agony
of tears she flung herself at the feet of the Empress, and
refused to rise, although Elizabeth twice urged her to do
so. "Let me go home to my parents!" she sobbed.—"How

---

[1] The best account of this memorable interview will be found in Solovev's
Istoria Rossy. Catherine's own account *(Mémoires)* is more circumstantial,
but appears to have been touched up to show herself off to the best advantage. As a matter of fact, it is Elizabeth who impresses us most favourably
on this occasion.

can I send you away?" replied Elizabeth kindly. "You forget that you are a mother, or have you no thought at all for your children?" [1]—"My children," replied Catherine, "are in your Majesty's hands, and I could not wish them in a better place."—At this the Empress was deeply moved and shed tears. She insisted, however, that Catherine should rise. "God is my witness," she added, "how I wept and grieved when, on your first arrival in Russia, you lay sick unto death. Had I not loved you as my own child, I should never have nursed you as I did.—But," she added, drawing still nearer to the Grand Duchess, "you think too much of yourself, you think nobody else has any mother-wit at all."— "If I ever thought such a thing," replied Catherine meekly, "my present position, and the words your Majesty has just addressed to me, are sufficient to cure me for ever of any such foolish presumption."—At this the Empress began pacing up and down the room again in silence. Presently her eyes fell upon the letters on her toilet-table, and she returned to the charge with a sudden access of acerbity. "Of late, Madam," said she, "you have not treated me with due respect. You interfere in affairs of state which do not concern you. I should never have dared to do in the reign of the Empress Anne, what you have done in mine.— How dare you send orders to Field Marshal Apraksin?"— "I send orders, your Majesty! Such an idea never entered into my head.—"What!" cried Elizabeth, angrily stamping her foot, "you persist in denying that you wrote to him, when your letters are actually staring you in the face?"— and she pointed to the toilet basin. "Were you not forbidden to write?"—"That is unfortunately true," replied

---

[1] In December, 1757, Catherine gave birth to a daughter who was christened Anne, and died twelve months later. The paternity of this child is very doubtful, and Count Vorontsov assures us that its decease saved the Court from a terrible scandal.

Catherine, "in that particular I did disobey your commands, and I humbly crave your Majesty's pardon for so doing. As, however, my three letters are there, they are my best proofs that I never sent him any orders. You can see for yourself that, in one of them, I simply tell him to execute your Majesty's commands more promptly, while the second merely congratulates him on the birth of a son, and the third is a New Year's greeting."—"But why did you write to him at all?" persisted Elizabeth.—"Because I liked him," replied the Grand Duchess.—"Bestuzhev says there were many more letters than these," observed the Empress.—"If Bestuzhev says that, Bestuzhev lies," retorted Catherine boldly.— "Very well," rejoined the Empress, now applying a little moral pressure, "if he has calumniated you, I shall send him to the Torture Chamber."—"It is in your Majesty's power to do whatsoever your Majesty may think fit," replied the dauntless little Grand Duchess, "but I maintain that I wrote only three letters to Marshal Apraksin."—To this the Empress made no reply, but began pacing up and down the room again. The Grand Duke, who hitherto had been gloating in silence over the distress of his wife, now thought fit to abuse her aloud, and a slight altercation ensued between the consorts till the Empress whispered to her nephew to hold his tongue, and not make a fool of himself. Catherine's words, and her whole bearing, had very favourably impressed the naturally equitable Elizabeth, she was softening visibly. Finally she approached Catherine again, and said to her in a low voice: "I have still a great deal more to say to you, but I don't want to quarrel with you any more, and it is now very late" (it was in fact past three o'clock in the morning) "and you look tired." The gentleness of her tone quite overcame Catherine. "I became all heart myself," she tells us. "And I also am at a loss for words," she exclaimed, "despite the yearning

desire I have to open my heart entirely to your Majesty."
Then Elizabeth's tears flowed once more, and Catherine
knew she was forgiven. At a subsequent interview, the
particulars of which are not recorded, the reconciliation
between the aunt and niece seems to have been completely
effected, and Catherine could breathe freely once more.
All confidence between them, however, was now at an end.

The Shuvalovs thus failed to implicate the Grand Duchess
in the supposed conspiracy, but all the more rigorously
were the proceedings against the other scapegoats, Apraksin and Bestuzhev, conducted. The Field Marshal protested
his innocence to the last; solemnly declared that the only
letters he had ever received from Bestuzhev and Catherine
had been to expedite his operations, and appealed for
mercy to the Empress in terms so abject as to make us
blush for his manhood. But his nerves were evidently
shattered by his misfortunes, and he evaded justice, as his
enemies would have said, by suddenly dying of apoplexy
on March 17, 1758. Bestuzhev's trial was protracted for
six months longer. More than once his enemies fancied
they had him completely in their power. Shortly after his
arrest, it came to light that he was carrying on a clandestine
correspondence with the Grand Duchess, the letters being
hidden in a brick-kiln near his house. They were, however,
found to be so utterly colourless that even his enemies
could make nothing out of them. Some months later the
Commission of Enquiry succeeded in unearthing, among his
confiscated possessions, a gold snuff-box adorned with
the portrait of the Grand Duchess. On being confronted
with it, the prisoner frankly admitted that it was a gift
from her, and even the Commission had not the face to assert
that he had no right to receive such presents. Finally, after
a fruitless enquiry of fourteen months, the ex-Chancellor
was found guilty of calumniating her Majesty to their

Highnesses, and egging them on against her; of opposing the execution of imperial decrees; of being privy to, and taking no steps to prevent, the retreat of Apraksin; of usurping autocratic power, and encouraging his creatures to do the same, and of revealing, while under arrest, state secrets. On these frivolous and mendacious charges, the fallen statesman was actually condemned to death; but the Empress mitigated the sentence to seclusion in his country-house at Goretovo in the Government of Mozhaisk. She had no further need of his services, but she took good care to snatch him away from the vengeance of his enemies. Bestuzhev was at least fortunate in the period of his fall. Had he been disgraced in the reign of Peter the Great, he would probably have been broken on the wheel; had he offended the Empress Anne, he would have been sent to Siberia for life. His fate, it is true, was altogether undeserved, but unfortunately, in those days, Russia had no civilized method of ridding herself of superfluous statesmen.

Bestuzhev and Apraksin were thus sacrificed to the resentment of Russia's Allies, who had been bitterly chagrined by the negative results of the campaign of Grossjägersdorf and were loud in their complaints of the dilatory strategy of the Russian generals. Elizabeth was naturally anxious to escape similar reproaches in the future, and the Conference of Ministers at St. Petersburg, both to restore the prestige of the Army, and also to oblige the Court of Vienna, ordered the new Commander-in-Chief to at once undertake a winter campaign for the purpose of occupying East Prussia. Apraksin's successor, Count Wilhelm Fermor, an honest, painstaking and conscientious officer, who, like most of his contemporaries, had served under Münnich and Lacy in Poland and Turkey without displaying any very superior ability, was now promoted over the heads of his five senior colleagues possibly because of his petty successes in the recent campaign. He had shared and supported all the views of Apraksin, and was therefore equally responsible for the measures which had led to the ruin of that unfortunate commander. On the other hand, being naturally self-distrustful, and with no powerful connections, he was a pliable tool in the hands of the Conference of Ministers, and this was considered a merit large enough to cloke all his shortcomings. Acting under instructions from St. Petersburg, Fermor had, at the end of December, 1757, set his thirty thousand men in motion, and marched into East Prussia a second time. The invasion being altogether unexpected, no serious resistance was anywhere encountered, and, by January 11th, 1758, nearly the whole Duchy, including the Capital, Königsberg, was in the hands of the Russians. Elizabeth at once converted it into a Russian Province, and appointed Fermor its first Governor-General. The rest of the winter was employed in introducing many necessary reforms into the army, restoring its discipline, and preparing it generally for the ensuing campaign which was intended to be decisive.

There can, indeed, be no doubt that the Russian army, at this period, was a very defective and clumsy instrument of warfare. All the foreign military *attachés*[1] who accompanied the army of Apraksin, agree in deploring the extraordinary abuses and anomalies which encumbered it, and tended to deteriorate the really excellent raw material of which it was composed. One of the most remarkable of

---

[1] Of course, there is some exaggeration in these reports, yet they seem to have been substantially true. Otherwise it is difficult to explain the unanimity of so many purely friendly critics. The Chauvinist Masslowski is much too sensitive on this point, and too hastily imputes wrong motives to these perfectly honest, if somewhat severe, animadversions.

these contemporary criticisms is the so-called "Letter from a traveller from Riga".[1] To begin with, this authority complains that no army was ever so overburdened with baggage as the Russian, a whole third of its effective strength, he says, had to be told off to feed and tend the horses and look after the stores. Every single captain was wont to appropriate the services of from ten to twelve men on the pretext of imperial business. Each regiment was in the habit of carrying along with it on separate wagons, numbers of gates and fences, wherewith, in case of need, to cover the whole front of the line, and so ward off the onslaughts of hostile cavalry. The chief strength of the army lay in its grenadiers. The men were sturdy and well knit together, but deficient in alertness and activity. The other regiments are described as very bad indeed, and but poorly equipped. The artillery is said to be numerous, but ill-served. The horses, we are told, are as a rule, too timid to be good for much. The horsemen did not even take their mantles along with them, but had them carried after them in wagons; indeed the cavalry seems to have had more wagons at its disposal than the infantry. The dragoons, says "The Traveller", did not deserve the name of cavalry at all, and their officers were so stupid that "as stupid as a dragoon" had become a by-word in the army. The hussars, however, made much better horsemen, but their officers also were very ignorant. The Calmucks were the best Russian irregulars. The Cossacks were only employed to harass and reconnoitre the enemy, and of these the Don Cossacks were the best. All the generals, except Villebois and Rumyantsev, are described in the most contemptuous terms; but it is interesting to note that this shrewd observer has already a very high

---

[1] The author, according to Masslowski, was a Captain Lambert.

opinion of the future hero of Catharine II's First Turkish
War, though he does not seem to have heard of the still
more illustrious Suvarov who was already serving his
apprenticeship in the army. Rumyantsev, he says, "is a
very young general who takes great pains to learn his
business, and has great theoretical knowledge. He is
indeed the best of all the Russian officers, his chief fault
being his impetuosity." [1]—This letter seems to have profoundly impressed the Russian Court. A translation of it
was sent to Fermor by the Vice-Chancellor Vorontsov,
who, at the same time, advised the Commander-in-Chief
"as a friend, to look and see in what our deficiences consist,
and what are the best means of remedying them without
loss of time."

The campaign of 1758 was retarded by a bad harvest,
and a cold and late Spring which prevented the grass from
growing, and rendered it very difficult to procure sufficient
forage. In June, Maria Theresa became urgent, and instructed Esterhazy to expedite the Russian armaments. Her
own arms, this year, had, so far, not been unsuccessful.
Frederick II's sudden attack upon the fortress of Olmutz
had been repulsed, and he was compelled (July 1) to raise
the siege and retreat across the Giants' Mountains back
into Silesia, if only Russia would move at once, the ruin
of the King of Prussia appeared to be certain. "Russia,"
wrote the Empress-Queen to her ambassador at St. Petersburg, "Russia now has it in her hands to deal our common
foe a mortal blow, and can do it all the more readily as
the Prussian King cannot collect sufficient forces to oppose
the Russian advance." Fermor, however, was now in a
very uncomfortable position. He knew from bitter experience
that it was impossible for the army to move rapidly while

---

[1] The Austrian *attaché* St. André, and the Swedish *attaché* Armfelt, be it
observed, are almost equally disparaging in their remarks.

the commissariat was in such a wretched state, and yet, if he did not move rapidly, the Austrian Court would cry out against him, and impute the failure of the Allies entirely to his tardiness.   In his extremity (for he had the fate of Apraksin constantly before his eyes) he piteously appealed to his friend Vorontsov for support.   " Inasmuch as my high position needs the utmost assistance of powerful patrons," he writes, "I venture to beg your Excellency to take me and the army committed to my charge, under your clement protection, and supply my shortcomings by your prudent dispositions."—A strange appeal, truly, from a commander-in-chief on the threshold of a decisive campaign!

It was not until the end of May that Fermor, acting under the directions of the Conference of Ministers at St. Petersburg, entered Pomerania.   His objective was Frankfort on the Oder. He was also to join hands, if possible, with the Swedish army, which was supposed to be advancing towards him from Stralsund, but which, as a matter of fact, did nothing at all.   On the 20th June, Fermor reached Posen, and, after remaining there eleven days, marched westwards into Bran-denburg, skirmishing all the way with the cavalry of the Prussian Commander, Count Dohna, who retreated steadily before him, reaching Meseritz on July 15th. It had been the original intention of the Commander-in-Chief to proceed thence to Frankfort, in order to unite there with an Austrian auxiliary corps under Laudon; but a Council of War, held at Meseritz, decided that, in view of the lack of forage, and the serious loss of horses and wagons in consequence of the heavy rains, the original plan was impossible, but that, instead of that, the army should cross the Warthe at Landsberg, and attack and capture the fortress of Cüstrin which would give Fermor the command of the Oder.   Rumyantsev was at the same time detached to cross the Oder lower down, at Stargard, where magazines were to be formed and the horses rested. On August 15th, Fermor reached the village of Gross Kammin, and pitched his camp there, about a mile distant from Cüstrin, which was bombarded on the following days with bombs and red-hot bullets, and soon the whole town was in a blaze. But the fortress itself, environed as it was by the rivers Oder and Warthe and by vast marshes difficult of access, proved impregnable by a sudden assault, so the Russians had to be content with blockading it. So far Fermor's operations had won the approval of his government. He was officially informed that what he had done hitherto had more than responded to the Empress's expectations, but he was warned, at the same time, to keep his eyes open, and in any case to establish his winter quarters in Brandenburg. Meanwhile, however, the King of Prussia was already flying to the relief of his hereditary estates, at the head of fourteen battalions of infantry and thirty-three squadrons of cavalry, marching no fewer than 120 miles in a fortnight. After effecting his junction with Count Dohna, Frederick crossed the Oder near Güstebiese (with the roar of the Russian cannon bombarding Cüstrin dinning in his ears) during a single night at an unguarded spot, without losing a single man, thereby cutting off Fermor from the corps of Rumyantsev (who was lower down the river in the direction of Schmedt), and immediately afterwards, with his usual celerity, set off to seek the main Russian army, and give it battle wherever he might find it.

It was only on August 23rd that the astonished Fermor learnt from Tököli's Servian Hussars that the whole Prussian army had already crossed the Oder, and was advancing against him. [1] Convinced at last that a decisive battle in the neighbourhood of Cüstrin was unavoidable, he at

---

[1] For Russian accounts of the Battle of Zorndorf see Masslowski II. 154—201; Bolotov and Solovev.

once marched in the direction of Zorndorf with his
42,590 fighting men,[1] and took up a position which, under
the circumstances, was the best that could have been
adopted by an army obliged to act on the defensive.
The ground he now occupied was an undulating plateau,
bounded on the north by the marshy Mietzel stream, only
fordable in a few places, on the west by the Oder, on the
south by the marshy Warthe, on the east by the upper
Mietzel. The whole district was surrounded by dense
woods. The position assumed by the Russian army was
almost unassailable in front, but strong as it was, it was
nevertheless liable to be outflanked, and Frederick had
resolved to outflank it. After uniting with Count
Dohna and crossing the Oder, as already mentioned, the
King of Prussia continued his march to the village of
Losau, where he encamped and rested his troops. On
the 24th the Prussian army proceeded to Darmitzel, and
at three o'clock on the morning of the following day,
Frederick resumed his march, passed the mill of Damm,
defiled by way of the forest of Massin, debouched into the
plain near the village of Batzlow, and thence continued his
march to the village of Zorndorf, thereby completely turning Fermor's position, and taking him in the rear. The
direction of the enemy's march did not escape the observation of the Russian light troops, and was communicated to the Commander-in-Chief, who now (between five
and six in the morning) could no longer doubt that his
position had been turned by his royal antagonist, and his
army thereby placed in so critical a situation, that nothing
short of victory could extricate him. Without losing a
moment, he endeavoured to reform his forces so far as the
nature of the ground permitted it. The Russians were

---

[1] Masslowski puts down the total force of Frederick at 32,760. Compare
Poll. Corr. Frederick II. Vol. XVI.

now drawn up in a sort of square formation facing out-
wards in every direction, with the whole of their artillery
grouped in batteries in front of their outmost lines, and
the cavalry on the wings. The right wing, under Fermor's personal command, stood on both sides of the Gal-
gengrund ravine. The left wing, under Browne, joined
close on to the right, and was also divided into two parts
by the swampy Hofbruch. As soon as the head of
Frederick's vanguard had passed Zorndorf, the King ordered
it to attack the Russian right flank forthwith. I will not
attempt to give a full description of a battle which, at a
very early stage of the engagement, degenerated into a
confused *mêlée*, almost every detail of which is still a
matter of dispute among military critics. Even Frederick,
only a week later, frankly owned that he had some
difficulty in understanding its separate details himself. "So
many unheard of things took place," he wrote to his brother,
Prince Henry, "that one must necessarily find it very difficult
to combine so many different facts."[1] Still, the main
features of the fight, apart from technical *minutiæ*, may
be briefly indicated. It lasted from nine o'clock in the
morning of August 25, till seven o'clock the same evening,
and was undoubtedly the most murderous engagement of
modern times.[2] Frederick himself describes the battle as
"uncommonly bloody," and his contempt for the Russian
commanders was considerably tempered by his respect for
the Russian soldiers. The battle began with the Prussians
attacking the Russian right wing where stood the newly
enrolled "Corps of Observation," which Peter Shuvalov

---

[1] *Pol. Corr.* Vol. XVI.

[2] See Dalhof-Nielsen: *Om Talene i Krig.*—34 % of the numbers engaged
at Zorndorf were placed *hors de combat*. At Aspern, which comes nearest
to it, the percentage of killed and wounded was 33. Waterloo and even
Borodino were far less bloody; at the former 24 %, at the latter 28 % were
placed *hors de combat*.

had presented to the Empress. This corps had never been under fire before. Nevertheless it withstood the charge of the Prussian Grenadiers without flinching, till the Prussian cavalry came to the assistance of the Grenadiers and scattered the Shuvalov Corps. At this point, moreover, the infantry of the Russian second line, unable to distinguish friend from foe amidst the enveloping clouds of smoke and dust, unfortunately fired into their own cavalry from behind, while Seydlitz, the famous Prussian cavalry-officer, attacked them in front, hurling them back upon their own infantry, so that Prussians and Russians were soon mingled together in a seething struggling mass. The right wing was still further demoralized by an outbreak of insubordination on the part of the hot and thirsty Shuvalov recruits, who flew upon the wine and spirit casks, despite all the efforts of their officers to prevent it, and soon lay drunk upon the ground by hundreds. At two o'clock, Frederick looked upon the Russian right wing as hopelessly beaten, and directed all his attention to their left. Here also, however, his first attack was repulsed with heavy loss, but then the gallant Seydlitz [1] came up with his horsemen, and again restored the fortunes of the day. Still, to the very last, the struggle was most desperate, and Frederick himself admits that three times in the course of the afternoon he was on the point of being totally beaten. [2] Even when the powder on both sides was exhausted, the men kept on fighting hand to hand, with swords, bayonets and the butt-ends of their muskets till nightfall, no quarter being given on either side. Both armies remained all night on the field of battle, so that neither of them can be said

---

[1] Seydlitz, amongst other exploits, captured one of the best Russian batteries with his cuirassiers, and turned its guns upon the Russians themselves.

[2] Letter to Finkenstein on the evening of the very day of the fight. *Pol. Corr.* Vol. XVI.

to have won the victory, though both claimed it. On the following day, indeed, Fermor was the first to retreat from his now impossible position; but, on the other hand, Frederick made no attempt to impede or molest him, and, later the same day, himself retired to Cüstrin. He could not afford to win another such victory. Both armies had suffered enormously. Masslowski puts down the Russian loss at 10,886 killed and 12,788 wounded, the loss of the Prussians has been variously estimated at from 1645 to 12,400.[1] The former figure is ridiculous, the latter probably much exaggerated. The Russians also lost more than 200 guns and 30 standards. Generals Saltuikov, Chernuishev and Browne, were all seriously wounded; three other generals were left in the hands of the enemy.

At first it was imagined at St. Petersburg that a signal victory had been gained by the Empress's forces, In her rescript, in reply to Fermor's bulletin, Elizabeth declares that to sustain a nine hours' combat with a superior foe[2] and remain on the field of battle four-and-twenty hours afterwards, were deeds which the whole world would hold in perpetual memory as redounding to the eternal glory of the Russian arms. But she was far less pleased with the subsequent proceedings of her general. At dawn, on August 27, in full sight of the enemy, the Russian army, in square formation, retreated to Gross Kammin, where an entrenched camp was hastily formed, and a Te Deum sung inside it.[3] Thence, still retreating, Fermor proceeded to Landsberg, where Rumyantsev's corps rejoined him, raising his effective

---

[1] Bolotov. Masslowski estimates the Prussian loss at 11,345.

[2] As a matter of fact the Russian army was superior to the Prussian, consisting as it did of 42,590 (*not* 70,000 as estimated by Frederick II) as opposed to 32,760. Fermor, however, both before and after the battle, held the enemy to be much stronger than he really was (45,000—60,000).

[3] The enemy had anticipated the Russian thanksgiving service by four hours. *Solovev.*

strength to 40,000, exclusive of hussars and cossacks, a force quite sufficient to have crushed the enfeebled King of Prussia. Nothing, however, in the way of pursuit seems to have been attempted, and the Empress, in another rescript, was obliged to express her displeasure at this strange lack of initiative. She also complains that Fermor's despatches are unintelligible, blames him for his reticence as to future operations, and expressly commands him to winter in Pomerania, so as to be able to live at the enemy's expense. He was also enjoined to capture, as soon as possible, the maritime fortress of Kolberg, which would greatly facilitate the re-victualling of the army from Russia, and exterminate the corps of Count Dohna, which Frederick had left behind to observe the Russians. "Avoid," concludes this imperial exhortation sarcastically, "avoid in future all such resolutions as have been adopted by your councils of war during the present campaign, avoid all such expressions in your despatches as 'if time, circumstances, and the movements of the enemy will permit.' Such resolutions are sheer irresolution. The real skill of a general consists in taking such measures as are independent of 'time, circumstances, and the movements of the enemy.'"—The wretched commander-in-chief was now in the same dilemma as his unfortunate predecessor. He also was no genius, but he was a soldier by profession, he was actually on the field, and was therefore in a much better position to grasp the situation than a council of civilians nearly a thousand miles distant from the theatre of operations. He begged for leave to retire to his magazines on the Vistula, and declared it was impossible to remain in Brandenburg. "If we stay on the Warthe," he wrote in desperation, "all the horses will die on the spot, and what is the army to do without horses?" To appease his critics, he adopted the middle course of invading Pomerania, besides detaching a

corps to besiege Kolberg; but nothing came of these operations, and, fortified by the approval of a Council of War,
he finally ventured, at the beginning of October, to retire
behind the Vistula, and so the campaign of 1758 ended as
abortively as the campaign of 1757.

Fermor seems to have been saved from the fate of
Apraksin by the growing conviction of the Empress and
her Ministers that the Court of Vienna was sacrificing the
Russian troops to its own particular interests. There can
be no doubt that very little assistance was rendered by
the Austrians to the Russians during the past campaign,
and the apologetic tone adopted by Maria Theresa seems
to show that Elizabeth had just cause for complaint.
The Empress-Queen pleaded as an excuse for her own
remissness the failure of the Court of Versailles to fulfil
its obligations to Austria. France, she said, instead of despatching the promised auxiliary corps of 30—40,000 men
to Austria's hereditary domains, had wasted her strength
in a fruitless struggle with England and Hanover. There
were, she added, symptoms of growing weakness in the
French Monarchy. Several times since the beginning of
the year, France had complained that the burden of the
war was growing intolerable and expressed a desire for
peace. Elizabeth's reply was both dignified and determined,
but it also shows that the French influence at St. Petersburg was at this time paramount. She protested that
France had taken a more active part in the war than any
other member of the league, and had, besides, the
additional merit of bringing Sweden into it. The alleged
infirmity of the French monarchy, assuming it to exist, was
only an additional reason for assisting it more strenuously,
and not allowing it to be sacrificed to England and Prussia. In the opinion of the Russian Empress, the war
must be prosecuted till the Most High had blessed the

righteous arms of the Allies with decisive success, and abated the pride and self-sufficiency of the King of Prussia.

Thus it was the unflinching firmness of Elizabeth which kept the anti-Prussian league at this stage from falling to pieces, and, towards the end of the year, the hands of the Russian Empress were strengthened by the accession to power in France of a new and vigorous Minister of Foreign Affairs, who fully shared her sentiments. The previous administration of Cardinal Bernis, the friend and *protégé* of Madame de Pompadour, [1] had been weak and vacillating, and his diplomatic tone was, generally speaking, querulous and despondent. Michael Bestuzhev had to listen to innumerable reproaches from his Eminence, who alluded to the retreat of Apraksin as if it were the sole cause of the discomfiture of the Allies. It was a thousand pities, he said, that the Russian Field Marshal should thus have left General Lehwaldt free hands in Pomerania, and thereby caused mischief not easily to be remedied. When, however, in the following year, the Russians again advanced and occupied whole provinces of Prussia, while the French, on the other hand, were routed at Crefeldt, and driven headlong over the Weser by Prince Ferdinand of Brunswick, Louis XV thought it necessary to send an autograph letter of explanation to Elizabeth, attributing the ill success of the French arms to failure of supplies, and assuring his " dear sister" that he would never quit the league till he had compelled the disturber of the peace of Europe to respect the laws of the Empire. Subsequently, indeed, at the end of November, 1758, Bernis bitterly complained of Fermor's failure to capture Kolberg, and protested that all the good intentions of the Tsaritsa were frustrated by the incompetence

---

[1] Madame de Pompadour's influence upon foreign affairs has been grotesquely exaggerated. Not her machinations, but the Treaty of Westminster brought about the Seven Years' War.

of her generals. This, however, was the Cardinal's last official communication, for he was now superseded by the able and resolute Étienne François de Stainville, Duc de Choiseul, the last really great statesman of the old French Monarchy. The first act of the new Minister was to inform Michael Bestuzhev that pacific overtures had been made to Great Britain through the Danish Court, with the object of isolating the King of Prussia, but that the English Ministers had steadily refused to separate their cause from his. Choiseul further informed the Russian Ambassador that Louis XV had given his solemn word never to make peace without the consent of his Allies, and Stahremberg, the Austrian Minister at Versailles, assured Bestuzhev that Choiseul could be absolutely depended upon. Bestuzhev's own description of the state of France at this period is gloomy enough. [1] He represents the poverty of the people as very great, the treasury as empty, trade as being in a state of stagnation; yet public credit was still good, and the enlightened energy of Choiseul succeeded in galvanizing the moribund body politic into something like fresh life again.

Golitsuin's despatches from London were, naturally, less satisfactory than those of Bestuzhev from Versailles. He reports " a fanatical enthusiasm of the whole nation for the King of Prussia," and a determination on the part of the English Ministers to make Prussia the leading German Power on the Continent instead of Austria. Frederick was even honoured with "the chimerical title of Defender of the Protestant Religion." [2] He goes on to say that the basis of England's foreign policy was hostility to France. Whoever is an enemy of France is a friend of England, and the damage done by Frederick II to the French Monarchy was no doubt at the bottom of England's respect for him.

[1] *Despatches of M. Bestuzhev,* cited by Solovev.
[2] *Despatches of Golitsuin,* cited by Solovev.

Russia dreaded most of all, at this time, lest England should send a fleet to the Baltic, but Golitsuin informed his Government that there was no fear of this, as Great Britain would thereby offend the Scandinavian Powers to the serious detriment of her own trade. On the other hand, the Court of St. James's resented the occupation of Prussian provinces by the Russians, and, according to the despatches of Obryezkov, [1] the Moscovite Ambassador at Constantinople, the English Minister there supported his Prussian colleague in his endeavours to induce the Porte to make a diversion against both Austria and Russia.

On the whole, then, the war in 1758 had proved as inconclusive as the war in 1757, and we may best summarize the political situation at the end of it, by quoting the memorable words, not without pathos, of Frederick the Great to Marshal Keith: "So our campaigning is over, and nothing has come of it for either side but the loss of many an honest fellow, the distress of many a poor soldier crippled for life, and the ruin of several provinces." [2]

---

[1] *Despatches of Obryezkov,* cited by Solovev.
[2] *Pol. Corr.* Vol. XVII.

CHAPTER XI.

THE CAMPAIGN OF KUNERSDORF.

1759.

INCREASING difficulties of the King of Prussia—The Conventions of Versailles, 30th and 31st. Dec.—Opening of the Campaign—Advance of Fermor—He is superseded by Peter Saltuikov—Causes of Fermor's supersession—Character of the new Commander-in-Chief—Advance of Saltuikov—Battle of Kay—Defeat of the Prussians—Saltuikov reaches Frankfort—Cautious counsels—Advance of the King of Prussia—Battle of Kunersdorf—Destruction of the Prussian army—Despair of Frederick—Attempted mediation of England in his favour—Proposed Peace Congress of the Hague—Elizabeth will not be separated from her Allies—Dissensions between Saltuikov and Daun—Obstinacy of Saltuikov—Angry diplomatic correspondence between the Courts of Vienna and St. Petersburg—Dignified tone of the Russian Empress—Maria Theresa reposes all her hopes in Elizabeth—Choiseul and Vorontsov.

THE outlook of the King of Prussia at the beginning of 1759 was gloomier than it had ever been before. After all his heroic efforts, after all his superhuman exertions, he had barely succeeded in retaining full possession of his hereditary domains and making head against the hostile coalition which was slowly crushing him in its iron grip. Want of money had already driven him to the desperate expedient of debasing the coinage, and the prudent craftiness of his foes, in refusing to exchange prisoners of war, had not only deprived him of a large portion of his ablest officers and veteran soldiers, but had also compelled him to increase the garrisons of his fortresses in order to guard his own prisoners, thereby materially reducing the effective strength of his army in the field. His very victories had been expensive object lessons for the ultimate benefit of his adversaries. They were beginning to guess the meaning of his tactics and anticipate the consequences of his strategy. "Last year," wrote Frederick to the English Minister, Mitchell,[1] "I deceived my enemies by acting when they did not expect me to act, and standing on the defensive when they expected me to make a push. Such stratagems may do for once, but they will not bear repetition. My enemies will learn at last to be on their guard, and take care to be strong everywhere, and then I shall have a bad time of it." This was only too true, and his enemies had already made their preparations for prosecuting the war during the coming year with redoubled energy. On the last two days of 1758, two fresh and very remarkable treaties had been concluded between the Court of Versailles and the Court of Vienna.[2] By the first of these treaties, signed on Dec. 30, France undertook to put 100,000 men in the field against Prussia and subsidize Sweden and Saxony. The complete restitution of the territory belonging to Austria is here represented as the final object of the military operations of the Allies. By Article XX the hereditary Prince of Saxony is to be recognised as the successor to the Polish throne, and by Article XXII the contracting parties undertake to engage Russia to accede to this treaty. On the following day, a still more important convention was signed between France and Austria, the particulars of which have only very recently been made known. By virtue of Article V of this second convention the two Courts

---

[1] May 20, 1757. *Pol. Corr.* Bd. XVIII.
[2] Martens: *Recueil des Traités, etc.*

mutually guaranteed to each other every territorial acquisition they might make at the expense of the King of Prussia. In April 1759, Esterhazy communicated to Vorontsov, who had, by this time, succeeded Bestuzhev as Grand Chancellor, a copy of the Treaty of Versailles of Dec. 30, 1758, at the same time inviting the Russian Empress to accede thereto; but neither then, nor subsequently, was the second, *secret*, convention of Dec. 31, 1758, communicated to the Court of St. Petersburg. Russia acceded to the first convention by the Treaty of St. Petersburg, March 7, 1760, of which more anon.[1]

It had been concerted among the Allies that the campaign of 1759 should commence early, and by the beginning of April the French had already begun operations. The Austrians, under Marshal Daun, were massing simultaneously in Bohemia for the purpose of clearing Saxony of the Prussians, which being done, they were to penetrate to the heart of Frederick's hereditary domains, while their Russian allies, reinforced by an auxiliary corps under Loudon, were to occupy the attention of Frederick's main army, and co-operate as soon as possible with their Austrian allies. The first shock of battle occurred in the West, where the ablest of the French commanders, the Duke de Broglie, won his Marshal's *bâton* by defeating the Prussians under Prince Ferdinand of Brunswick, at Bergen (April 13). This unexpected reverse was a premonition of coming disaster to the King of Prussia. By the end of April, Fermor and his 90,000 men were also on the march, the financial difficulties [2] of the Government

---

[1] See Chap. XII.

[2] It was with the utmost difficulty that the Russian Government could obtain a loan of 1,000,000 efim ducats from the bankers of Dantzic and Warsaw. About 500,000 rubles had also been borrowed from the higher clergy, and at the suggestion of Peter Shuvalov 2,000,000 of debased copper money had been issued at the end of 1758. Solovev: *Istoria Rossy.*

having made it impossible for the Russian army to take the field earlier. Fermor's instructions were precise and explicit. Leaving all his invalids behind the Vistula, to guard the baggage, recover their health, and form the nucleus of a fresh army-corps of 40,000, which, it was hoped, would be available in the early summer, he was to proceed straight to Posen, and thence to Saxony, to co-operate with the Austrians. Fermor crossed the Vistula on May 1, and reached Posen on June 21st. On the 27th news was received that the Prussians had also entered Poland, and, three days later, Fermor was ordered to resign his command to his senior officer, Peter Saltuikov. Ever since the opening of the campaign, there had been incessant friction between the cautious general and the impatient Council of Ministers at St. Petersburg, the Russian Cabine' expressing its displeasure at his dilatoriness and general incapacity in the shape of sharp and sarcastic imperial rescripts. They want to know, for instance, why he has ordered the enormous quantity of 70,000 quarters of corn in Posen, when more than sufficient corn was already on its way to the army by sea from St. Petersburg. They have no particulars of a payment of 56,000 rubles to the Jew Baruch for yet another consignment of corn. At this rate the occupation of Prussia will mean the bankruptcy of Russia. They cannot understand why 4,000,000 rubles were spent in provender alone in 1758, when 2,000,000 sufficed in 1757. Last of all came the rescript of May 19, which deprived Fermor of the supreme command, but he was instructed, at the same time, to remain at his post and assist his successor with his counsels. Poor perplexed Fermor was only too delighted to be relieved of his perilous dignity. "The lowest of your Majesty's slaves is full of gratitude for this fresh proof of your Majesty's beneficent condescension," was his obsequious reply to the decree of degradation.

The appointment of the new Commander-in-Chief caused universal astonishment, and not a little derision. Those who knew Count Peter Semenovich Saltuikov personally, not only had no great hopes of him, but could not even imagine him doing anything at all.[1] Fermor, with all his faults, had at least had *some* military experience, Saltuikov had had none. In his extreme youth, he had served in the Guards, and Peter the Great had sent him to France for twelve years,[2] to master the science of navigation, which he had quite failed to do. Subsequently he had served under Münnich without distinguishing himself in the least. As a relative of the Empress Anne, he was a *persona ingratissima* at the Court of Elizabeth, and had been allowed to vegetate for years in the distant Ukraine, where he had been occupied mainly in drilling the local militia. His very personal appearance provoked good-natured *badinage.* He was a tiny, grey-headed, rather silly-looking old fellow, whose kindliness and artlessness endeared him to his friends; but he had no brilliant record, no ostensible talents, and was generally regarded as "a regular little old goose."[3] Frederick the Great communicated this new appointment to his brother, Prince Henry, with more than his usual caustic acerbity. "Fermor," he writes contemptuously,[4] "has received by way of appendage one Soltykoff, [*sic*] who is said to be more stupid and imbecile than anything else in the clodhopper line which Russia has yet produced." Yet this "goose," this "clodhopper," was within three weeks to bring about the one overwhelming catastrophe of

[1] Bolotov: *Zapiski.* Compare Solovev: *Istoria Rossy.*
[2] Bantuish–Kamensky: *Biografy russkikh generalissumesov.*
[3] *Sushchaya Kurochka,* Bolotov: *Zapiski.*
[4] June 16, 1759. *Pol. Corr.* Bd. XVIII.

Frederick's career, and reduce the disdainful King of Prussia to the last extremity.

Although thus suddenly pitted against the most redoubtable captain of the age, without having ever commanded an army in his life, Saltuikov seems to have accepted his tremendous responsibilities without the slightest hesitation. Passing through Königsberg, where his simplicity of dress and manners excited some surprise, and even dismay among those who had been accustomed to the solemn dignity of Fermor and the luxurious magnificence of Apraksin, the new Commander-in-Chief reached headquarters at Posen on July 9th.[1] At first the army did not know what to make of the apparition of the little old man in the simple unadorned white kaftan of the Ukraine Militia, but, by his energy and promptitude, Saltuikov very soon inspired his subordinates with respect. Immediately upon his arrival, he held a Council of War, at which it was resolved to march at once towards the Oder, so as to effect a junction with the Austrian auxiliary Corps under Laudon, which was advancing from Silesia ; and accordingly, after reviewing his forces, Saltuikov set off for Krossen on Oder without delay. Now a junction between the Austrian and Russian forces was the very thing which Frederick feared the most, and all his strategy was directed towards preventing it. He had already detached Count Dohna to attack the advancing Russians, but Dohna, failing to carry out his instructions with sufficient promptitude, was somewhat abruptly superseded by General Wedell. Wedell, a comparatively young officer, and eager to justify his master's confidence, only two days after his arrival at headquarters, and, seemingly, without taking proper precautions, attacked the Russians (July 23) as they were marching along the high

---

[1] I here follow, for the most part, Bolotov and Solovev.

road towards Krossen to meet the Austrians, between the villages of Pattsig and Kay, not far from Züllichau. The battle, which was most obstinately contested, lasted from 4 o'clock in the afternoon till 7 o'clock at night, and resulted in a signal Russian victory. The Prussians were compelled to retreat with the loss of 6,000 men, [1] Saltuikov's light cavalry pursuing the routed foe till nightfall. The moral effect of this victory was immense. The army was now full of confidence in its new Commander-in-Chief, who throughout the fight had displayed the utmost sangfroid, joking with his officers, and flipping with his whip at the bullets which whizzed around him.

Saltuikov now felt his way cautiously along in the direction of Frankfort on Oder. The most contradictory rumours met him on his march as to the whereabouts of the King of Prussia, who at one time was reported to have already crossed the Oder and to be only a few miles off, and at another was said to be still watching Marshal Daun opposite Landshut. Daun himself was more than usually cautious, and his persistent inaction while the Russians were advancing and winning victories caused deep dissatisfaction both at Vienna and at St. Petersburg. He even sent a courier to Saltuikov, demanding a reinforcement of 30,000 men, which the Russian general prudently refused. On August 1st, Saltuikov reached Frankfort, and received the keys of the city from General Villebois, who had been sent on before to occupy it. It was here, too, a few days later, that he was joined by the Austrian Auxiliary Corps of 20,000 men, mostly cavalry, under Laudon, who with great skill had evaded the vigilance of Frederick, and brought his contingent safely through Lusatia, without losing a man. The news of Saltuikov's victory

[1] Bolotov: *Zapiski.* Solovev: *Istoria Rossy.*

had been received with some incredulity by the Russian garrisons posted in the occupied provinces, but the authorities at St. Petersburg were delighted with their new general, and praised his conduct warmly. He was instructed, however, to proceed with the utmost caution in future, and the whole tone of the Imperial Rescript addressed to him is pervaded by a salutary fear of the enterprising King of Prussia. Saltuikov, "despite the egotism and insincerity of Austria," [1] is to act in concert with Daun if he draws nearer and the occasion imperatively requires it, so long as he does not unnecessarily expose his own army. If "the affair of Count Daun with the King of Prussia" prove indecisive, Saltuikov is to act so as best to preserve his own army. If the King of Prussia attack Daun, Saltuikov is to act with the utmost circumspection, bearing in mind that Daun is skilful in choosing impregnable positions, and the King of Prussia apt to make sudden assaults. He is to be very cautious even if the King of Prussia stands over against him with quite a small army. In case he crosses the Oder, he is never to be more than a three days' march away from it. Even if he defeat the King of Prussia, he is to recross the Oder immediately after his victory.

And the King of Prussia was to more than justify his reputation for alertness and celerity. For the last two months he had been engaged in warily observing "my sanctified blockhead of a Daun, who won't stir a stump," [2] opposite Landshut, cutting off the Austrian supplies, and awaiting an opportunity to turn him and drive him back into Bohemia, which the proverbially careful Daun never once gave him. The unlucky accident of the Battle of

[1] Solovev: *Istoria Rossy.*
[2] "Ma grosse tête bénite de Daun ne remue ni pied ni patte." To Dohna, June 18, 1759. *Pol. Corr.* Vol. XVIII.

Kay, however, dislocated all his plans, and compelled him to protect Brandenburg and quit the Austrians in order to thrash the Russians.   He accordingly ordered all the troops he could muster to instantly converge on the Oder, and himself hastened to join Wedell.   Although his whole army did not exceed 48,000 men, while the combined Russians and Austrians numbered at least 60,000, he resolved to attack them forthwith.   He was resolved that, this time, the Russians should be not merely defeated, but annihilated, and so certain was he of success, that when a courier brought to him, while on his way to meet Saltuikov, news of Prince Ferdinand of Brunswick's great victory over the French at Minden (Aug. 1) he detained the messenger with the words: "Wait a while, Sir, and we will send you back with another compliment to the Prince of the same sort." [1]   On hearing of the King's approach, Saltuikov took up as strong a defensive position as he could discover among the wooded hills near the village of Kunersdorf, not far from Frankfort on the Oder. [2]   His right wing extended almost to the Oder, [3] his left wing was hard by the village of Kunersdorf, extending to where the wooded heights came to an end, and thence across a small stream flowing in the midst of meadows.   The right wing consisted of the 1st Division under Fermor, and some regiments of the vanguard under Villebois; Rumyantsev was in the centre with the 2nd Division, and on the left wing was placed a newly formed Division under Prince Golitsuin. Laudon's corps was placed behind the Russian right wing, the narrow space preventing it from forming into line.   The light troops under Todtleben were in front of the right wing.

---

[1] Bolotov: *Zapiski.*

[2] Hence the Russians always allude to this battle as the Battle of Frankfort.

[3] Saltuikov's bulletin quoted by Solovev.

The Russian army faced the Oder in the direction whence it was expected the enemy would appear, [1] and its whole front was covered by deep and almost impenetrable marshes crossed by a single bridge. Its rear extended to the town of Frankfort, and was also covered by difficult ground— ravines and gullies. Kunersdorf was now in the centre of the army. Both wings were strongly fortified by entrenchments and batteries mounted by more than one hundred large guns. So advantageous indeed was the position taken up that, although the enemy approached from an altogether different direction to what was anticipated, so as to take the Russians in the rear, as had been done at Zorndorf, Saltuikov saw no reason to alter his dispositions, [2] but placidly awaited the arrival of his Prussian Majesty's forces. It was Frederick's intention to attack the Russians at dawn, and, accordingly, before the short August night was over, his army was already on the march. But the boggy forest roads were so difficult that his progress was unusually slow, and it was past nine o'clock before he came in sight of the Russians, whose position was very much stronger than he had anticipated. It was necessary, first of all, to plant a heavy battery on the hill overlooking the enemy, and it was not till 12 o'clock [3] that, under cover of its fire, the Prussians advanced to the attack. Saltuikov had already burnt down the single bridge across the marshes already mentioned, thereby making his threatened right wing almost unassailable, wherefore the Prussians now concentrated their attack on his left, which was defended with entrenchments mounted with eighty guns. [4]

[1] Bolotov: *Zapiski.*
[2] Bolotov.
[3] Saltuikov's report cited by Solovev. Frederick, writing in the confusion of disaster, says 11 o'clock. *Pol. Corr.*
[4] Bolotov.

But the keen eye of Frederick had here detected the weak spot in the Russian line, which was defended by only two regiments. The Russian position was here covered by a river bed or chasm, [1] and the ground was so difficult all around, that no attack was expected. It was just here that the Prussian Grenadiers broke through, forming into columns as they emerged from the wood, and charging through the river's bed straight upon the enemy's batteries. The two unsupported Russian regiments were wiped out in an instant, and two batteries captured. Still advancing, over most difficult ground, the Prussian Grenadiers tried to force their way clean through the Russian army, so as to cut it in two, supported by a terrible fire from all their batteries. There was not a square yard on the whole plateau where the bombs and bullets did not fall upon the cramped Russian ranks, which were pressed so tightly together that they had not sufficient space wherein to deploy. Step by step, despite the energetic resistance of Rumyantsev and Golitsuin, and the well-directed fire of the Shuvalov howitzers, the Prussians continued to drive the Russians before them, till they were forced *behind* the village of Kunersdorf, which, at the beginning of the battle, had been in their centre. By five o'clock the battle seemed irretrievably lost to the Russian Generals, and even "our little old man," [2] in an agony of despair, dismounted from his horse, fell on his knees, and, forgetting all else, raised his hands to Heaven, and, in the presence of his entire staff, implored the Almighty, with tears in his eyes, to help him in his extremity, and save his people from destruction. "And the prayer, coming from a pure heart and mind," says the pious Bolotov, "must have been heard,

[1] Bolotov.
[2] Bolotov. He means Saltuikov of course.

18

for a very short time afterwards an unexpected and impossible change took place." By six o'clock, the Prussians had captured all the batteries on the Russian left wing, and were in possession of 180 guns, [1] and thousands of prisoners. Frederick had already despatched couriers to Berlin and Silesia, with the tidings of his signal victory. But, as already mentioned, it was not merely the defeat, but the annihilation, of Saltuikov's army that he had resolved upon. The Russians still held stubbornly several strongly fortified positions, notably the Spitzberg and the Jewish Cemetery near Frankfort, where they had turned at bay upon their pursuers, and mauled them terribly. [2] These positions Frederick determined to capture at any cost. In vain his guards implored him to be satisfied with the victory already won, in vain they represented to him that his soldiers, exhausted by a seven hours' combat following hard upon a forced march of nine hours, were scarce able to breathe, or put one foot before another. He was inexorable, and ordered both the Spitzberg and the Jewish Cemetery to be captured at once. But Laudon, with his fresh troops, had already reinforced the Russians both in the Jewish Cemetery and on the Spitzberg, and again and again the valiant but worn-out Prussians were hurled back into the ravines and gullies surrounding these impregnable positions, with terrible loss. General Puttkammer was killed at the head of his white hussars. Prince Eugene of Wurtemberg, Generals Finkenstein and Hilsen were dangerously wounded. Frederick himself had three horses killed under him; his hat and coat were riddled with bullets, and only a little box that he carried in his pocket saved his leg from being smashed by a bullet. At

---

[1] Bolotov.

[2] Le cimetière nous a fait perdre une prodigieuse monde [*sic*]. Fred. to Finkenstein. Aug. 12. *Pol. Corr.* Vol. XVIII.

about 7 o'clock the King ordered Seydlitz to quit his post of observation over against Laudon, and rally his horsemen for a final effort, thus relieving the Austrian general, who at once threw the whole weight of his own hitherto un-engaged cavalry upon the exhausted Prussians. In an instant the whole Prussian army broke in wild confusion. "We were unfortunate," wrote Frederick a week later, "because our infantry grew impatient a quarter of a hour too soon." Impatient! Exhaustion had reached its ex-treme limit and human nature could do no more. All Frederick's endeavours to stay the flight of his panic-stricken warriors were fruitless. He was no longer master of his own men. They scattered in every direction, hotly pursued by the Russian and Austrian light-horse. He him-self was only saved from death or captivity, in the general stampede, by the devotion of Rittmeister Pretwitz and forty hussars. Late the same evening, three thousand repentant fugitives rallied to his standard, all that now remained to him of a host of 48,000 men. Mortal indeed had been the hug of the "Bears of the Holy Roman Empire." [1]

"Your Imperial Majesty must not be surprised at our serious casualties," wrote the triumphant Saltuikov to the Empress on the following day, "for you know that the King of Prussia always sells victory dearly. Another such vic-tory, your Majesty, and I shall be obliged to plod staff in hand myself to St. Petersburg with the joyful news, for want of messengers." [2] When the news of this astounding victory was brought to Elizabeth at Tsarkoe Selo, she at once hastened to the capital, and offered up her thanks-

---

[1] The name given by him to the Russians at the end of the year when he had somewhat recovered from the shock of "this horrible catastrophe," as he elsewhere calls it. The total Prussian loss on the field is generally estimated at 19,000 men, besides 182 guns and 28 standards. As to the Russians and Austrians, Solovev admits a loss of nearly 16,000.

[2] Bolotov.

giving to the Almighty, in the Chapel of the Winter Palace, while joyous salvos rang out from all the guns of
the Citadel and the Admiralty.   The victors were lavishly
rewarded.   Saltuikov received the Marshal's *bâton* from his
own Sovereign, and a diamond ring, a jewelled snuff-box,
and 5,000 ducats from Maria Theresa.   Generals Fermor
and Browne were rewarded with estates in Livonia; Golitsuin was made a full General; Rumyantsev was decorated
with the Order of St. Alexander Nevsky; Laudon was
presented with a sword covered with brilliants.   Michael
Bestuzhev gave a grand banquet at Versailles, in honour
of the victory, at which Choiseul and eighty of the most
distinguished men in France, drank Saltuikov's health in
bumpers of Imperial Tokay.   Nor were these rejoicings at all
exaggerated.   At that moment the ruin of the King of Prussia
seemed imminent and inevitable.   For the first time in
his life Frederick himself absolutely gave way to despair.
"I shall not survive this cruel reverse," he wrote to the
faithful Finkenstein, on the very evening of the battle.
"The consequences of this affair will be worse than the
affair itself.   I am at the end of my resources, and, to
speak the plain truth to you, I believe that everything is
lost.   I will not survive the ruin of my country." [1]   For
the next three days [2] he remained in a sort of stupor,
and left the command of the *débris* of the army to Finkenstein, after giving instructions that Berlin should be
evacuated as indefensible, and the royal family and the
public archives removed to Magdeburg. [3]   But on the
evening of Sept. 1st a glimmer of courage springs up

---

[1] To Finkenstein, *Pol. Corr.*

[2] From the afternoon of the 13th to the evening of the 15th or 16th
Aug.   Then, if at all, he must have taken the poison he is said to have kept
in his ring.   "Eine schwere Krankheit," he himself called his temporary despair
and apathy.   *Pol. Corr.* Bd. XVIII.

[3] Bolotov.

anew in that unconquerable breast. "So long as I can keep my eyes open," he writes to another friend, "I will sustain the State, as in duty bound ... Picture to yourself," he concludes, "all that my soul suffers in this cruel crisis, and you will readily judge that the torments of the damned are as nothing to it." He no longer deludes himself, however, with any hope of ultimate victory. "Our affairs hang, day by day, on a mere hair," he wrote to Finkenstein on Sept. 7th; "the multitude of our enemies is overwhelming us." And again, the same day, to Prince Ferdinand of Brunswick: "My affairs are worse than ever. Except for a miracle or your assistance, I am lost without resource."[1] His own idea now was to come to terms with Russia, and endeavour to separate her from her Allies.[2] He was well aware that the friction between Russia and Austria was increasing daily; he was in hopes that Elizabeth's well-known horror of bloodshed would prove stronger than her personal resentment against himself, and he formally authorized the English Government to use whatever influence it possessed with the Russian Court in his favour. Once released from the pressure of the Moscovite, he hoped to be able to come to terms with his remaining adversaries.

In June, 1759, Frederick had already written to George II, proposing the assembly of a Peace Congress at the Hague, to put an end to the war, a proposition warmly adopted by the English Government.[3] After Kunersdorf, however, more urgent expedients were needed. "Only a miracle can save us," wrote Finkenstein to Kneiphausen,

---

[1] *Pol. Corr.* Vol. XVIII.

[2] Despatch of the English Minister, Mitchell, to the English Government, of Nov. 25, immediately after an interview with Frederick. *Pol. Corr.* Bd. XVIII.

[3] Solovev: *Istoria Rossy.*

the Prussian Minister at London, a few days after the
catastrophe. "Speak to Pitt not merely as a Minister but
as a friend. Represent to that great man the terrible
danger to which the most faithful ally of England is exposed. Possibly he may be able to procure us a peace."
Great Britain took instant action in the matter, and Robert
Keith, the English Minister at St. Petersburg, was instructed
to make pacific overtures to the Russian Chancellor, Vorontsov, and inform him that the Kings of England and
Prussia were ready to renew their former alliances with
Russia. The Empress, he was to say, could legitimately
contract such an alliance independently of her Allies.
Subsequently Keith showed Vorontsov the copy of a declaration which the English and Prussian Kings were
prepared to submit to the plenipotentiaries of Russia, Austria
and France, at the proposed Peace Congress to be held
at the Hague. On Dec 12, the Empress delivered her
reply to these pacific overtures. She said she deeply deplored the effusion of so much innocent blood, but if peace
depended upon amicable assurances only, it was still, in
her opinion, a very long way off. In any case she could
not make peace without the consent of her Allies, and
could listen to no terms which did not amply satisfy the
demands for compensation of the injured parties. She declared, at the same time, that she and her Allies were
equally desirous of peace, but of a peace that was honourable, durable and profitable. Such a peace, she opined,
was impossible if things were allowed to remain on the
same footing as they were before the war. After this it
was plain to the English Ministers, that no more could be
said for the present, and the war must proceed.

Frederick's case would have been desperate indeed if
the operations of the Russian armies had been as vigorous and decided as the language of the Russian Empress.

Fortunately for him and for Prussia, at the precise moment when his political existence hung upon a hair, the long smouldering differences and dissensions between the Russian and Austrian Commanders, burst into an open flame, and their mutual jealousies ruined the military plans of the Allies.

Ten days after the Battle of Kunersdorf, Saltuikov set off for Guben on Neisse, a town some miles south of Frankfort on Oder, where he met the Empress-Queen's Commander-in-Chief, Count Daun. The Austrian Field Marshal was very polite to his Russian colleague at this first interview. The Russians, he said, must now rest upon their well-earned laurels, and allow the Austrians to do the work, whereupon Saltuikov at once professed his willingness to unite his forces to those of Daun, and end the war by promptly crushing the King of Prussia and his brother, Prince Henry, in detail. They separated apparently the best of friends, but there their friendship ended. It seems to have been arranged [1] at the Conference at Guben, that the Russians should remain in the Prussian provinces on the left bank of the Oder, and be well supplied with food by Daun, till he had returned from capturing Dresden, when both armies were to go into winter quarters in Silesia, preparatory to wresting the King of Prussia's last conquests from him in the ensuing year. Daun, however, does not seem to have kept his promise to Saltuikov. Doubtless he found it impossible to support the large Russian army as well as his own, out of the diminished resources of the sadly impoverished province of Lusatia, which had been supporting four armies [2] for many months before. Anyhow, Saltuikov was soon compelled

---

[1] Bolotov: *Zapiski.*

[2] The King of Prussia's, Prince Henry's, Daun's and Fermor's... Finally Daun offered Saltuikov money wherewith to purchase supplies, but Saltuikov tartly replied that his soldiers couldn't eat hard coin, but must have bread.

to wander further afield in search of supplies. Presently
he was alarmed by persistent rumours that Frederick had
rallied his forces, and was approaching to attack him again.
These rumours proved false, but now he received a despatch
from Daun, requesting him to proceed to Lüppen, to prevent
Frederick from entering Saxony, while he, Daun, marched
against Prince Henry. Saltuikov, however, refused to run
the risk of having his army cut off from its supplies at Posen,
and, not content with this, sent back an insolent message
to Daun, to the effect that it was high time for the Austrians to do something now after lying idle the whole summer.
On August 29, Saltuikov received an Ukaz from St. Petersburg, with an elaborate plan of campaign, the chief features of which were that Daun should operate vigorously
against Prince Henry, cutting him off from the King,
shutting him up in Upper Silesia, and capturing the fortresses of Glogau, Liegnitz and Schneidnitz, while Saltuikov
and Laudon were to act against Frederick in Brandenburg,
and keep him there. This done, Saltuikov was to winter
between the Oder and the Bober, with Glogau as his
centre of operations. So far from attempting to carry
out this plan, Saltuikov wasted the ensuing six weeks in
marching aimlessly about between the Neisse, the Oder, and
the Bober, in search of forage, sending, from time to time,
curt sarcastic messages to Daun, demanding supplies and re-
inforcements, which were frequently promised but never sent.
The summer was now at an end, and the prospect of
crushing the King of Prussia that year as remote as
ever. Frederick had cautiously followed upon the heels of
Saltuikov and Laudon, with his little army, wherever they
went, yet never once had they tried seriously to attack
him, although he could only oppose 24,000 to their 48,000. [1]

[1] "We missed repeated opportunities of attacking him at this period when
he was quite incapacitated by gout, which caused him hellish tortures, so

The Cabinet of St. Petersburg, naturally very dissatisfied with its general, at last addressed to him (Oct. 9) an angry rescript, blaming him severely both for his inaction and his discourtesy towards his Austrian Colleagues, and urging him to use every endeavour to fall upon the King of Prussia and beat him. He was, furthermore, ordered not to retire to the Vistula (the favourite asylum of anxious and uncertain Russian Commanders during this war) unless things went badly with Daun, or Laudon had to leave him. An animated correspondence ensued. The victor of Kay and Kunersdorf could not allow himself to be brow-beaten, like an Apraksin or a Fermor, and not only replied with spirit, but even presumed to disobey categorical commands. He boldly asserted that his operations had had the good effect of detaining the King of Prussia in Silesia, and preventing him from sending a single regiment to Prince Henry, who was being hard pressed by Daun in Saxony. He refused point-blank to remain in Silesia a day longer than October 15; after that date he *must* take up his winter quarters on the Vistula. The preservation of his army, he said, was his primary consideration, and if he wintered in Silesia, "the Russian army would have to snatch its forage out of the enemy's hand, and live precariously."[1] It must have been about this time, too, that he addressed to his "sole protector," Ivan Shuvalov, a long rambling tirade against Daun,[2] which is an odd blend of the naïve simplicity natural to him and the megalomania which undoubtedly took possession of him shortly after the Battle of Kunersdorf and completely changed his character, developing ultimately, as we shall see, into downright hysteria.

---

that he could not sit on horseback. Never had he feared us so much as he did then." Bolotov: *Zapiski.*

[1] *Saltuikov's Despatches* cited by Solovev.

[2] *Iz bumag I. I. Shuvalova.* It takes up 280 lines in the original Russian.

"I had flattered myself," concludes the old ex-militia-man, "that, after this campaign, I should have been esteemed fortunate, and now I see that I have nothing to look for but dishonour. I deserve gracious approbation, not reproaches. I am plunged into confusion and know not what to be at! 'Tis a hard thing for an honourable man to enjoy the favour of his Sovereign in important matters, and to be overwhelmed with rebukes and reproaches for mere trifles. My only sin is my zeal for her Majesty's interests, and especially her army."—It now became clear that Saltuikov either could or would not do anything more in the course of this campaign. Rescript after rescript was sent, forbidding him to indulge in sarcastic comments on his Austrian Colleagues, and urging him to attack the King of Prussia— all with little or no result. Thus the rescript of Oct. 18, counsels oblivion of past differences, and abstention from dry and irritating refusals of co-operation. His offensive expressions, he is told, are very far from representing the tenderness of the Empress's sentiments towards her Allies. The rescript of Oct. 24, again insists upon the adoption of a bolder and more enterprising strategy. "As the King of Prussia has already attacked us four times," wrote Vorontsov, "the honour of our arms demands that *we* should attack *him* at least *once*, as it is always more honourable and advantageous to attack than to defend, especially when our army is much larger than the army of the King of Prussia... Attack him but once, and he will keep away from you, and you will be able to say that you *wished* to adopt more energetic measures, but the enemy would not give you the chance." [1] Nevertheless Saltuikov had his own way. At the beginning of November he deliberately marched back to his magazines at Posen, and

---

[1] Solovev: *Istoria Rossy.*

when Laudon asked him what he was to do with his
auxiliary corps, the Russian Commander-in-Chief curtly
replied: "What you like," [1] whereupon Laudon had nothing
for it but to return to Daun.

It must be admitted that the Empress and her Ministers
dealt very leniently with a Commander-in-Chief who persistently refused to obey the most explicit instructions. No
doubt they felt that much might be forgiven the victor of
Kay and Kunersdorf, but there were also diplomatic reasons for their forbearance. The relations between the
Courts of Vienna and St. Petersburg had become somewhat strained during the autumn. If the Russian Empress
was disappointed with the strategy of her own generals,
she was by no means satisfied with the strategy of the
generals of her Imperial sister. If Saltuikov had been over
cautious, Daun had certainly not been too impetuous. Nay,
it is evident, that Elizabeth and Vorontsov thought, with
Saltuikov, that the Austrian Government was "up to its
old game of ascribing its ill-luck to the blunders of its
allies," and was trying "to put out the fire with other peoples
fingers." [2] On the whole, then, they took the part of their
Generalissimo, who, after all, had two signal victories to his
credit, while Daun had done nothing, and a lively correspondence ensued between the two Courts, full of ac-
rimonious recrimination. When Esterhazy complained to
Vorontsov of the inactivity of the Russian army, and the
impossibility of getting any definite answer from Saltuikov, who
kept even the Austrian Chancellor, Kaunitz, waiting a whole
month for a reply to his letters, Vorontsov, while excusing
Saltuikov's remissness, retorted that the proposals made to
Saltuikov by the Austrian generals, were "enough to upset
the patience of the most phlegmatic of philosophers."

[1] Bolotov: *Zapiski.*
[2] Saltuikov to Ivan Shuvalov. *Iz bumag I. I. Shuvalova.*

When, late in the autumn, the Austrian Government proposed that the Russian troops should undertake a winter
campaign in Silesia, or that, at least, an auxiliary corps of
30,000 men should be sent to Maria Theresa's hereditary
domains, both demands were summarily rejected as impossible. When Esterhazy had the impudence to insinuate
that Saltuikov had been acting under secret orders from
his own Government, at the instigation of Great Britain,
the Russian Government took no pains to conceal its honest
indignation. Elizabeth, in reply, described such an insinu-
ation as " offensive to us, and unworthy of the Empress-
Queen." " We have never," she pursued, " given the
slightest occasion for a reproach of double-dealing; we have
never promised anything that we have not striven to perform in very deed; and if, through any selfish designs of
our Allies, we should be obliged to depart from our present
system, we should openly say as much to our Allies, and
withdraw our armies; but never would we allow the glory
won by the precious blood of our subjects, to be obscured
by any suspicion of bad faith." [1]

As a matter of fact, the " offensive " language of Austrian diplomatists was due to their nervous apprehensions
lest Russia should be induced by England to accede to the
proposed Peace Congress of the Hague. When all doubts
were removed on this head by the spirited remonstrance
of Elizabeth, the Court of Vienna at once became penitent,
and even apologetic. Maria Theresa instructed Esterhazy
to assure her " dear sister," the Russian Empress, that she
placed all her hopes in the Tsaritsa's unshakable constancy.
She protested, moreover, that she would never consent to
make peace till Russia had received ample satisfaction for
all her exertions. It might be advisable, however, she added,

[1] Solovev: *Istoria Rossy.*

to consent to the meeting of a Peace Congress, in order to delay matters, and sow dissensions between Great Britain and the King of Prussia, with a view of isolating the common enemy.

The relations between Russia and the other principal member of the league, France, naturally became more and more amicable as Russia proved herself to be more and more indispensable to the common cause. The Duc de Choiseul even went so far as to reproach the Austrian Ambassador, Count Stahrenberg, in Michael Bestuzhev's presence, for the conduct of his Court in sparing its own army, in order to exploit the Russians, whose valour he exalted to the skies. On the other hand, Choiseul blamed Vorontsov for sparing the territories of the King of Prussia, instead of utterly impoverishing them, as Frederick himself was wont to treat any country occupied or traversed by him. "At this rate," concluded Choiseul, "the King of Prussia can go on warring for ever." Vorontsov, in reply, read his French Colleague a lesson in humanity, which does him honour. The inhabitants of the occupied Prussian provinces, he said, were quite unable to pay the contributions levied on them, and even if they were able, concluded the Russian Chancellor, "it is not for us to imitate, in this respect, the bad example of his Prussian Majesty."

CHAPTER XII.

THE LAST YEARS OF ELIZABETH.

1760—Jan. 5th, 1762.

ELIZABETH her own Minister of Foreign Affairs—Frederick to be crushed—
His despair—Attempts to bribe the Shuvalovs—The Austro-Russian
Conventions of May, 1760—Futile diplomacy of France—England's
apprehension of Russia's territorial aggrandizement—Saltuikov's plan
rejected—Campaign of 1760—Austrian successes—Saltuikov superseded by Buturlin—Occupation of Berlin—Battle of Torgau—General
desire for peace—Resolute attitude of Elizabeth—She rejects all
pacific overtures—Her direct and secret negotiation with Louis XV—
The question of a Peace Congress—Pitt and Golitsuin—Frederick's
projects—Campaign of 1761—The new Russian Commander-in-Chief,
A. B. Buturlin—His utter incompetency—Operations in Silesia—
Scathing rescripts of the Empress to Buturlin—Laudon and Chernuishev capture Schweidnitz—Siege and capture of Kolberg by
Rumyantsev—Frederick abandons all hope—The last illness and
death of Elizabeth—Reflections.

IT is not too much to say that, from the end of 1759 to
the end of 1761, the unshakable firmness of the Russian
Empress was the one constraining political force which held
together the heterogeneous, incessantly jarring elements of
the anti-Prussian combination, and prevented it from collapsing before the shock of disaster. This is a fact which
has hitherto escaped the attention of historians, and yet is
absolutely, demonstratively true. From the Russian point
of view, Elizabeth's greatness as a statesman consists in her

ELIZABETH PETROVNA.

Ætat. 53.

steady appreciation of Russian interests, and her determination to promote and consolidate them at all hazards.
It may also be maintained, without fear of contradiction,
that, after the removal of Bestuzhev, she was *obliged* to
become, to a great extent, her own Minister of Foreign
Affairs. It is impossible to imagine the timid Vorontsov,
and his equally pusillanimous coadjutor, Ivan Shuvalov,
(both of them already weary of the war,) inditing the
vigorous and stimulating ukazes and rescripts, which, during
1760 and 1761, were so persistently addressed to backsliding
Russian generals and bewildered Russian diplomatists.
Vorontsov and Shuvalov were but the instruments of the
overruling will of their Imperial Mistress, their facile pens
gave eloquent expression to her sentiments; but their hearts
were no longer in their work, and they obeyed the Empress's
instructions reluctantly and mechanically.

Elizabeth insisted throughout that the King of Prussia
must be rendered harmless to his neighbours for the future.
The only way to bring this about was to curtail his dominions and reduce him to the rank of a Kürfürst. The
bulk of his territories must necessarily be partitioned among
his adversaries, and Russia's share was to be the province
already in her possession, Ducal Prussia, certainly a very
moderate compensation for her enormous sacrifices and her
preponderating services. We smile now, perhaps, at the bare
idea that the destruction of the vigorous young Prussian Monarchy could ever have been even a contingent possibility. We
have been fascinated by the glamour of Macaulay's rhetoric,[1]
we have been overpowered by the boisterousness of Carlyle's

---

[1] "Europe in arms was unable to tear Silesia from his iron grasp." As
a matter of fact, Frederick held but a part, and a small part, of that Province
at the end of 1761, and, to hold it at all, he had been practically obliged
to abandon the rest of his domains. Not his own doggedness, splendid as
it was, but the death of Elizabeth alone saved him from utter destruction.

hero-worship. The fact remains that from the Battle of Kunersdorf to the death of Elizabeth, Frederick's position was absolutely hopeless, and he himself frankly recognised that it was so. "I am at the end of my resources," he writes at the beginning of 1760, "the continuance of the war means for me utter ruin..."[1] Things may drag on, perhaps, till July, but then a catastrophe *must* come..."[2] I tremble as I look forward to the opening of the campaign.[3] I have already wrought miracles, but the worst of modern miracles is that they have to be done all over again."[4] Nevertheless, he was quite resolved never to consent to a dishonourable peace, that is to say a peace involving cession of territory, however insignificant. His sole ambition now, he said, was to perish on a field of battle. Yet, first of all, he made one last attempt to bribe the Russian Court to, at least, keep its forces "inactive" during the coming campaign. The dignitary he proposed to approach on this occasion was Count Peter Shuvalov, and his secret intermediary was Robert Keith, the English Ambassador at St. Petersburg, in whose hands he placed 400,000 écus.[5] But the attempt failed utterly, as might have been anticipated. Shuvalov was far from being "the only man in Russia who has any power at all," as Frederick imagined. Besides, if Count Peter's greed was great, his prudence was still greater, and so he declined the dangerous gift. An attempt, at the end of the same year, to corrupt young Ivan Shuvalov with a gift of 1,000,000 rixdollars, to be conveyed to him through his uncle Peter's German physician, Bodenhaupt, for the same consideration, also

---

[1] *Pol. Corr.* Jan. 1, 1760.
[2] To Fink., Jan. 10.
[3] March 19.
[4] May 7.
[5] To Kneiphausen, Feb. 16, 1760. *Pol. Corr.*

led to nothing. [1] Frederick might, indeed, have saved himself the trouble in both cases. But disbelief in the higher motives of humanity was one of the radical defects of this acute but somewhat oblique observer of his species, and he never seems to have been able to realize that his enemies might be at least as patriotic as himself. [2] Thus the King of Prussia was reduced to the fatal necessity of depending entirely on the faults and blunders of his enemies in the ensuing campaign, and maintaining, with demoralized or inferior troops, a defensive warfare which the Allies were preparing to make as difficult for him as possible.

And now it was that the spirit of the Russian Empress stimulated the confederate courts to a fresh, and, as it was hoped, a final effort to crush "the disturber of the peace of Europe." When the Austrian Ambassador, Prince Esterhazy, on Jan. 1, 1760, presented his New Year congratulations to the Tsaritsa, and expressed the hope that her Majesty would make still further sacrifices for the common cause, Elizabeth replied · "I am always a long time making up my mind, but when once I have decided what ought to be done, I stick to my opinion. I mean to continue this war in conjunction with my Allies, even if I am compelled to sell all my diamonds and half my clothes." [3] But if Elizabeth was quite willing to make heavy sacrifices for the common cause, she was equally determined that the just claims of Russia should be no longer ignored. Now, hitherto, while both France and Austria had been ready enough to use to the uttermost the military resources of Russia, for their own purposes, they had been singularly reticent as to the prospective reward of their loyal and zealous ally. Although, as early as 1757, the Court of

[1] Dec. 16, 1760.
[2] Hence his complete misunderstanding of Bestuzhev's character, for instance.
[3] Solovev: *Istoria Rossy.*

St. Petersburg had pressed the Court of Vienna for a definite settlement of the indemnification to be allowed to Russia out of the common spoil, Maria Theresa and her Ministers, up to the beginning of 1760, had continued to evade the question. But now the time had come when Russia would not be put off any longer with vague promises, and accordingly, when Esterhazy, at the beginning of 1760, proposed that the two Imperial Courts should prepare a joint plan of campaign for the ensuing year, Vorontsov informed him that his wishes should be complied with, provided that Russia was formally guaranteed the future possession of Ducal or East Prussia, which had been conquered by her arms, and was actually in her power. On March 1, 1760, a pro-memoria was remitted from Vienna to Esterhazy at St. Petersburg, to which was annexed the draft of a new treaty of alliance, and Esterhazy took this opportunity of informing the Russian Chancellor that the Austrian Court was willing to sign a declaration solemnly engaging to completely satisfy the claims of Russia at the conclusion of a general peace. But with this "solemn declaration" the Court of St. Petersburg was not content. The Empress insisted upon a formal engagement to the effect that Ducal Prussia should be annexed to Russia, at the same time that the Empress-Queen recovered possession of Silesia. The Court of Vienna was much perturbed. Maria Theresa was well aware that France would never consent to the aggrandizement of Russia, and yet she herself could not afford, at this crisis, to alienate that Power. What was to be done? Even the Austrian Chancellor, Kaunitz, who admitted that the interests of Russia and Austria were identical, did not deem it possible to concur, by any formal act, in the annexation of Ducal Prussia to Russia. But Elizabeth would accept nothing less than a formal guarantee, and Vorontsov persuaded Esterhazy, on April 1, to sign a new treaty of alliance in place of the Convention of 1746, and a special Convention providing for the continuance of the war with Prussia. By Article V of this special Convention, Silesia and Glatz were to be restituted to Austria, and Ducal Prussia was to be annexed to Russia. Esterhazy was moved to take this most important step, not so much by the arguments of Vorontsov, as by his own intimate persuasion that Austria had absolute need of the succour of the Russian troops. The tidings of the signature of these Conventions very much disconcerted the Court of Vienna, for Esterhazy had received no instructions to conclude any such engagements, and had clearly exceeded his powers in so doing. Esterhazy, therefore, was severely rebuked for his presumption,[1] and copies of the Conventions were submitted to the French Court, Austria, by the Treaties of Versailles, not being at liberty to contract any alliances without the consent of France. Louis XV categorically refused to accept the Austro-Russian Conventions in their existing form, and, finally, Maria Theresa was reduced to the humiliating expedient of striking out the article relating to the cession of East Prussia to Russia, and substituting therefor a general clause to the effect that *some* indemnity should be ultimately conceded to Russia. At the same time, however, a secret clause, *never communicated to the Court of Versailles,* specifying East Prussia as the indemnity so to be conceded, was added to the amended Conventions, which, together with the secret clause, were ratified by the Empress-Queen on May 21, 1760.[2]

The real sentiments of the Court of France towards Russia, at this period, are most plainly discernible in the instruc-

---

[1] He was superseded in 1761 by Mercy d'Argenteau.

[2] The annexation of East Prussia to Russia, was, however, made contingent upon the recovery of Silesia and Glatz by Austria. Compare Martens: *Recueil des traités, etc.;* Solovev: *Istoria Rossy.*

tions given to the new French Envoy to St. Petersburg, Louis Auguste Le Tonnelier, Baron de Breteuil, who superseded L'Hôpital in the beginning of 1760. The incompetence of the latter had now become glaringly patent, and Louis XV considered him "bien cher." The new Ambassador was a dashing young cavalry officer of seven-and-twenty, of elegant manners and some political experience, but more reliance seems have been placed upon his handsome face [1] than upon his diplomatic dexterity. It was impressed upon him that it would be highly dangerous to allow Russia too great an increase of territory, especially as Poland might suffer thereby, indeed the problematical advantage of maintaining intact the anarchical independence of the headless Polish Republic, and assuring to France a preponderating influence in that helpless and hopeless realm, seems to have completely blinded Louis XV to the far more urgent necessity of stifling in its germ the menacing greatness of Prussia. Never in the history of the monarchy had French diplomacy been so futile, so vacillating, and so perverse. It has well been said that the policy of Louis XV aimed at nothing higher than throwing obstacles in the way of his own allies, and that he was content to let Prussia escape certain ruin, rather than see her perish by the hands of Russia. [2]

The British Ministers were as apprehensive as the Ministers of France, lest Russia should claim any territorial compensation from Frederick II, for, in view of the unyielding disposition of the King of Prussia, such a claim meant the interminability of the war, or, which was even

---

[1] He was to obtain the recall of Poniatowski to St. Petersburg, to gratify the Grand Duchess, or take Poniatowski's place, if his recall were impossible. Elizabeth very promptly put a stop to all such intrigues. Vondel: *Louis XV et Elisabeth;* Solovev: *Istoria Rossy.*

[2] Vondel.

worse, and far more probable, the speedy and complete
collapse of the Prussian Monarchy. Pitt asked Golitsuin
point-blank whether Russia intended to keep her conquests.
"I always thought," said he, "that the magnanimous purpose of assisting the King of Poland was the sole reason
why your Sovereign embarked in this war." Golitsuin replied that the intentions of the Empress were unknown to
him, but that all dispassionate people "must recognise her
right to compensation." [1] Golitsuin reported to Elizabeth
that the British Court and people, and Pitt himself, were
all convinced of the justice of Russia's claims, but when
Ivan Shuvalov, at St. Petersburg, sounded Keith as to the
opinion of the English Court concerning the retention of East
Prussia by Russia, Keith at once replied that, if Russia
had resolved to keep her conquests, the war would not be so
soon over as some people imagined, as the King of Prussia
was determined to bury himself beneath the ruins of his
last town, rather than consent to such humiliating conditions
of peace. "I cannot understand," replied Shuvalov, "why
the annexation of such a small district should have such
a prodigious effect."

Frederick himself tells us, in his own *Mémoires*, [2] that
in 1760 the Russians had only to step forward in order
to give him the *coup-de-grâce*. Elizabeth was equally well
aware of this, and the New Year was not three days old
when she summoned Saltuikov to the Capital, to draw up
a plan of campaign. The plan he finally submitted was
simplicity itself, and may best be described as an ingenious
method of avoiding a general engagement at all hazards,
and keeping out of harm's way as much as possible. "In
this way," Saltuikov triumphantly argued, "the glory of
her Majesty's arms will not be tarnished, and the army

[1] *Despatches of Golitsuin,* cited by Solovev.
[2] II. Ch. 10.

will be preserved intact." The Empress and her Ministers thought differently. The old man's plan was summarily rejected, but, at the same time, his vanity was soothed by the assurance that it was plain he regarded the situation simply from the point of view of "a skilful general," without having regard to paramount political considerations. Russia's obligations to her Allies, he was furthermore informed, demanded a more aggressive, adventurous strategy, and, after the experience of Kunersdorf, there was no longer any reason to be afraid of "hazarding our army in an engagement with the King of Prussia, however desperate and bloody."—"Our Allies," concluded the imperial rescript, "show signs of weariness and exhaustion; only the hope of terminating the war in another campaign has inspired the Empress-Queen to rally her last resources." Elizabeth's plan was that Saltuikov should proceed at once to Silesia, to coöperate there with Laudon, who, at her particular request, had been appointed to an independent command on the Oder, and was there holding Prince Henry of Prussia in check, while Marshal Daun, with another Austrian army, stood face to face with Frederick in Saxony. Moreover, before quitting Posen for Silesia, Saltuikov was to detach 15,000 men to besiege for the second time the maritime fortress of Kolberg on the Persante, as a first step towards conquering Pomerania. Saltuikov set out for the army early in the Spring, and nothing beyond captious criticisms, dolorous complaints of want of cash and want of forage,[1] and obscure and perplexing accounts of insignificant skirmishes with the enemy's cavalry, was heard of or from him for the next three months. And while the Russian Commander-

---

[1] *E.g.*, "How the game will end, I know not. We are roaming about pretty widely, and have no place of refuge. God grant that we alone shall not be made to pay the piper." Saltuikov to I. Shuvalov. *Iz bumag I. I. Shuvalova. Sb. of Imp. Hist. Soc.* Vol. IX.

in-Chief was thus idly making his moan, news reached St. Petersburg of brilliant Austrian victories in Silesia. On June 23, Laudon attacked and annihilated the army corps of the Prussian general, Fouqué, at Landeshut, and captured the fortress of Glatz. Laudon had received instructions to suspend further operations [1] till the Russians had reached the Silesian frontier, but, elated by his first success, and seeing no sign of the Russians, he attempted to take the still more important fortress of Breslau, but was repulsed with serious loss. In the middle of July, two sharp rescripts spurred Saltuikov on his way to Silesia at last, but the mere intelligence of Frederick's victory over Laudon at Liegnitz (Aug, 15) at once drove the nervous Russian Commander-in-Chief back into Polish territory. In excuse he wrote that he was ill, and did not want to expose his whole army to the danger of a defeat. Simultaneous reports from General Chernuishev informed the Empress that the whole army was in an anarchical condition, and the Commander-in-Chief could do nothing but go about wringing his hands and shedding tears. It was now evident that Saltuikov's mind had become unhinged by his responsibilities, and he was suffering from acute melancholia. He was accordingly superseded (in the beginning of September) by the senior officer in the service, Field Marshal Alexander Borisovich Buturlin, who, however, only arrived on the scene in time to lead the army back behind the Vistula. The closing incidents of this abortive campaign were the occupation of Berlin [2] (Oct. 9-12) by Chernuishev and Todtleben, which caused great rejoicings at St. Petersburg (although, as Solovev well observes, it was

---

[1] Bolotov: *Zapiski.*

[2] On this occasion the Russian Commanders honourably distinguished themselves by preventing their Austrian and Saxon colleagues from pillaging and burning the city.

a financial rather than a military operation, the heavy contributions levied on the Prussian Capital helping to fill the depleted Russian Treasury), and the second siege of Kolberg which proved an expensive failure. On the other hand, Frederick the Great succeeded in wresting almost the whole of Saxony, except the capital, from the hands of Marshal Daun, by the victory of Torgau, Nov. 3.

If France and Austria had only with the utmost difficulty been persuaded to continue the war at the end of 1759, it may be imagined with what feelings they faced the prospect of yet another campaign at the end of 1760! Even in Russia itself there was now a very general desire for peace. The customary New Year illuminations in front of the Winter Palace at St. Petersburg gave eloquent expression to this desire. The principal transparency represented a winged genius (the New Year) with a gift in his hand, to wit, a laurel wreath intertwined with an olive branch, standing upon captured standards, cannons and other military trophies, with the keys of Berlin in front of him. The contemporary Russian Gazettes also emphasized the rumour that " Our most gracious Sovereign has expressly stated that the only object of the glorious triumphs of her arms is the restoration and the maintenance of peace." But peace was only obtainable by fresh exertions; fresh exertions desiderated plenty of money, and where was the money to come from? The new Commander-in-Chief had demanded 2,031,000 rubles for putting the army on a war footing and only 1,465,000 of that amount was available. Even by such desperate expedients as employing Cossacks instead of hussars, filling up the infantry ranks with conscripts from the conquered provinces, paying the last penny of the million thalers levied upon Berlin into the army chest, and feeding the army by mercilessly levying contributions upon the enemy's territory was the vigorous prosecution of the war conceivable.

And there was yet another difficulty. The Allies of Russia were fast approaching the limits of their endurance and were becoming clamorous for peace.

On the evening of Jan. 22, 1761, Breteuil, the French Ambassador at St. Petersburg, presented to the Russian Chancellor a despatch from Choiseul to the effect that the King of France, by reason of the condition of his dominions, absolutely desired peace. He added that it was notorious that the King of Prussia was so exhausted that if England had not helped him with subsidies, he would have been constrained to come to terms long ago. Nevertheless, despite the aid of England, he was now at the end of his resources and therefore would doubtless listen to any reasonable propositions. "Would her Imperial Majesty therefore consent to sacrifice her particular interests to the common cause?" On the following day, Esterhazy, acting in concert with his French colleague, likewise presented to Vorontsov a rescript from Maria Theresa, declaring that peace was indispensable, and if obtainable in the course of the winter the Empress-Queen would be content with a portion only of Silesia. The Russian Empress's reply was delivered to the two Ambassadors on Feb. 12. It was inspired by the most uncompromising hostility towards the King of Prussia. Elizabeth would not consent to any pacific overtures until the original object of the league had been accomplished. If, she argued, the King of Prussia is able in the midst of the most savage and exacting of wars to fill up the gaps in his regiments and make head against his enemies, a couple of years of peace would enable him, with his present resources undiminished, terribly to avenge himself on all his enemies in the Reich. If he loses little or nothing on the conclusion of peace he will be haughtier and more mischievous than ever. Russia indeed, had nothing to fear from his vengeance. Her territories were so vast that she might be harassed and annoyed, but could never be endangered by her neighbours. Very different was the situation of the Empress-Queen. She could always be attacked in the very heart of her hereditary domains from more quarters than one. The essential and permanent crippling of the King of Prussia should therefore be regarded as the sole basis of peace. Even if Austria could not obtain all that she had a right to, she should at least retain possession of her actual conquests in Silesia. The King of Poland should also be compensated for the inhuman devastation of his lands, by the principality of Magdeburg and all the Prussian possessions in Lusatia. Sweden's Pomeranian frontier should also be "advantageously rectified", likewise at the expense of the King of Prussia. Russia demanded no more for herself than the Province of East Prussia, or, in default thereof, adequate compensation elsewhere from her "loyal allies." This reply was duly delivered to Esterhazy by the Russian Foreign Office, accompanied by a letter from Elizabeth to Maria Theresa, rebuking the Court of Vienna for its want of candour in negotiating with France behind the back of Russia, and threatening, in case of a repetition of such violation of treaties, to treat with the King of Prussia directly and independently. [1]

Whilst this correspondence was still proceeding, Elizabeth had caused to be privately conveyed to Louis XV through Vorontsov and Tercier, a French Secretary of State at Paris, a confidential letter [2] in which she proposed the signature of a new treaty of alliance of a more comprehensive and explicit nature than the preceding treaties between the two Powers, without any intermediary and without the knowledge of Austria. Elizabeth's object in this mysterious

---

[1] This letter was, at the earnest solicitation of Esterhazy, exchanged for another, similar in purport, but milder in tone.

[2] Vondel: *Louis XV et Elisabeth.*

negotiation seems to have been to reconcile France and Great Britain, in return for which signal service France was to throw all her forces into the German War and energetically cooperate with Russia in Poland and elsewhere. This project, which certainly lacked neither ability nor audacity, foundered upon Louis XV's invincible jealousy of the growth of Russian influence in Eastern Europe and his fear of offending the Porte. So far, indeed, from falling in with the Empress's views, he addressed a haughty letter to Breteuil, explicitly forbidding him to enter into any explanations with the Russian Ministers as to the policy of France in Poland.

We have seen that Elizabeth categorically refused to entertain any project for a general pacification injurious to the interests of Russia or her Allies, but she was not averse to a peace congress sitting while the war still went on, and the Congress Question occupied the diplomatists of Europe during the greater part of 1761. France and Austria were in favour of a double congress sitting at Paris and London simultaneously, the Paris Congress to compose continental differences, and the London Congress to put an end to the maritime war between Great Britain and France. It was proposed by Breteuil that Prince Golitsuin, the Russian Ambassador at London, should take the initiative in the matter by "using any means whatsoever" to induce Great Britain to open direct negotiations with Russia. An alternative proposition of the French Court was the holding of a Congress at Augsburg, or any other German town more agreeable to England and Russia, accompanied by a suspension of hostilities as long as the Congress was sitting. Elizabeth, however, strongly opposed anything resembling a truce as being likely to be extremely useful to the King of Prussia, and on this point Maria Theresa concurred with her. Nevertheless, on April 22, Breteuil returned to the charge, and demanded of Vorontsov that P. G. Chernuishev, the new [1] Russian Ambassador at Paris, should be authorised to consent to a truce if proposed by England and Prussia, but Vorontsov rejected the proposition as inopportune. Then, at last, France yielded, and in her pacific declaration forwarded to London in the course of the spring, no mention was made of a truce. It was now arranged between the Allies, that their envoys at Paris should fix a date, between July 1 and July 15, for the assembling of a Congress, and that in the meantime the war should be vigorously prosecuted. This was entirely due to the uncompromising attitude of Russia, who was now assuming the lead of continental affairs, not only in war, but in diplomacy also. A fresh Russian note in the beginning of May laid it down as an imperative necessity that France should leave America and the Indies alone for a time, and concentrate all her attention upon the Continent. Every effort was at the same time to be made to detach Great Britain from the Prussian alliance; the settlement of the King of Prussia's affairs was to be left entirely to Austria and Russia, and Golitsuin at London was to be entrusted with the conduct of the negotiations between the two Empresses and the court of St. James's. In the course of the summer Golitsuin had several interviews "with the famous Pitt", who told him that sincerely as Great Britain desired peace, she nevertheless could not desert the King of Prussia. "He tried in his usual way," writes Golitsuin, [2] "to prove to me by ingenious and eloquent representations, that England's interests were inseparable from those of Prussia. I said that the King of Prussia as soon as he had recovered from his losses would again be the first to disturb the peace of Europe—would England guarantee Europe against the consequences of such a disturbance?" [3] Pitt affected to see in the preponderance

---

[1] Michael Bestuzhev had died at Paris in February 1761.
[2] *Despatches of A. M. Golitsuin*, cited by Solovev.   [3] Ib.

of Russia the best guarantee for the peace of the future. 'Your Empress,' said he, 'having no longer any occasion to fear that monarch, has no motive, surely, for partitioning his domains?' Pitt further observed that France was already so exhausted that Great Britain was in a position to exact the most advantageous terms from her whenever she chose, and he denied the right of those Powers which had neither fleets nor colonies to intervene as mediators in the purely maritime, colonial war between Great Britain and France. 'France,' concluded the great commoner, 'must not flatter herself that Hanover will serve as a road for her to America and India.'" On July 31, Golitsuin further reported that Bute [1] and Newcastle had told him that the Prussian Minister at London had been instructed to inform them that his master would never surrender an inch of territory. [2] "The obstinacy of this monarch," exclaims Golitsuin, "somewhat disquiets the present Ministry, which is convinced that peace will be difficult if concessions be not made to the injured parties. The *result of the present campaign* will determine the attitude of the Anglo-Prussian courts towards the German War."

Golitsuin was right, the equally uncompromising attitudes of Prussia and Russia rendered another campaign inevitable, a durable peace could only be arrived at through the decisive arbitrament of battle. Despite the enormous odds against him, three to one at the lowest estimate, Frederick had braced up his drooping energies for a final struggle. His tone at the beginning of 1761 was a trifle less gloomy than it had been at the end of 1760, but the hopelessness of

---

[1] He was instructed to deal with Bute rather than with Pitt, as the former was less prejudiced in favour of the King of Prussia.

[2] According to Bolotov, however, Frederick was ready to exchange East Prussia and Westphalia, outlying provinces, for Saxony, which would make his territory more compact.

his position is best gauged by the desperate expedients to
which he now clung as a drowning man clings to straws.
During the previous year he had confidently relied upon
the intervention of the Porte, this year he hugged himself
with the still more chimerical notion of an alliance with the
Tartar Khan.   Rexin, his envoy at Constantinople, was
intrusted first of all with these fantastic negotiations, [1] but
secret emissaries, principally renegade Poles and Moldavians,
seem to have been moving to and fro all the summer
between Warsaw and the Ukraine, with the view of obtaining
from the Khan some thousands of savage horsemen, who,
under the direction of Prussian hussars, were to systematically
ravage Austria's hereditary states. [2]   He had also succeeded
in bribing Todtleben, one of the ablest cavalry-officers in
the Russian army, to supply him with secret information
of the movements of the Russian troops, and well-paid
Jewish spies also kept him informed of what was going on
in the Russian camp.   As, however, despite all his efforts,
he could only oppose 96,000 to 230,000, he was driven to
act strictly on the defensive.   He proposed with the pick of
his army to closely observe Laudon in Silesia and, if possible,
prevent his junction with the Russians, leaving his brother,
Prince Henry, to oppose Daun in Saxony, and Prince Ferdinand
of Brunswick to operate against the French in Westphalia.
The plan of the Allies was for the Russians to unite with
the Austrians and drive Frederick out of Silesia, while Daun
kept Prince Henry busy in Saxony, and Rumyantsev proceeded to Pomerania to besiege Kolberg for the third time.
The new Russian commander-in-chief, Alexander Borisovich

---

[1] We know from the despatches of Obryezkov, the Russian Minister at
the Porte, that the Turks never had the slightest intention of aiding the King
of Prussia.

[2] *Pol. Corr.* June 23, Oct. 3 and Dec. 17, 1761.   Frederick was ready to
pay as much as 300,000 crowns for this barbarous accommodation.

Buturlin was one of the last surviving 'fledglings' of Peter the Great, and had seen more service than any other officer in the army. He had accompanied Peter through his Swedish and Persian campaigns, served against the tribes of the Caucasus in 1735, and subsequently fought under Münnich in the Turkish War of 1737—1740. He had been a brave soldier in his day, but his abilities in his best days had been of a very mediocre order, and he was now a crapulous septuagenarian whose stupidity was as notorious as his debauchery.[1] He enjoyed, however, the personal friendship of the Empress,[2] and as an old and faithful servant of her beloved father she esteemed him far more highly than he deserved. His instructions were to join Laudon in Silesia without a moment's delay, and it was impressed upon him that if the campaign were not prosecuted with the utmost vigour the consequences would be disastrous. The Court of St. Petersburg awaited with the utmost impatience tidings of the junction of Buturlin with Laudon and the consequent defeat of the King of Prussia, preliminary to the assembling of the projected peace-congress at Augsburg; but week after week passed by and still there was no intelligence of anything important. Not till July 11th did Buturlin quit his magazines at Posen,[3] and so leisurely did he proceed on his way to Silesia, that he did not reach Breslau till August 11. His grenadiers captured the heights surrounding the fortress, his light horse penetrated into the suburbs up to the very gates; but although the garrison was comparatively insignificant and the King of Prussia still far away, not a single member of the Council

---

[1] According to Bolotov he was either drunk or sleeping off his drunken debauches the whole time, and could not pass a tavern without going into it with his grenadier boon-companions.

[2] He had been one of her lovers 30 years before.

[3] *Bolotov.*

of War held by Buturlin to consider the advisability of an
assault upon the fortress itself, "had the manliness to look
the alleged difficulties fairly in the face." [1] "If the place
could have been taken by assault," wrote the indignant
Empress, "firmness and courage, not Councils of War, were
necessary. When our ministers have to be firm in order
to keep our Allies firm, they are placed in a pitiable position
if the progress of our arms does not correspond with their
professions. If something of importance does not happen
during this campaign it will be difficult to find the money
for another. The attitude of Denmark [2] also depends on
the issue of this campaign." — Stimulated by these
sarcasms, Buturlin on Aug. 14, crossed the Oder and
captured the fortress of Liegnitz; but Frederick, who
had been accurately informed beforehand as to the
character of the Russian Commander-in-Chief, played
upon his fears by harassing him incessantly, and for two
days skilfully prevented the junction of Buturlin and Laudon,
which finally took place at Striegau on Aug. 23. As the
combined armies were now 132,000 strong, while Frederick
could only muster 50,000 against them, [3] he cautiously retired before them in the direction of the great fortress of
Schweidnitz. The Allies, however, followed so hard upon
his heels that in no very long time he was placed in a
more awkward predicament than he had yet been in during

---

[1] Imperial rescript to Buturlin of Aug. 25, 1761.

[2] Denmark which now had an army of 20,000 men at her disposal, caused
the Allies considerable anxiety during 1760—1761. Denmark feared that the
Grand Duke Peter, as Duke of Holstein, might, on his accession to the Russian throne, be injurious to Danish interests. Only with great difficulty did
Choiseul and Vorontsov between them prevent an outbreak of hostilities on
the part of Denmark in favour of Prussia, which, in view of the impotence
of Sweden and the exhaustion of France, might have turned the scale against
the Allies. Frederick hoped at one time that the intervention of Denmark
might save Kolberg.

[3] *Bolotov.*

the whole course of the war. He durst not attack them as he could no longer afford the luxury of a victory however signal, while the far more probable contingency of a defeat would have meant absolute ruin. In his extremity he resolved to do what he had never done before, convert his camp, which he had pitched at Bunzelwitz, into a fortress and defy the Allies to attack him behind his trenches. He was materially assisted at this crisis by the dissensions and the vacillations of the allied commanders. The energetic Laudon was for giving battle to the King of Prussia at once, but Buturlin could not be got to consent to anything of a decisive character, and in the meantime Frederick's soldiers, working night and day in relief gangs, had in the incredibly short space of three days, surrounded his whole camp with strong redoubts and high walls, which he mounted with 460 guns and surrounded with a triple trench, within which he had laid down 182 mines. The approaches to this improvised and almost impregnable fortress were protected by a whole network of streams and morasses. While Frederick had been working, his adversaries had been deliberating, and the final result of their deliberations was a determination to fall upon him; but when they came within sight of his position another council of war was held, at which Buturlin refused point-blank to assault such a stronghold, although Laudon insisted that it was worth taking the risk as success would mean the utter annihilation of the Prussian army and the consequent termination of the war. During the following fortnight a blockade was attempted, but as Frederick had taken the precaution to ravage the whole country mercilessly beforehand for miles around, the besiegers suffered more severely than the besieged; and when the news reached the camp of the Allies, that General Platen had pounced upon the Russian magazines at Gostyn and totally destroyed them, Buturlin, apprehensive lest the principal

Russian dépôt at Posen should also be destroyed, abruptly quitted Laudon, leaving behind Zachary Chernuishev with a corps of 20,000 men to assist him in his subsequent operations, and recrossed the Oder, vaguely announcing his intention of proceeding against Glogau, " or *some other place.*"

"We will not conceal from you," wrote the Empress to Buturlin, on receiving intelligence of this disgraceful stampede, "that the news of your retreat has caused us more sorrow than the loss of a battle would have done... We have documentary evidence before us from our Allies, that an assault [on Frederick's position at Bunzelwitz] was at first quite feasible, yet after marching but ten miles you required a prolonged rest... Without wasting any more words, we command you to proceed forthwith to Berlin, occupy it and lay upon it a larger contribution than before, and if Prince Henry throws himself in your way you are to attack him at once without any more councils or delibera-tions. There have been so many councils-of-war in this campaign, that the very word " council-of-war " has become an abomination to us. If anybody in future dares to say that our army is not fit for attacking strongholds, he is instantly to be arrested and sent hither in chains."

Buturlin did *not* occupy Berlin after all, yet Frederick would have considered the blackmailing of his Capital a second time a lesser evil than the two fresh calamities which befell him at the end of the year. Three weeks after the departure of Buturlin from Silesia, Laudon, vigorously sup-ported by Zachary Chernuishev and his twenty thousand Russians, suddenly turned upon the fortress of Schweidnitz, the strongest in Silesia. The Commandant, General Zast-row, sold the place dearly, the assailants losing 1,000 men, but Chernuishev's grenadiers fought like lions and, after a fierce three hours' combat, the fortress which every Prussian had deemed impregnable was captured by assault. At

first Frederick himself refused to believe the news. "You
have heard of the misfortune which has happened to me
at Schweidnitz," he wrote to Prince Henry four days after
the event, [1] "... Zastrow and the garrison seem to have
played the man, but Laudon used his men as if they were
fascines in order to force his way in." And, at the very
end of the year, another virgin fortress was forced to
open her gates to the enemy.

At the end of August the Russians undertook the siege
of Kolberg for the third time, with the assistance of their
own and the Swedish fleets. The operations against the
fortress were most vigorously conducted throughout September, but the defence was equally stubborn, and in the
beginning of October a violent tempest shattered the coöper-
ating fleets and compelled them to raise the blockade. Still
the Russian commander, Rumyantsev, held on from the land
side. Although reinforced with 12,000 men from Buturlin, he
could not prevent General Platen from forcing his way into the
fortress with 6,000 fresh troops, but, on the other hand, he
succeeded in capturing 2,000 of the besieged who, under
General Knoblauch, had made a sortie in the direction of
Trepow in search of provisions. By the time the first
snows began to fall the garrison was reduced to eating
horseflesh and using the roofs of the houses for fuel; but
the Russian soldiers also suffered terribly in their tents, for
the winter had set in early with exceptional severity, the
sentries being frequently found frozen to death at their
posts. An attempt made by the Prince of Wurtemberg to
relieve the place at the end of November was repulsed,
but fresh hope arose in the hearts of the starving garrison
when a merchant vessel, bound from Königsberg to Amsterdam and laden with provisions, was driven ashore by a storm

---

[1] *Pol. Corr.* Oct. 5, 1761.

close to the harbour of Kolberg. Moreover, the gallant commandant, Major von Heyden, rejected every summons to surrender and converted the walls and bastions of the fortress into a sheet of solid ice by flushing them with water. But nothing could shake the dogged obstinacy of Rumyantsev, who swore he would have Kolberg if it cost him 10,000 men. And at last his patience was rewarded. On Christmas Day, O.S., 1761, Kolberg opened its gates and Rumyantsev sent the keys of the fortress to the Empress as a New Year's gift.

And now, at last, Frederick the Great was absolutely at the end of his resources. Ever since the rout of Kunersdorf, for all his heroic efforts, he had been unable to recover himself. That "horrible catastrophe," as he called it, had forced him to abandon an offensive for a defensive strategy; but now he had no longer the means to even stand upon the defensive with any prospect of success. His treasury was depleted, his land ravaged, his army decimated. His best officers were either slain or captives. He could no longer shut his eyes to the fact that his enemies were, slowly, perhaps, but irresistibly, attaining their object. The struggle for existence was becoming a death-agony, yet how could he prevent it? A peace honourable to the Allies would mean to him degradation. It would mean the breaking to pieces of all that he had so patiently, so painfully welded together. It would mean the loss of Silesia, of Pomerania, of East Prussia, the loss of the very provinces to which he owed his royal title. And now, too, his one effectual ally, Great Britain, seemed about to abandon him in his extremity. In the autumn of 1761 Pitt, his zealous friend, had been compelled to retire from the cabinet, and Great Britain, shortly afterwards, had embarked in a war with Spain, so that, as Golitsuin, the Russian Ambassador at London, shrewdly observed, she had no more money to waste upon the King of Prussia. Nor could he dare to

reckon, as heretofore, on the sluggishness of the foes he
feared the most, "the Bears of the Holy Roman Empire."
The timid incompetency of the first four Russian Commanders-
in-Chief had materially simplified his strategy.   They had
moved with mechanical deliberation in a fixed direction, in
obedience to the wire-pulling of a council of civilians 1,000
miles off; they had sustained, stubbornly but unintelligently,
the impact of any enemy that might happen to cut across
their line of march; and they had been amazed after the
engagement to discover, sometimes, that they had won a
great victory without being aware of it.   But they had
never taken any steps to follow up their purely fortuitous
triumphs, and at the slightest rumour of danger, at the
slightest suspicion of scarcity, they had retreated to their
dépôts behind the Vistula.   But now there were ominous
indications that even in the Russian ranks the lessons of
a five years' warfare were beginning to produce good scho-
lars.   Foreign military experts already spoke highly of
Zachary Chernuishev, and the talents of young Rumyantsev,
the victor of Kolberg, were universally recognised.   There
could be little doubt that Rumyantsev would be the next
Russian Commander-in-Chief, and it was equally certain that
his strategy would be of a very different order to the
strategy of a Fermor, a Saltuikov or a Buturlin.   His
one fault was extreme impetuosity, but this was of itself
a distinction in an army of sluggish phlegmatics.   Yes,
Frederick, was now indeed in evil case, and his correspondence at this period is a melancholy reflection of his
despair. "It seems to me," he wrote to Finkenstein on
Jan. 6, 1762, [1] "that we ought now to think of preserving
for my nephew, [2] by way of negotiation, whatever fragments
of my possessions we can snatch from the avidity of my

[1] *Pol. Corr.* Bd. XXI.
[2] The heir to the throne.

enemies. Be persuaded that if I saw a gleam of hope, even
by running the greatest risks, of re-establishing the state
on its ancient foundations, I would not use such language,
but I am convinced that, morally and physically, it is
impossible." This means, if words mean anything, that
Frederick was resolved to seek a soldier's death on the
first opportunity and thus remove the principal obstacle to
a peace for want of which Prussia was perishing. But
he was spared this heroic sacrifice. A fortnight later he
received from Warsaw the news of "a great event"
which made him rapturously exclaim to Prince Ferdinand
of Brunswick. "The sky begins to clear. Courage, my dear
fellow!"—This great, this joyous event which suddenly
snatched him from destruction was the death of the Russian
Empress. [1]

Throughout 1761 Elizabeth had been slowly dying. At
the beginning of the year she was confined to the Palace,
with swollen legs, unable to walk without assistance and
obliged to listen and reply to despatches as she lay upon
her couch. Occasionally she was conveyed in a litter to
the apartments of Alexius Razumovsky or Ivan Shuvalov,
where she would make a pretence of supping, and listen to
current gossip, [2] but even this was becoming an effort. Her
sole relaxation now was to nurse the little Grand Duke
Paul to whom she was tenderly attached, and whose rooms in
the Palace adjoined her own. She was never weary of
listening to the prattle of the child, and took a keen interest
in his education. In the course of the summer she was
conveyed with the utmost difficulty to Petershof, whence,
late in the autumn, she was brought back to the capital
more dead than alive. Imprudence in diet since her last

---

[1] "Morta la bestia, morto il veneno," he wrote to Kneiphausen on Jan. 22,
1762.

[2] Vasilchikov: *Semeistvo Razumovskikh.*

serious illness in 1757,[1] despite the repeated warnings of her skilful French and Greek doctors, undoubtedly hastened her end, but it was anxiety which actually killed her. For it was in the dismal company of tormenting apprehensions, failing hopes and disappointed expectations that the daughter of Peter the Great was about to close her eyes. It had been the desire of her latter days to dwell, if but for a short time, in the splendid palace which the genius of Rastrelli had raised at her command, but the depleted treasury could not supply the funds necessary to complete the edifice. At the very beginning of the year the vacillation of the Court of Versailles had threatened to traverse her steadily pursued and patriotic endeavours to put a curb upon the rapacious and disquieting King of Prussia. This obstacle her unshakable firmness had with difficulty surmounted, and now the incompetence of her Commander-in-Chief had scattered the fruits of her diplomacy to the winds. In midsummer, moreover, a terrible conflagration had destroyed stores to the value of one million sterling, which had laboriously been got together in the earlier part of the year, and there were no means of making good the loss. And the burden of her responsibility was all the more grievous because she had to bear it alone. Her nephew and designated successor, the weak-witted Grand Duke, was a Prussian at heart and would, no doubt, reverse her whole policy (the policy of a life-time) before her body was yet cold. The Grand Duchess she distrusted and avoided. Her Ministers, with their eyes fixed upon the near future, durst not perform the will of a Sovereign whose days they knew to be numbered. The ablest of those Ministers, Count Peter Shuvalov, was himself dying.[2] The most virile of

---

[1] We hear of *Perigord pâtés* and other indigestible delicacies being sent to her, from time to time, from Paris by Michael Bestuzhev.
[2] He survived her but 12 days.

them, Prince Shakovsky, the Procurator-General, professed to be at the end of his resources. The most eminent of them, the Grand Chancellor Vorontsov, had found the heritage of the disgraced Bestuzhev too heavy for his puny shoulders, and went about wringing his hands, threatening resignation and complaining bitterly of the all-consuming cost of "this accursed war." The members of the Conference met in fear and uncertainty only to wrangle with one another, and no resolution would ever have been arrived at had not Secretary Volkhov frequently taken it upon himself [1] to draw up protocols which often contradicted the unstable opinion of the fluctuating majority.—And then there was the ever present dread of Death, and the haunting fear of secret plots and a midnight revolution similar to that to which the Empress herself owed her elevation to the throne. It is said that, during the last few weeks of her life, nobody dressed in mourning clothes was allowed to pass in front of the Palace, and the deaths of distinguished personages were sedulously concealed from her. A dismal and melancholy picture! Yet flashes of the old masterful spirit burst forth from time to time, and it may confidently be affirmed that whatever of energy the Government displayed was inspired by the dying Empress. Thus on Dec. 14th Elizabeth's cabinet secretary, Olsufiev, appeared in the Senate, with an angry rebuke from her majesty, upbraiding the ministers for their neglect of public business and dictating what course was to be pursued in various current matters, because they "would not or could not come to a decision of their own accord." Nine days later Elizabeth was seized with a fit of coughing, accompanied by violent and persistent hemorrhage. The three doctors in attendance, very much alarmed, blooded her

---

[1] *Despatches* of the Austrian Minister, Mercy d'Argenteau, who superseded Esterhazy in 1761.

copiously, and again her vigorous constitution responded to their efforts and she rallied. [1] On Dec. 28, Olsufiev again appeared in the Senate with a special ukaz signed by her Majesty, remitting various pains and penalties for fiscal offences; mitigating the severity of the Salt-tax and ordering the release of several persons who had been imprisoned for defrauding the Treasury. Elizabeth continued to improve till January 2, 1762, but on Jan. 3, at 10 o'clock in the evening, she had a dangerous relapse, and the doctors considered it their duty to inform her that her life was in danger. She at once sent for her confessor, who shrived and communicated her, and on the following day the Sacrament of Holy Chrism was also administered. The same evening she requested that the *Otkhodnaya*, or Prayer for the departing, should twice be said over her, and she repeated the most touching passages after the priest, with great fervour. Then the agony began, and lasted all that night and the greater part of the following day. The Grand Duke and the Grand Duchess, the two Razumovskys and a few other Dignitaries who were also personal friends, remained with the dying woman to ease her last moments, but the timid Chancellor on being summoned to her side, to receive certain private instructions, feigned illness and took care to keep his bed till all was over. [2] The antechambers leading to the Empress's bed-chamber were thronged by Senators, Ministers, Generals, high ecclesiastics and court functionaries from an early hour. All present took no pains to conceal their sorrow at their approaching bereavement, and most of them were on their knees praying for her whom they regarded more as a mother than as a

---

[1] It is characteristic of her, that, hearing at this time that her jeweller was seriously ill, she bade her doctors leave her and attend to him.

[2] Vorontsov's poltroonery was all the more shocking because he had been the friend and playfellow of the Empress from his earliest years.

mistress. At 4 o'clock in the afternoon of Christmas Day (O. S.) 1761, the folding doors leading into the imperial dormitory were suddenly thrown open, and then everyone knew that the end had come. Immediately afterwards, the senior Senator, Prince Nikita Trubetskoi, appeared in the doorway, and above the tempest of sobs and weeping which instantly burst forth, rose the old man's high thin voice: "Her Imperial Majesty Elizabeth Petrovna [1] has fallen asleep in the Lord—God preserve our Most Gracious Sovereign, the Emperor Peter III."

* * *

It is the peculiar glory of Elizabeth Petrovna that she consolidated once for all the life work of her illustrious father. During the first fifteen years after the death of the great political regenerator, his stupendous creation, Russia, (before him we only hear of Muscovy,) was frequently in danger. The reactionary boyars who misruled the infant empire under Peter II would have sacrificed both the new capital and the new fleet, the twin pivots upon which the glory and the prosperity of the new state may be said to have turned; the German domination under the Empress Anne, directly contrary as it was to the golden rule of Peter, "Russia for the Russians," threatened the nation with a western yoke far more galling than the Eastern or Tartar yoke of ruder times. From this reaction, from this yoke the daughter of Peter the Great set the nation free, and beneath her beneficent sceptre Russia may be said to have possessed itself again. All the highest offices of state were once more entrusted to natives and to natives only, and whenever a foreigner was proposed for the next highest, Elizabeth,

---

[1] Elizabeth died in the 52nd year of her age and the 20th of her reign.

THE GRAND DUKE PETER.

Ætat. 33.

before confirming the appointment, invariably enquired:
"Is there then no capable Russian who would do as well?"
Moreover, she inherited from her father the sovereign gift of
choosing and using able councillors, and not only did she
summon to power a new generation of native statesmen and
administrators, but she constrained them to work harmoniously
together despite their mutual jealousies and conflicting ambitions. She herself had advantageously passed through the bitter
but salutary school of adversity. With all manner of dangers
haunting her path from her youth upwards, she had learnt the
necessity of circumspection, deliberation, self-control; she had
acquired the precious faculty of living in the midst of people
intent on jostling each other, without in any way jostling them;
and these great qualities she brought with her to the throne
without losing anything of that infinite good-nature, that
radiant affability, that patriarchal simplicity which so
endeared her to her subjects and made her, deservedly,
the most popular of all the Russian monarchs. It does not
fall within the scope of this work to allude to the internal
reforms introduced into Russia under Elizabeth, many and
important as they were; but, as regards her foreign policy,
it may be safely affirmed she laid down the deep and
durable foundations upon which Catherine II was to build
magnificently indeed, but too often, alas! so flimsily. The
diplomacy of Elizabeth, on the whole, was not so confident
or so daring as the diplomacy of her brilliant successor;
but, on the other hand, it was more correct, equally dignified
and left far less to chance. It must also be borne in
mind that the energy and firmness of Elizabeth considerably facilitated the task of Catherine by rendering Prussia,
Russia's most dangerous neighbour, practically harmless
to her for the remainder of the century. This of itself
was a political legacy of inestimable value, and it was not
the only one. All the great captains, all the great diplo-

matists of the "ever victorious Catherine," men like Rumy-antsev, Suvorov, Ryepnin, Bezborodko, the Panins and the Golitsuins, were brought up in the school of Elizabeth. Excellent was the use which the adroit and audacious Catherine made of these instruments of government, these pioneers of Empire, but it should never be forgotten that she received them all from the hands of the Daughter of Peter the Great.

THE END.

INDEX. *

A

Abo, Treaty of, Aug. 7, 1743, 83—4.

ADADUROV (Vasily Evdokimovich), 101, 144, 240.

ADOLPHUS FREDERICK, *Crown Prince of Sweden,* 83, 100, 163.

Aix-la-Chapelle, Treaty of, Apr. 30, 1748, 129.

ALLION, see DUSSON.

AMELOT DE CHALLEUX (Jean Jacques), 33, 50, 72, 84.

ANDREEVNA (Elizabeth), 67.

ANNE, *Duchess of Holstein,* 9, 97.

ANNE, *Empress of Russia,* accession, 10; last illness and death, 17—20; 138, 139, severity, 150.

ANNE LEOPOLDOVNA, early career, 15—16; plots against Biren, 26—30; character, 31; dissoluteness and sloth, 40—42; shyness and incompetence, 42—3; quarrel with Elizabeth Petrovna, 52—3; arrest, 57—8; last years and death, 124—125.

ANTHONY ULRIC, *Prince of Brunswick Bevern,* marriage, 16; public humiliation, 23—4; 26, generalissimo, 31; 40, 41; banished to Kholmagory, 125.

APRAKSIN (Fedor Matvyeevich), 209.

APRAKSIN (Stephen), 47, 127, extravagance, 141; 201, 203, appointed Commander-in-Chief, 208; early career and character, 209—210; sloth, 211; strategy in 1757, 212—214; tactics at Grossjägersdorf, 215—20; retreat, 221—222; 235, trial, 236—7; 241, 242, 246, death, 247; 260.

APRAKSINA (Agripina Leonteevna), 236.

AUGUSTUS II, *King of Poland,* 119.

AUGUSTUS III, *King of Poland,* 32, 166, 167, 207, 238.

* All place names (*e. g.* treaties and battles) are indicated by Italics.

B

BAKKOW, *General*, 237.

BARRIDIAN, 144.

BEKETOV (Nikita Afanasievich), liaison with Empress Elizabeth, 158—9.

BEKHTYEEV (Theodor Dmitrievich), mission to Paris, 198—9; 222, 226, 229.

BELLEISLE, *Maréchal de*, 34, 199.

Bergen, Battle of, Apr. 13, 1759, 265.

BERGEN, *Lieut*, 92.

BERNIS, *Cardinal*, 182, 228, 230, timorous policy, 1758, 260.

BESTUZHEV-RYUMIN (Alexius Petrovich), *Count, Chancellor*, helps Biren to regency, 17—18; 20, arrested, 1741, 29; recalled to court, 48; 59, early career and character, 77—80; 82, 83, 85, cautious policy, 88; 96, 99, 107, Frederick of Prussia's fear of, 108—9; expels Trotti from Russia, 112—113; made chancellor, 113; anti-Prussian policy, 114—117; ib. 1745, 119—120; 121, political duel with Frederick, 122—124; predilection for England, 125—6; 127, 128, 129, brilliant triumphs, 130—131; 141, 144, 145, 150, 151, protects Beketov, 158; 159, 160, 162, 164, 165, Polish policy, 166—7; Frederick II's hatred of, 168; peevishness, 168; rupture with brother Michael, 168—170; difficulties, 1753, 171; obtains loan from England, 171—2; promotes Anglo-Russian Alliance, 172—178; out-witted, 185—6; loses influence, 1756, 187; cultivates friendship with Grand Duchess Catherine, 187—188; ib., 193—4; 194, 195, advises establishment of Council of State, 195; intrigues with Williams, 200—202; 211, 212, correspondence with Apraksin, 213; fall of, 234—40; trial, 241—2; 246, sentence, 247—8, 312.

BESTUZHEV-RYUMIN (Michael Petrovich), *Count*, early career and character, 76—77; 85, 91, 92, 93, 96, 114, romantic attachment to Madame von Haugwitz, 168—170; mission to Paris, 1758, 229—30; despatches from Paris, 1758—60, 260—261; celebrates Kunersdorf, 276, 285.

BESTUZHEV (Peter), *Count*, 10.

BESTUZHEVA (Anna Gavrilovna), 79, character, 91; arrest, 92; trial, 93—95.

BIREN (Ernst Johann), *see* ERNEST John, *Duke of Courland*.

BIREN (Peter), 16.

BODENHAUPT, *General*, 288.

BOLOTOV, description of battle of Grossjägersdorf, 216—19.

BOTTA, *Marquis de*, 33, 69, 84, 87, 92, 93, 94, 108, 114, 115.

BOURBON, *Duc de*, 69.

Breslau, Treaty of, June 11, 1742, 80.

BRETEUIL, *Baron de, see* LE TONNELIER.
BREVERN, *Count,* 59.
BROGLIE, *Duc de,* 269.
BROWNE, *Fieldmarshal,* 207.
BRUMMER, 89, 99.
BUTURLIN (ALEXANDER BOROSOVICH), *Fieldmarshal,* 76, supersedes Saltuikov, 295; early career and character 302—3; incapacity, 303—4; refuses co-operation with Laudon, 1761, 305—6; 307.

C

CANTEMIR (Antiochus), *Prince,* 34, 84.
CARLYLE (Thomas), 287.
CASTELLANE, *Marquis de,* 72, 84.
CATHERINE I, *Empress 'of Russia,* 3, accession, 4—5; reign, 5—6; foreign policy, 9; 68.
CATHERINE II, *Empress of Russia,* arrival in Russia, 101; serious illness, 101—103; received into Orthodox Church, 103; betrothal, 103; marriage, 104—106; her description of Elizabeth Petrovna, 153; her description of A. Shuvalov, 157; character and early married life, 187—192; 200, intrigues with H. Williams, 202; 210, 212, 237, 238, alarm at arrest of Bestuzhev, 240; 241, appeals to Empress Elizabeth, 243; midnight interview with Elizabeth, 1758, 243—247; 313.
CHARLES VI, *Kaiser,* death, 32.
CHARLES VII, *Kaiser,* 116.
CHARLES, *Prince, of Lorraine,* 115, 222.
CHÂTEAUNEUF, *Marquis de, see* L'HÔPITAL.
CHEREGORODSKAYA (Catherine), 243.
CHERKASKY (ALEXIUS MIKHAILOVICH), *Prince,* character, 11—12; 17, 18, 31, Grand Chancellor, 35, 74; 87, death, 88.
CHERNUISHEV, *Count, Ambassador,* at Berlin, 96; 124, 125, at London, 164; 173, despatches, 299—300.
CHERNUISHEV (Ivan Grigorievich), *Count,* extravagance, 140.
CHERNUISHEV (Zachary Grigorievich), *Count,* 257, 295, 306, 309.
CHESTERFIELD, *Earl of,* 127.
CHOGLOKOVA (MARIA SEMENOVNA), 188.
CHOISEUL, *Duc de, see* STAINVILLE.
Crefeldt, Battle of, 1758, 260.

D

DASHKOVA, *Princess,* account of Elizabeth Petrovna, 136.
DAUN, *Count, Fieldmarshal,* 222, 223, 265, 269, 270, differences with Saltuikov, 279—80; 281, 294, defeated at Torgau, 296; 302.

D'EON DE BEAUMONT, *Chevalier*, mission to Russia, 197—8 and 228—29.

DEVIER, *General*, 67.

DICKENS (Guy), Frederick II's opinion of, 167; negotiations in Russia, 173—4.

DOHNA, *Count*, 252—3, at Zorndorf, 255—7; 258, 268.

DOLGORUKI (Vasily Vladimirovich), *Prince*, 60, 117.

DOUGLAS (Mackenzie), missions to Russia, 1755—56, 197—198.

Dresden, Peace of, Dec. 25, 1745, 119.

DULYANSKY, *Father*, 143, 144.

DUSSON (Jean Louis), *Marquis de Bonac-d'Allion*, 82, 85, 89, 95, 112, 124.

DUVAL, 140.

E

ELAGIN (Ivan Perfilievich), 144.

ELIZABETH IVANOVNA, 137.

ELIZABETH PETROVNA, *Empress of Russia*, discontent of, under Ivan VI, 45; political intrigues with La Chetardie, 46; popularity, 46; hatred of Ostermann, 47; 50, friendship with the Guards, 50—51; quarrel with the Regent Anne, 52—53; overthrows government of Ivan VI, 54—61; earlier years, 66—71; character, 71—72; 81, patriotism, 82; concludes peace with Sweden, 83; 87, saves the Bestuzhevs, 1744, 96; affection for her nephew, 97—99; tenderness to little Princess of Zerbst, 102; marries her nephew to Catherine, 103—106; cajoled by Frederick II, 108; hostile to Prussia, 117—119; causes of her dislike of Frederick, 120; dismisses Princess of Zerbst, 121; distrustful of England, 126; personal appearance, 134; amiability, 134—136; equity, 136; indolence, 137; ignorance, 137; devotions, 138; extravagance, 138—140; marriage, 143; pilgrimage to Kiev, 1744, 148—149; fondness for drama, 152; in male attire, 152; skill as a dancer, 153; mode of life, 154; liaison with Ivan Shuvalov, 155; liaison with Beketov, 158—9; 167, 170, kindness to Bestuzhev, 171; negotiations with England, 1755, 175—178; friendship with Catherine, 192—3; institutes the Conference of Ministers, 195; anti-Prussian policy, 196—203: accedes to Treaty of Versailles, 1756, 204; 210, 222; description of, by L'Hôpital, 227—228; 231, serious illness, 1758, 232—33; orders arrest of Bestuzhev, 239; 241, threatens Bestuzhev with torture, 242; 243, midnight interview with Catherine, 1758, 244—47; 249, differences with Maria Theresa, 259; firmness, 260; refuses mediation of England, 1759, 278; rescripts to Saltuikov, 282; sharp reproaches to Maria Theresa, 284; tenacity of purpose, 286—7; anti-Prussian policy,

287—9; demands E. Prussia guaranteed, 290—91; prepares for campaign of 1760, 293—4; refuses peace, 297—8; private negotiations with Louis XV, 298: 299, indignant rescripts to Buturlin, 1761, 304—6; last illness, 310—312; death, 313—4; appreciation of, 314—16.

ELIZABETH, *Princess of Zerbst*, arrival in Russia, 100—101, a Prussian spy, 109; expulsion from Russia, 120—121; 123.

ERNEST JOHN, *Duke of Courland*, early career and character, 10—11; 16, intrigues for regency, 17—18; proclaimed regent, 22; regency, 23—25; overthrow, 26—30, 61, 65, 166, 167.

ESTERHAZY (Nicholas), *Prince*, 147, 199, 223, 235, 236, 237, procures fall of Bestuzhev, 238—39; 242, 265, 283, 284, 289, 290, 291, counsels peace, 297.

ESTRÉES, *Maréchal d'*, 223.

EUGENE, *of Wurtemberg, Prince*, 32, 274.

F

FERDINAND, *Duke of Brunswick*, 260, 265, 271, 277, 302, 310.

FERMOR (Wilhelm), strategy in 1757, 212—13; 216, 217, 237, character, 248; winter campaign, 1757, 249; 251, 252, campaign of 1758, 252—55; at Zorndorf, 255—7; subsequent operations, 258—9; campaign of 1759, 265—6; superseded by Saltuikov, 266—7; 271, 276.

FINCH (*Hon.* Edward), 41, 42, 47, opinion of Ostermann, 48; 49, 64, gloomy opinion of Russia, 72—3; 86.

FINKINSTEIN, *Count*, 124, 274, 277.

FLEURY, *Cardinal*, abandons Maria Theresa, 34; fear of Russia, 38.

FOUQUÉ, *General*, 295.

FREDERICK II, *King of Prussia*, First Silesian War, 32—33; cajoles Münnich, 35; 80, 89, 96, 100, dread of Russia, 107—8; plots against Bestuzhev, 109—110; 2nd Silesian War, 114; reverses in Bohemia, 115—116; invades Saxony, 117—119; alienates Russia, 120; plots against Bestuzhev, 122—123; advises Empress Elizabeth to banish Brunswickers, 124—5; fear of Bestuzhev, 129; 130, 131; universal distrust of, 162; Swedish policy, 163—65; diplomatic rupture with Russia, 165; opinion of Guy Dickens and Hanbury Williams, 167—8; hatred of Bestuzhev, 168; 172, 173, Treaty of Westminster, 1756, 182—84; 191, 196, 202, 203, disbelief of Franco-Austrian Alliance, 204—5; mistaken as to Russia's policy, 206; ultimatum to Maria Theresa, 206; invades Saxony, 1756, 207; 222, 223, Rossbach and Leuthen, 224; Olmutz, 251; campaign of 1758, 253—5; Zorndorf, 255—7; 258, 260, Defender of Protestant Religion, 261; 262, sarcasms against Saltuikov, 267; gloomy prospects, 1759, 267—72; Kunersdorf, 272—5; after Kunersdorf,

276—7; begs mediation of England, 277—9; 280, 285, 287, desperate position, 1760, 288—9; 292, supported by England, 293; Liegnitz, 295; Torgau, 296; 1761, 301; desperate expedients. 302; Bunzelwitz, 305—6; 307, utter despair, 308; meditates death, 309—10.

G

GAGARINA, *Princess*, 92.
GEORGE I, *King of England*, 8, 9, 78.
GEORGE II, *King of England*, 203, 231, 277.
GOLDBACH, 112.
GOLITSUIN (Alexius Mikhailovich), *Prince*, despatches from London, 200—203; ib. 230—31; ib. 261—62; interviews with Pitt, 1760, 293; negotiates for a peace-congress, 299—300; interviews with Pitt, 300—301; despatches, 1761, 308—9.
GOLITSUIN, *Prince, General*, 271, 276.
GOLITSUIN (Peter), *Prince*, 113.
GOLOVKIN (Michael Vasilevich), *Count*, 31, 35, character, 47; 56, 62, 64.
GOLOVKIN, *Admiral*, 77.
GROSS, *Ambassador*, 163, 164.
Grossjägersdorf, Battle of, Aug. 30, 1757, 215—9.
GUROWSKI, *Ambassador*, 166, 167.

H

Hastenbeck, Battle of, July 26, 1757, 223,
HAUGWITZ, *Frau von*, romantic attachment to M. Bestuzhev, 168—70.
HENRY I, *King of France*, 68.
HENRY, *Prince of Prussia*, 255, 267, 279, 281, 294, 302.
HESSE-HOMBURG, *Princess*, 106.
HEYDON, *Major von*, 308.
HOLDERNESSE, *Lord*, 200, 231.
HOLSTEIN, *Prince of*, 216, 218.
Hunnersdorf, Battle of, 119.
HYNDFORD, *Lord*, 116, 119, 127, 128, description of Elizabeth Petrovna, 136; ib. 153; 165.

I

ILINICHAVA, 67.
IVAN VI, *Emperor of Russia*, birth, 15; accession, 22; description of, 41; deposition, 58; 89, banishment, 125; 202.
IZMAILOVNA (Nastasia), 137.

K

KAUNITZ (Wenzel Anton von), *Prince*, counsels change of political system for Austria, 180—181; chancellor, 182; 235, 283, 290.
KAYSERLING, *Ambassador*, 124.
KEITH (James), 83, 209, 262.
KEITH (Robert), 184, 238, 278, 293.
Kesselsdorf, Battle of, 119.
KLINGGRAEFFEN, *Ambassador*, 205, 206.
Kloster-Zeven, Capitulation of, 223.
KNYPHAUSEN, *Ambassador,* 205, 277.
Kolin, Battle of, 223.
KRUSE (Cornelius), 6.
Kunersdorf, Battle of, Aug. 12, 1759, description of, 270—75.
KURAKIN (Ivan Ivanovich), *Prince,* 78.
KURBATOV, 113.

L

LACY (Peter), *Fieldmarshal,* 12, early career and character, 15; Finnish campaigns, 1741, 39—40; declares for Elizabeth, 58; 83, 117, 127, 209.
LA CHETARDIE, *see* TROTTI.
LAMBERT, *Captain,* Account of the Rumain Army, 1757, 249—51.
LANCZYNSKI, *Ambassador,* 80, 94.
Landeshut, Battle of, Jan. 23, 1760, 295.
LAUDON, *Fieldmarshal,* 252, campaign of 1759, 269—74; at Kunersdorf, 275—7; 276, 280, 281, 283, 294, at Landeshut, 295, 302, 303, 305, captures Schweidnitz, 306—7.
LEFORT (François), 2.
LEHWALDT, *General,* strategy, 1757, 212—214; at Grossjägersdorf, 215—220; 223, 260.
LENOIR, *Mdlle.,* 67.
LESTOCQ (Armand), *Count,* 54, aids Elizabeth in her *coup d'état,* 54—59; 60, early career and character, 74—75; influence, 76; 78, 81, venality, 88; plots against the Bestuzhevs, 89—96; 99, 100, 109, 129, fall of, 130—132.
LE TONNELIER (Louis Auguste), *Baron de Breteuil,* embassy of, to St. Petersburg, 1760, 292; counsels peace, 297; 299.
Leuthen, Battle of, Dec. 5, 1757, 224.
LEVENHAUPT, *Swedish General,* 53.
L'HÔPITAL (Paul Gallucio), *Marquis de Châteauneuf,* character, 226; mission to Russia; 227—8, ruins Bestuzhev, 228—9; 235, 236, 237, 242, recall, 292.
Liegnitz, Battle of, 295.

LILIENFELD, 92.

LOCATELLI, *Architect*, 151.

LOEWENWOLDE, *Count*, 62, 90, 92.

LOPUKHIN (Ivan Stepanovich), 90, arrest, 92; 94.

LOPUKHIN (Stepan Vasilevich), 90, arrest, 92; trial, 93; 94.

LOPUKHIN (Vasily Abramovich), 217.

LOPUKHINA (Natalia Fedorovna), character, 90—91; arrest, 92; trial, 93—4.

LOUIS XV, *King of France*, 68, 85, contracts Austrian alliance, 183—4; 260, 261, refuses to aggrandize Russia, 1760, 291; perverse anti-Russian policy, 292; refuses closer alliance with Elizabeth, 298—9.

LOUISA ULRICA, *Queen of Sweden*, 163; 205.

Lowosowitz, Battle of, Oct. 1, 1756, 207.

LYNAR, *Count,* liaison with Anne Leopoldovna, 40—42; 87.

M

MACAULAY (Thomas Babbington), 287.

MALTZAHN, 207.

MANFREDINI, 151.

MANSTEIN, *General,* 28.

MARDEFELT, *Ambassador,* 37, correspondence with Frederick II, 107—109; 110, 111, 117, 122, 123, recall from St. Petersburg, 124.

MARIA THERESA, *Empress-Queen,* 32; attacked by Frederick II, 1740, 33—34; signs treaty of Breslau, 80; 87, defends Botta, 95; 107, appeals for help to England, 114; finally relinquishes Silesia, 119; 128, 170, advised by Kaunitz to change Austrian system, 180—82; 184, 199, 205, ambiguous reply to Frederick II's ultimatum, 206—7; 225, urges on Russian armaments, 1758, 251; irresolution, 259; rewards victors of Kunersdorf, 276; unwilling to aggrandize Russia, 290—1; desires peace with Frederick, 297; 298, peace negotiations, 299—300.

MARWITZ, *von der, General,* 114.

MARY, *Princess of Saxony,* 99.

MARY, *Leszczynska, Queen of France,* 69.

MASSLOWSKI, 218, account of battle of Zorndorf, 254—7.

MAURICE, *of Saxony, Fieldmarshal,* 166, 167.

MENGDEN (Bina), 41.

MENGDEN (Julia), extraordinary influence over Anne Leopoldovna, 41; connives at her adultery, 41—42; 57, 58.

MENGDEN, *Baron,* 56, 62,

MENSHIKOV (Alexander Danilovich), *Prince,* character, 2; training, 3; 4, 10, 68, 69.

Minden, Battle of, Aug. 1, 1759, 271.

Moys, Battle of, Sept. 7, 1757, 223.
MÜNNICH (Burkhard Christoph), *Fieldmarshal,* early career and character, 14; helps Biren to Regency, 17—18; overthrows Biren, 26—30; Premier-Minister, 30—31; vanity and rapacity, 31—32; cajoled by Frederick II, 35; resignation, 35—36; arrest, 57; trial, 62; on scaffold, 63—4; exiled, 64—65.

N

NADARSLY (Ferencz), 223.
NARUISHKIN (Sergius), extravagance, 140.
NARUISHKINA (Ekaterina Ivanovna), *see* RAZUMOVSKAYA.
NEWCASTLE, *Duke of,* 164, 173, 200, 301.
NIODINI, 151.
NIVERNOIS, *Duc de,* 183.
NOLCKEN, *Swedish Ambassador,* 45, 51.
Nymphenburg, Convention of, May 28, 1741, 34.

O

OBRYEZKOV, *Russian Diplomatist,* despatches from Constantinople, 262.
OLSUFIEV, 312, 313.
OSTERMANN (Andrei Ivanovich), *Count,* early career and character, 6—7; Peter the Great's eulogium of, 8; 9, political system, 12—13; diplomatic successes, 13—14; 19, 22, 30, 31, 35, supreme, 36; foreign policy, 37—38; successes, 39—40; 42, 44, 47, 48, 49, arrest, 56; trial, 61—62; on scaffold, 63—4; exiled, 64—5.
OSTERMANNA (Martha Ivanovna), 7.
ORLEANS, *Duc d',* 68.

P

PANIN (Nikita Ivanovich), *Count,* diplomacy of, at Stockholm, 162—4.
PANIN (Peter Ivanovich), *Count,* 220.
PAUL PETROVICH, *Grand Duke,* birth, 193, 241, 310.
PETER I, *Emperor of Russia,* death, 1; 9, 67.
PETER II, *Emperor of Russia,* reign, 9—10.
PETER III, *Emperor of Russia,* early career and character, 97—99; betrothal, 103—104; serious illness, 104; marriage, 104—106; 139, early married life, 189—92; 193, 200, 201, 210, 239, 244, 313, accession, 314.
PEZOLD, *Saxon Diplomatist,* 73, 78.
PITT (William), *Earl of Chatham,* averse to Russian aggrandisement, 293; endeavours to aid King of Prussia, 300—1; 308.
PLATEN, *General,* 305, 306.

PODEWILLS, *Prussian Statesman*, 163.
POMPADOUR, *Madame de*, 260.
PONIATOWSKI (Stanislaus), liaison with Grand Duchess Catherine, 201, 238, 240, 242.
Prague, Battle of, May 6, 1757, 222.
PRASSÉ, *von*, 237.
PUTTKAMMER, *General*, 274.

R

RAZUMOVSKAYA, *Countess*, 106.
RAZUMOVSKAYA (Ekaterina Ivanovna), 145.
RAZUMOVSKY (Alexius), *Count*, 54, 60, 109, extravagance, 140; early career and character, 142—3; marries Empress Elizabeth, 143; 144, privileges, 145; common sense, 146; piety, 148; 151, 155, 158; made Fieldmarshal, 210; 310, 313.
RAZUMOVSKY (Cyril), *Count*, 106, extravagance, 140; educated abroad, 144; marriage, 145; anecdotes of his generosity, 146—148, 313.
REXIN, *Prussian Diplomatist*, 302.
RONDEAU (Claudius), 10, 40.
ROSENBERG, Count, *Austrian Diplomatist*, 114, 115.
Rossbach, Battle of, 5 Nov., 1757, 224.
RUMYANTSEV (Peter Aleksandrovich), *Count*, 219, 250, 251, 252, 253, at Kunersdorf, 271—73; 276, 302, captures Kolberg, 1761, 307—8; 309.
RYEPNIN, *Prince*, 127; march to Rhine, 128—9; 209.

S

Saint-Petersburg, Treaty of, Dec. 9, 1747, 128.
Saint-Petersburg, Treaty of, Feb. 1, 1756, 177.
Saint-Petersburg, Treaty of, 1760, 265 and 290—1.
SALTUIKOV (Peter Semenovich), *Fieldmarshal*, 266, appointed Commander-in-Chief, 267; early career and character, 268; at Kay, 268—9; subsequent operations, 269—70; at Kunersdorf, 270—275; made Fieldmarshal, 276; quarrels with Daun, 1759, 279—80; 281, obstinacy, 282—3; plan of campaign, 1760, 293—4; superseded by Buturlin, 295.
SALTUIKOV (Sergius), 194.
SCHWARZ, 58.
SÉCHELLES, *General*, 199.
SEREBRYAKOV, 218.
SEYDLITZ, *General*, 256, at Kunersdorf, 275.
SHAFIROV, *Vice-chancellor*, 7, 8.
SHCHERBATOV, *Prince*, 139, 141.

SHEREMETEV (Peter Borisovich), extravagance, 141.

SHUBIN (Alexius Nikiforevich), 70, 143.

SHUVALOV (Alexander), *Count,* 54, extravagance, 141; character, 157; 201, 237, tries Bestuzhev, 241—2; 244.

SHUVALOV (Ivan Ivanovich), *Count,* liaison with Empress Elizabeth, 155; character, 157—8; pacific nature, 159—60; 243, 244, 281, 287, refuses bribes from Frederick II, 288; 293, 310.

SHUVALOV (Peter), *Count,* 54, 60, 135, extravagance, 141; origin and character, 155—57; treachery, 159; 210, 237, 239, 255, refuses bribes from Frederick II, 288.

SHUVALOVA (Mauro Egorovna), 137, 145.

SOPHIA AUGUSTA FREDERICA, *of Anhalt-Zerbst, see* CATHERINE II, *Empress of Russia.*

STAHREMBERG, *Austrian diplomatist,* 182, 198, 261, 285.

STAINVILLE (Etienne François de), *Duc de Choiseul,* French For. Min., 1758, 260—61; reproaches Vorontsov, 285.

STANISLAUS LESZCZYNSKI, *King of Poland,* 12, 69.

STAMKE, *Councillor,* 238.

STEHLIN, *Academician,* 190.

STROGANOV, *Count,* 137.

SUMARAKOV (Alexander Petrovich), 144, 151.

SUVOROV (Alexander Vasilievich), 251.

T

TARAKHANOVS, 143.

TEMERYAZEV, 63.

TERCIER, 198.

THEODORSKY (Simeon), 101, 102.

TODTLEBEN, *General,* 271, 295, 302.

TOLSTOI (Peter Andryeevich), *Count,* 3, 4, 10.

Torgau, Battle of, Nov. 3, 1760, 296.

TRAUN, *General,* 115.

TROTTI (Joachim Jacques), *Marquis de la Chetardie,* 33, 35, 39, character, 43—44; blunders, 44—45; intrigues on behalf of Elizabeth, 45—47; 50, 51, 76, popularity in Russia, 81; recall from Russia, 84—5; return thither, 96; 109, expulsion, 111—113, 132.

TRUBETSKOI (Nikita), *Prince,* 22, 62, character, 74; 76, 83, 90, 109, 132, brutality to Bestuzhev, 240; tries Bestuzhev, 240, 314.

U

USHAKOV, *General,* 23, 24, 76, 113.

USUPOV (Boris Grigorievich), 151.

V

VALORY, *Marquis de*, 92, 205, 207.
Versailles, Treaty of, May 2, 1756. 183—4.
Versailles, Treaty of, Dec. 30, 1758, 264.
Versailles, Treaty of, Dec. 31, 1758, 265.
VILLEBOIS, *General,* 250, 269, 271.
Vilmanstrand, Battle of, 40.
VOLKHOV, *Secr.,* 312.
VORONTSOV (Alexius), *Count,* 152.
VORONTSOV (MICHAEL LARIONOVICH), *Count, Chancellor,* at *coup d'état,* 1741, 54—59; 76, 89, Vice-Chancellor, 114; 117, a Prussian spy, 122—123; discomfited by Bestuzhev, 124—5; 127, 129, 131, in danger, 1748, 132; 169, 170, 177, 187, 197, negotiates secretly with France, 198—199; 202 203, 222, 226, 228, 239, Chancellor, 265; 278, 283, 287, 290, carries through Treaty of St. Petersburg, 1760, 291; 298, 299, 300, 312, poltroonery, 313.
VORONTSOVA (Anna Karlovna), 76, 137.

W

WAGER, *Admiral,* 9.
Warsaw, Convention of, Jan. 8, 1745, 116.
WARENDORFF, *Prussian Diplomatist,* 165, 168.
WEDELL, *General,* defeated at Kay, 268—9; 271.
Westminster, Treaty of, Jan. 16, 1756, 178.
WILLIAMS (*Sir* Hanbury), diplomacy of in Poland, 167; negotiations of in Russia, 1755, 175— 8; flippancy, 185; 197, intrigues of at Russian Court, 202—204; 227, 231.
WINTERFELD, *General,* 223.
Worms, Compact of, Sep. 13, 1743, 107.
WYCH (*Sir* Cyril), 87, 88, 89, 139.

Y

YAGUZHINSKAYA (Nastasia Pavlovna), 92.
YAGUZHINSKY (Paul Ivanovich), 3.

Z

ZASTROW, *General,* 306, 307.
Zorndorf, Battle of, Aug. 25, 1758, account of, 253—57.
ZUIBIN, *General,* 217.

Printed by the Motley Press: London Office, 18 Eldon Street, E.C.